Pope John XXIII: 101 Facts & Trivia

By The Same Author

SNA: Theory and Practice

Reengineering IBM Networks

Integrating TCP/IP i-nets with IBM Data Centers

Corporate Portals Empowered with XML and Web Services

Web Services: Theory and Practice

Popes and the Tale of Their Names

The Next Pope

The Next Pope 2011

The Last 9 Conclaves

The Last 10 Conclaves: 2013 to 1903

The Election of the 2013 Pope

Pope Names for the 2013 Conclave

Comet ISON, C/2012 S1 (ISON)

Comet ISON, C/2012 S1 (ISON) Quick Reference

Comet ISON for Kids

Comets: 101 Facts & Trivia

Devanee's Book of Dwarf Planets

Matthew's Book of 4 Vesta the Would be Planet

Teischan's ABC Book of Great Artists

A Pup is NOT a Toy

Pope John XXIII: 101 Facts & Trivia

Anura Gurugé

Edition One
March 2014

WOWNH LLC
New Hampshire
USA
www.wownh.com

First published by WOWNH LLC in March 2014 as a Kindle eBook.

First paperback edition March 2014.

ISBN-10: 149612491X

ISBN-13: 978-1496124913

Printed in the United States of America

This book is printed on acid-free paper.

PHOTOGRAPHIC CREDITS: Most of the images used in this book, including the cover image, are public domain material. Most photographs published in Italy prior to 1963 are now no longer subject to copyright. The *'Papa Giovanni'* Website, www.papagiovanni.com, run by the *Pontificio Istituto Missioni Estere* (PIME) [Pontifical Institute for Foreign Missions], kindly gave me permission to use all of their photographs. These will be attributed to 'PIME'. Mariotti Carlo & Figli S.p.A. of Rome was kind enough to grant me permission to use the picture of the *'Domus Mariae'* that appears on page 4.

To

Philip P. Bonafide,

my lawyer from 1997 to 2014

(when he retired);

of proud Italian descent

and a good Catholic.

CONTENTS

Joannes P. P. XXIII

Pope Saint John XXIII (#262), October 28, 1958 to June 3, 1963.

FOREWORD

Pope John XXIII: A Personal Recollection

by:

Father Anthony Churchill, S.T.L.

Parish Priest of
Our Lady of Sorrows Church,
Bognor Regis, West Sussex
Dean of the Arundel Cathedral Deanery

I remember vividly when we learnt that Pope Pius XII was dying. I was eleven years old and had just begun attending Wimbledon College, a Jesuit Grammar School. It was a Catholic school run by the Jesuits; a Catholic school within the State system.

Pope Pius XII died on Thursday October 9th, 1958. It was hard to imagine anyone else as the Pope. On the evening of Tuesday October 28th I had just got home from school in time to see the famous *'white smoke'* from the Sistine Chapel and to hear the announcement that the Patriarch of Venice, Cardinal Angelo Roncalli was the new Pope, and that he had chosen the name of John XXIII. The Newspapers said that he would be a *'transitional pope'*. His task, so they thought, was to restore some order to the Roman Curia which had been somewhat neglected by his predecessor, and to keep the seat warm for a much younger pope next time. How wrong they were.

I can remember watching the Coronation of the new Pope on television. It was broadcast live from Rome on the BBC. I remember my father, just a few years earlier, struggling to hear on Vatican Radio the canonization of Pope St. Pius X. Now just a few years later we could watch the Coronation of the new Holy Father on live television. For him and for my mother it was an exciting moment. My father had been to Rome once in 1954. My mother never imagined that she would ever get there, and for both of them television brought the Pope into our home. We always prayed for him. During those years, as television was coming into its own, we saw quite a lot of Pope John. It made him a much more familiar figure than previous popes could ever have been. He was certainly a much loved Pope.

Within a hundred days Pope John had announced his intention to call a Diocesan Synod for Rome, to undertake a complete revision of the Code of

Canon Law and, the biggest surprise of all, to convoke an Ecumenical Council. Any of these projects would be daunting, but to undertake all three at the age of 77 was stunning.

Angelo Roncalli was in office for some four and a half years only, but his pontificate was perhaps one of the most significant in many centuries. The Council marked a turning point in the history of the Catholic Church. Even now, almost fifty years since it ended, it is much too soon to write a definitive history of the Council and its impact, not only on the Catholic Church but on Christianity as a whole. The Council is an on-going process. It is as they say *'a work in progress'*.

For me as a schoolboy with a lively interest in the Church it was an exciting time as it became clear that this *'transitional'* Pope was determined to shake things up. We watched so many *'firsts'*. The visit by Geoffrey Fisher, Archbishop of Canterbury was a historic event. No Anglican Primate had been to Rome since before the Reformation. More and more Church leaders from other denominations made their way to Rome to meet the Pope. The Catholic Church began to enter into the ecumenical movement under the direction of the German Jesuit Cardinal Augustin Bea.

I cannot pretend that as a young teenager I understood the implications of all that was going on, but then I wonder if Pope John himself could see how profoundly his decision to call a General Council would have an impact on the Church. I suspect that he did understand that his personal approachability and his gentle friendliness could help to bring about a much needed thaw in relations between the Catholic Church and those outside. During his years as Nuncio in Paris, and earlier in Bulgaria and Turkey, he had proved a most effective diplomat and had reached out to all sorts of people who were traditionally suspicious of, if not actually hostile, to the Church. This he continued with remarkable success as Pope.

I had the good fortune to see Pope John XXIII in Rome in 1962. I was 15 years old and was in Rome with a school party from Wimbledon. We saw the Pope at a general audience in St Peter's on the Wednesday, and then again at the Papal Mass on Easter Sunday. I could not believe the size of the Basilica or the huge crowds taking part, but I can still see the gentle smiling face of Papa Roncalli as he came past where we were standing.

My mother eventually got to Rome in 1976 when I was studying there, and she was able to see Pope Paul VI at a General Audience. Later she was at Mass with me in Westminster Cathedral in London in 1982 when we received Holy Communion together from Pope John Paul II.

In England, a country with a long history of anti-Catholicism, it was amazing to see the impact Pope John had in changing the relations between the churches, and among ordinary people at large.

My parents were friends with a married couple who used to go regularly to Rome. In those days that was not as common as it is today. They had seen Pope Pius XII on several occasions and had a tremendous devotion to him. I remember that at first they found the contrast between Pius XII and Pope John quite difficult. It took them a little time to get used to the informal style of the new Pope. Within a short period they came to love him and to admire his sheer goodness.

This was very obvious in the last months of his life when he was visibly dying from cancer, and especially in the last few days. I well remember how from May 30th when it became clear that the end was near, until his death on the evening of June 3rd, reports from Rome led the Radio and TV news bulletins and made the headlines in the newspapers. Following his death the Queen ordered flags to be flown at half-mast in tribute. Such had been his impact that even in Britain, a country with a strong Protestant tradition, this was widely seen as an appropriate response to the death of a much revered world figure. The decision to lower the flags reflected the Queen's own sensitivity to a changing world.

On April 27th Pope Francis will declare both John Paul II and John XXIII to be Saints. I don't think my mother would have been surprised.

With the passage of the years I have learnt much more about Pope John, and it will be a great thrill for me to be in Rome, God willing, for his Canonization on April 27th. Inevitably John Paul II is a more immediate memory for most of us. Through the good fortune of studying in Rome, and later because of my work, I had the privilege of meeting him, however briefly, on several occasions and speaking with him. And so, I have vivid memories of him and especially his sense of humor. There is no doubt that he was a remarkable human being and a tireless traveler preaching the Gospel.

I think, however, that John Paul II would be the first to recognize that his historic pontificate could not have happened without the extraordinary events set in motion by Pope John XXIII.

It can be said of both of them that the Church would never be the same after them. They illustrate for me that we must never underestimate the importance of individuals in human affairs. Angelo Roncalli was certainly a unique and wonderful individual whose impact on the Church and the world was profound.

Anthony Churchill
November 8th 2013

PREFACE

"Men are like wine - some turn to vinegar,
but the best improve with age."

"Jacqueline!"
Greeting U.S. First Lady Jacqueline Kennedy, on March 11, 1962,
having been unable to decide whether to call her
'Madame President', 'Mrs. Kennedy' or just 'Madame'

-- **Pope John XXIII** (#262)

To say that this book resulted from an epiphany would border on hyperbolic. But, a flash of inspiration was definitely involved. It happened one morning in early October 2013, while I was on my near-daily 2.5 mile jog on a deserted mountainous dirt road in rural, central New Hampshire. In July 2013 I had published my first *'101 Facts & Trivia'* book. It was about comets and rounded off the four books I had written about comets that year. I found the *'101'* concept very appealing. It appeared to have promise in today's social-media-centric, short-attention-span, very-mobile society, where so many prefer to gleam information from Twitter, Facebook, subject-specific apps, Wikipedia, PowerPoint presentations and 24x7 cable news as opposed to traditional printed books. The *'101'* concept, with its self-contained Tweet-like bullet-points, is meant to satisfy those that just do not, any longer, have the time or the desire to wade through a conventional 'chapter' book.

I was so enamored with this *'101'* concept that I wanted to write a series of such books. So, in mid-September once I had finished my work on comets I started, at once, to work on *'Popes: 101 Facts & Trivia'* with the first chapter devoted to the Ecumenical Councils. Given my penchant for papal history and the wealth of research data on popes that I have amassed since 2005 I knew that just one *'Popes: 101'* would not suffice. So in my mind I already had a series of such books, each book with at least two chapters, with a minimum of fifteen bullets a chapter, on specific popes. In the first book I was going to cover Popes Pius XII (#261) and John XXIII (#262). I was going to cover Francis (#267) and one of the John Pauls in the next. I had already finished chapter 1 of the book and was starting on chapter 2 when I had the realization, on my run, that a mere fifteen or sixteen bullet points on John XXIII would be a travesty –

especially now that he is to become a Saint as of April 27, 2014. I shelved the *'Popes:101'* and that very day, in early October, started working on this book. So, now you know how and why this book came to be.

This book, of course, is not meant to be a conventional, narrative form biography of the *'Good Pope'*. There are plenty of those around, in multiple languages. Nonetheless, this book will still provide you with a very solid and sound, albeit succinct, account of the pope's entire life – and even the canonization process that followed. In quite a few instances, especially when it comes to his election and papacy, you are likely to find unique insights and analysis, this being my forte as I have already demonstrated in my prior seven papal books (not to mention my 'popes-and-papacy' blog).

What sets this book apart from the conventional biographies is that it is designed to give the readers the freedom and flexibility to pick-and-chose what they want to explore. The 'Q&A' style I have employed is, in addition, meant to make the whole experience more interactive and personal – a point that has been borne out by the few people who helped review this book. Though grouped into nine chapters to provide chronological structure and separation, each of the 101 *'nuggets of knowledge'* is totally self-contained. So readers can, and should, hop around at will. This book is meant to be dipped into; readers fishing out and savoring a few nuggets on each dip.

Given that I am known for my generosity when it comes to facts, I find it impossible to restrict myself to just *'101 facts & trivia'* despite what it says on the title! In the Comets *'101'* book I augmented each of the 'nuggets' with at least one other piece of data. So that book could have been called *'202 facts & trivia'* without me ever being in danger of misrepresentation. Ditto when it comes to this book. I haven't counted and I don't intend to, but I know that I included way more than 101 bits of information, especially since I started each of the chapters with a preamble studded with facts.

With this, my twenty-first book as the sole-author, I lucked out. I had a small cadre of trusted collaborators who read each chapter as soon as they were written and notified me of the various *faux pas* and typos that they encountered. This was a tremendous help since my middle name is 'typo'. Two of these, Father Churchill who wrote the Foreword and Mark Trauernicht, have helped me out in various ways over a long period of time – we having met on the Web through my papal blogs. Father Churchill, who was too modest to mention in his Foreword that he concelebrated Mass with Pope Benedict XVI in

Westminster Cathedral in London in 2010, and assisted at Mass in Rome with Pope Paul VI and Pope John Paul II on many occasions, including on one occasion the consecration of a number of bishops from around the world, is my expert on theology, Church structure and historical insights -- as well as a generous provider of stunning pictures of Roman churches to grace my work. Mark, who lives in the D.C. area, is an accomplished papal historian, a noted *cognoscente* of papal coinage and an exceptional proofreader.

Another Mark, viz. Mark Delaplaine, from Texas, who I only met last year, knows his popes and is very good at spotting my typos. Though he has helped me, online, over the years, with an enormous amount of data and guest posts for *'popes-and-papacy'*, I actually do not know my fourth collaborator on this book! He wishes to remain anonymous. But, he has a wealth of knowledge and is another fine proofreader. I also need to thank Dr. David W. Tschanz, a fellow author, a polymath and a Pius XII aficionado, who over the last few years has unselfishly helped me out with much research and findings, for supplying me with a number of invaluable leads pertaining to John XXIII's canonization and making sure that I portrayed Pius XII in the right light in Chapter 1. I thank all five of these intrepid souls from the bottom of my heart. They helped make this book so much better and put my mind at rest that we managed to catch quite a few of the typos.

While my wife, Deanna, as ever, will do a final read through I am sure that I will, per my reputation, still manage to have some typos here and there. As far as I can tell, thanks to my collaborators, there should be no major howlers when it comes to the facts. I am fairly good at getting those nailed. I, however, apologize, as I always do, beforehand for the typos. If they bother you, please return the book and ask for your money back, in full – ideally though after you have finished reading it and maybe even lending it to a friend or two.

There is not much more that I need to bore you with at this stage. There is really nothing complicated about the structure of this book. The chapter headings are quite self-explanatory.

I hope you enjoy this book and that it gives you a well rounded appreciation of this extraordinary pope – arguably the most popular pope ever. Thank you.

Anura Guruge
Lakes Region, New Hampshire
February 4, 2014

I.
THE *PAPABILE*

Pope Pius XII (#261), who had been unwell for weeks and ailing since 1954, died of acute heart failure, in the early morning hours of **October 9, 1958**, in Castel Gandolfo, the papal summer residence. He is believed to have also suffered at least two strokes earlier and had, in addition, contracted pneumonia. His interment, at St. Peter's Basilica, with considerable pomp, took place four days later – following a large, a record for the time, funeral.

The *sede vacante* following his death, including the conclave to elect the next pope, was governed by his Apostolic Constitution *Vacantis Apostolicæ Sedis* which had been published on Christmas day 1945. This Constitution superseded **Pius X's** (#258) landmark 1904 *Vacante Sede Apostolica* which consolidated and formalized all the various *sede vacante* and conclave related protocols which had come to be the norms, typically via papal edicts, since the 16th century.

This 1904 Constitution, also published on Christmas day, incorporated Pius X's pivotal *Commisum Nobis* decree, from January 20th of that year, which famously and decisively put an end to *Jus Exclusivæ* (right of exclusion). This was the imperial papal veto controversially claimed by the sovereigns of France, Spain and Austria to eliminate candidates from consideration at a conclave. Pius XII's *Vacantis* in essence propagated much of the 1904 Constitution, albeit with two noteworthy notifications.

It included **Pius XI's** (#260) empathetic *Cum proxime motu proprio* of 1922 which mandated that future conclaves should start fifteen full days after the start of the *sede vacante*, as opposed to ten, with the option, if need be, of a further three day postponement. This was to ensure that all cardinals, particularly those from afar, had ample opportunity to get to Rome on time. The other change was Pius XII innovation. He, to the surprise of many, overrode what had been the sacrosanct *two-thirds* electoral majority that had been specified in canon #1 of the **1179** 'Third Council of the Lateran.' Per Pius XII, the majority at all times had to be *two-thirds plus one* (the two-thirds rounded up if the number of electors was not exactly divisible by three).

The need for the additional vote was to preclude the possibility that a candidate may have obtained the two-thirds majority by voting for himself – balking the then norm that explicitly forbade 'self-voting'. Increasing the majority by one precluded the need for the ballots cast at a conclave to contain an identification mechanism in case there was an accusation of self-voting (as had happened, unjustly, at the 1914 conclave). This change, however, was to be transitory. On September 5, 1962, 46 months into his papacy, with the start of Vatican II just five weeks away, **Pope John XXIII** (#262) with his *Summi Pontificis electio motu proprio* overturned Pius XII's *two-thirds plus one* requirement and reinstated the centuries old two-thirds majority (rounded up when necessary). Typical of that pope's magnanimity, there was also no explicit admonishment against self-voting. [Interestingly this majority requirement would get flipped back-and-forth twice more: first by **Paul VI** (#263) and then by **John Paul II** (#265).]

In accordance with the 'fifteen full days after the start of the *sede vacante'*, as required by *Vacantis*, the conclave to elect Pius XII's successor began on the afternoon of Saturday, **October 25, 1958**. The cardinals participating in the conclave (bar the *Camerlengo*) were housed in the lower floor of the Apostolic Palace, with the voting, per the norm, taking place in the Sistine Chapel.

Figure 1: Cardinal Angelo Giuseppe Roncalli when Patriarch of Venice.

1) When did the future pope arrive in Rome for **Pius XII's** (#261) funeral and where did he stay in Rome prior to the conclave?

Cardinal Angelo Giuseppe Roncalli, Patriarch of Venice, arrived in Rome, by train, on the morning of Monday, October 13, 1958 – the day of Pius XII's funeral. He had left Venice on October 11th after having celebrated a High Requiem Mass for the departed pope at his cathedral, St. Mark's Basilica.

The Patriarch was accompanied by his private secretary, **Fr. Loris Francesco Capovilla** [b. October 14, 1915] and the devoted and versatile **Guido Gusso** [b. 1931]. He was the Patriarch's multi-tasking 'Man Friday' factotum; valet and driver for a start. These two would be his conclavists. At the time each cardinal was typically permitted two conclavists; the most senior cardinals, as well as those very elderly, sick, or from the nobility allowed another. [**Paul VI's** (#263) 1975 Constitution *Romano Pontifici Eligendo* eliminated the practice of conclavists. Rather than each cardinal bringing his own personal aides a communal support staff was to be present within the conclave to collectively take care of all those present. *Capovilla, now an archbishop and in his late 90s, was created a cardinal on February 22, 2014.*]

Cardinal Roncalli stayed at the *Domus Mariae*, on Via Aurelia 481, about a mile and a half southeast of the Vatican, from October 13th till the start of the conclave. *[See Fig. 2.]* This was a large, salubrious multi-function facility that belonged to the *Gioventù Femminile di Azione Cattolica* (Young Female Catholic Action) – an arm of the then strident Italian Catholic Action movement which in the 1950s had a lay membership in the millions. Nearly forty years earlier, while a priest in Bergamo, he had been assigned to work with this group when it was in its infancy. *[q.v. #37].* The *Domus Mariae* was built between 1949 and 1954, Pius XII in 1948 having consecrated its foundation stone. A part of this tall, multi-story building, which consisted of two identical rectangular wings, each with a sizeable courtyard within, served as the headquarters for the *Gioventù Femminile.* It also housed a self-contained, well-appointed conference center with attached lodging facilities. Cardinal Roncalli had a room in the conference center section. Today, this elegantly imposing building is a 4-star hotel, the *Domus Mariae Palazzo Carpegna*.

2) Who was the ***Camerlengo* of the Holy Roman Church** in charge of the 1958 *sede vacante* and when had he been appointed as such?

The 1958 *Camerlengo* was Italian Cardinal Bishop, **Benedetto Aloisi Masella** [b. June 29, 1879]. He, as of October 27, 1954, had been the Prefect of the Sacred Congregation for the Discipline of the Sacraments and the Archpriest of the Papal Archbasilica of St. John Lateran. He was the nephew of Cardinal Gaetano Aloisi Masella [1826 to 1902; created 1887]. He had first served as a secretary to his uncle prior to joining the curia, in 1906, within the Secretariat of State. He was a Domestic Prelate to the pope from 1917 to 1919. He had been the nuncio both to Chile and Brazil and was often the papal legate sent to coronations.

He was appointed *Camerlengo* on **October 9, 1958**, soon after the death of **Pius XII** (#261)!

Yes, he was not appointed *Camerlengo* by a pope. Instead he was appointed by the cardinals present in 'Rome' the day of the pope's death – at the instigation

Figure 2: The *Domus Mariae* where Cardinal Roncalli stayed prior to the 1958 conclave. Judging from the parked Fiat 128 in the forefront this picture was taken in the early 1970s.

source: Mariotti Carlo & Figli S.p.A.

of the Dean of the College of Cardinals, French Cardinal Bishop, Eugène Tisserant. Tisserant had deputized as the makeshift *Camerlengo* and had verifed, as is mandatory, the pope's death. The ability to elect a *Camerlengo*, interregnum, being a special prerogative afforded due to necessity to the College of Cardinals, if one is not available during a *sede vacante*, either due to a prior vacancy or an unexpected incapacitation. The new pope obviously having the right to continue with the *sede vacante* appointee or to appoint a different replacement.

Pius XII was elected pope on March 2, 1939, his birthday; the only known instance of a birthday election. He was the *Camerlengo* of the conclave that elected him – only the third pope to have been a *Camerlengo* upon election. He had also been his successor's Secretary of State – yet again only the third pope to have been the previous S.S. upon election. Uniquely, Pius is the only pope, so far, to have been, when elected, *both* the last Secretary of State and the *Camerlengo*.

On December 11, 1939, nine months after his election, Pius appointed 75-year old, Italian Cardinal Priest, **Lorenzo Lauri** as the new Camerlengo; he a longtime nuncio and the Grand Penitentiary as of July 1927. Cardinal Lauri, in

February 1939, had heard the last confession of **Pius XI** (#260). He had also been the *Camerlengo* of the Sacred College of Cardinals from June 1936 to December 1937; that a very separate post to that of the *Camerlengo* of the Holy Roman Church.

Figure 3: The canopied *sede vacante* coat of arms of Cardinal Aloisi Masella, the Camerlengo of the 1958 conclave. The canopy indicates that the Church is being governed, temporarily, on a collegiate basis by the College of Cardinals.

[The *Camerlengo* of the Sacred College of Cardinals is the treasurer for the College, in charge of managing its revenues and assets. This post ceased to be as of 1995. The duties of the treasurer are now performed by the Deputy Secretary of the College of Cardinals – who is typically the deputy to the Secretary of the Congregation of Bishops. Pius, as Cardinal Pacelli, had also held this post. Actually, he took over directly from Lauri and also held this title, in parallel to the others, when elected pope. Tisserant (1958 – 1960) and Masella (1962 – 1964) would also go onto hold this post; typically a short-duration appointment rotated among the members of the College.]

Lorenzo Lauri was to die October 8, 1941, after 667 days as *Camerlengo*.

Pius XII did not deem it necessary to appoint a replacement. Given that Pius was pope for nineteen years, seven months and one day [7,161 days] he did not have a *Camerlengo* for 91% of his papacy. A similar scenario was also true when it came to the Secretary of State.

Pius XII, eight days into his pontificate, appointed Italian Luigi Maglione, his Secretary of State. He had attended college with 'Pius' and they had gone onto become fellow curialists. Maglione died on August 22, 1944, of a heart attack.

The pope did not bother to appoint a replacement. Instead he opted to perform the duties of the S.S. himself assisted primarily by two (cardinalate spurning) *monsignori*: Domenico Tardini (who under John XXIII was S.S. and a cardinal) and Giovanni Battista Enrico Antonio Maria Montini (the future **Paul VI** (#263)).

That Pius, known for his need to be 'in control' and as an ex-S.S. himself, decided to be his own S.S. is somewhat understandable and even defensible. But, why he refused to appoint a *Camerlengo*, especially after 1954 when he had been so sick, remains yet another mystery surrounding this very private, diffident, aloof and enigmatic pope.

3) Starting the day after Pius XII's funeral, i.e., October 14, Cardinal Roncalli, wearing the obligatory purple cassock, started attending the daily pre-conclave, 'general congregation' meetings that were held in the Vatican's Consistory Hall. All cardinals in Rome are expected to attend these collegial, cardinals-only gathering where they deal with all of the logistical issues pertaining to the *sede vacante*, in particular the conclave. [General congregations prior to the funeral would have dealt with the funeral arrangements.] The general congregations attended by Cardinal Roncalli had to deal with a rather unusual and quite unappealing 'problem' – that most of the time would have been outside their normal purview. What was this 'problem' that they as a group handled with aplomb on October 20th, five days prior to the conclave?

The cardinals, in congregation, demanded the immediate resignation of Dr. Riccardo Galeazzi-Lisi [b. July 26, 1891], who had been Pius XII's *Archiatra Pontificio* (pope's personal physician) since 1939. The cardinals did not blame him, in any way, for the pope's death or the treatment he had received. Though he retained his title and the privileges to access the papal chambers he had not been involved in treating the pope during the last year of the pope's life. Neither was he blamed, explicitly, for the experimental, *'the same as that used with Jesus Christ'*, embalming procedure he had performed on the pope's body, with the help of a qualified embalmer from Naples – though the embalming went horribly awry with disastrous, extremely unpleasant results. It appeared that he had been trying to honor the pope's wishes of wanting his body and organs intact in the manner in which they had been created by God.

What rankled the cardinals and prompted this rare interregnum dismissal of a papal appointee was Dr. Galeazzi-Lisi's insistent and unabashed attempts to profit financially from the pope's death. He had sold photographs of the dead pope with an account of his death to the French *Paris Match* and to an Italian publication. He was known to be trying to sell a diary that he had compiled of the pope's last four days, along with pictures of the pope during these last days. He had also given a lurid and lengthy press conference on the exact details of how the pope's body had been embalmed. This was all too much for the cardinals. They did not wait, as would typically have been the case, for the next pope to take the necessary action. Galeazzi-Lisi acquiesced to this august body and tendered his resignation, that very same day, as had been requested. He was permanently banned from entering the Vatican City.

4) What single action by Cardinal Roncalli in the early days of his pre-conclave stay in Rome has since been interpreted as proof positive that he was indeed aware and sensitive to the possibility that he would be the next pope?

He had written a letter to his 31-year old nephew, Fr. Battista Roncalli [the son of his younger brother Giovanni Francesco] instructing him not to come to Rome. The cardinal did not want the presence of his nephew to be negatively interpreted as a precursor to the Roncalli clan descending on Rome in anticipation of what they hoped was about to transpire. Cardinal Roncalli apparently was anxious not to be seen as a hopeful; aware, no doubt, of the adage: *'he who enters the conclave as pope comes out a cardinal'*. Nepotism, particularly so with the rapacious, institutionalized 'cardinal nephews' (a euphemism in some instances for even tighter bonds) during the Renaissance era, had been a long running scourge that had marred many a papacy.

Pius XII's family, the Pacellis, were *bona fide* 'Black Nobility' – Roman aristocracy (who in this case had served the Holy See for decades) that had remained stoutly loyal to the popes during and after the Italian unification. Pius XII's older brother, Francesco [1872 to 1935], was a legal advisor to **Pius XI** (#260). He had played a key role in successfully negotiating the **1929** *Lateran Treaty* that among other things resulted in the creation of the autonomous, sovereign Vatican City State. The pope, Pius *XI*, rewarded him for his services by granting him the hereditary title of *Marquis*. The King of Italy, posthumously, made him a 'prince'. So, his three sons, Pius XII's nephews, were 'princes'. Though these titles were awarded prior to the Pacelli papacy, he, as one of XI's favorites and the Secretary of State since February 1930, was, nonetheless, indubitably, in a position to influence matters. Consequently, even before 'Pius' became pope, there was talk of resurgent nepotism.

Francesco's oldest son, Prince Carlo, during the time of his uncle's papacy, was the legal adviser to the government of the Vatican City State. He was also a member of the pope's 'kitchen cabinet' which consisted of: his longtime German housekeeper, Mother Pascalina Lehnert [1894 to 1983], his physician Galeazzi-Lisi, Galeazzi-Lisi's half-brother, two German Jesuits and German priest cum ex-politician Ludwig Kaas. The latter three were designated as the pope's secretaries and assistants. Post 1954 as the pope became increasingly unwell there was growing rumors and resentment as to the role of this kitchen cabinet in running the Vatican. Carlo, given his official role in the administration of the City State and often chosen as a papal legate, was seen, negatively, as a re-emergence of the once despised 'cardinal nephew'.

At the time of Cardinal Roncalli's letter to Don Battista, asking him to stay away from Rome, Roncalli was not a front-line *papabile*. To be fair, however, there were no clear-cut front runners during this entire *sede vacante*. Probably because of this Rome seethed with intrigue. Shrewdness was one of the cardinal's many virtues. He was also an astute analyst of Vatican politics; with three decades of hard-earned experience, some of it bruising, to hone his skills. From the start he knew that the six French cardinals favored his chances. Though his prospects as a *papabile* only started to gain traction during the second week of the *sede vacante*, the cardinal, though giving all outward appearance of indifference, appears to have realized that he may not be going back to Venice.

Three other letters written closer to the start of the conclave, one to Archbishop Montini in Milan [i.e., the future **Paul VI**], the other to Bishop Giuseppe Pazzi of Bergamo [his 'hometown'] and the third to Bishop Giuseppe Battaglia of Faenza [his nephew's bishop], do indicate that the cardinal did have some inclination that he could end up as pope. To Bishop Pazzi he said: *'but it matters little whether the new pope be of the Bergamo region or not. ...'.* To Bishop Battaglia he confided: *'... to say on no account should he* (i.e., his nephew) *move until he has my approval ...'.* He sought prayer from Archbishop Montini noting that: *'... I have great need of the help of the Saints. ...'.* Though he appears to have been pensive at the prospect, there is a definite sense that he, deep down, was not averse to the possibility, this late in his life, of being able to make a mark in the Church he so cherished.

5) During the afternoons of his pre-conclave stay in Rome, following the general congregations in the mornings, Cardinal Roncalli would try to visit some of his favorite churches in Rome. Having spent eight years in Rome, from 1900 to 1904 and 1921 to 1925, first as a young seminarian and then as a curialist, Angelo Roncalli had a history with some of the Roman churches. Early on in the *sede vacante* he visited two churches. First, **Santa Maria (Regina Cœli) in Montesanto** [St. Mary (Queen of Heaven) on the Holy Mountain], the church facing the northern gate of the Aurelian Walls, where he had been ordained 54 years ago, on August 10, **1904**. Then, the minor basilica of **(Sant'Ambrogio) e Carlo al Corso** [a church dedicated to St. Charles (Carlo) Borromeo], on Via del Corso, where he had been consecrated as the titular **Archbishop of Areopoli** on March 19, **1925**. On Wednesday, October 22, 1958, he visited the crypt of St. Peter's where he had celebrated his first Mass the day after his ordination. *[q.v. #31]* What were the last two churches that he was known to have visited, on Thursday, October 23rd, two days prior to the start of the conclave?

That Thursday, with the conclave starting on Saturday, Cardinal Roncalli visited *Sant'Andrea della Valle* (the mother church of the Theatines order) and **(Il) Gesù** [i.e., **Santissimo Nome di Gesù all'Argentina**] (the main church of the Jesuits) – two of the three celebrated 17th century 'preaching churches' in Rome. As a young seminarian Angelo Roncalli used to visit these two churches when he felt the need to unwind and be re-inspired.

More than five decades later, with much on his mind, his name getting mentioned with increasingly regularity as a *papabile*, the 76-year old future-pope was indulging in some nostalgia to brace himself for what lay ahead.

6) What were the prevailing sentiments ahead of the 1958 conclave vis-à-vis the selection of the next pope?

Pius XII's (#261) 19.6 year papacy had not only spanned the entirety of WW II but had also witnessed, to the Vatican's consternation, the rise of communism in Europe. Though he had labored, in his own diffident manner, for peace and the opposition of communism, there were many, inside and outside the Church, that felt that he had not been adequately resolute or assertive – and therefore efficacious. He had gained a reputation for being somewhat conservative, dogmatic, high-handed and aloof. He, a career curialist, had also not been very decisive in curtailing attempts by the curia to extend their degree of control over the Church. The last four years of his reign, once his health started to deteriorate, had been particularly trying for those in the upper echelons of the Church. The pope had appeared to be inconclusive and, furthermore, unwilling to deal with personnel matters. Elevations or for that matter terminations were at a virtual standstill. The Church hierarchy was allowed to stagnate.

By the time of the conclave, there was a prevailing sentiment that what the Church now needed was a compassionate, spiritual and gentle pope; one who would be more inclusive, less dogmatic, restrain the curia and favor outreach in its most universal form. They basically were looking for a new pope who would be very different from the prior one. Though Cardinal Roncalli, most likely because he was nearly 77, was not initially a *papabile*, he was an exact match to what most Catholics, including many of the cardinals, were seeking.

Pius' reign, the 11th longest to that point, had lasted nearly two decades. There were some who believed that they did not want a new pope who could also potentially have a lengthy papacy. So the option of a 'short-term,' transitional pope was also a consideration. Roncalli's age, ironically, was a positive in this scenario. At the start of a conclave, the cardinals hear a homily from a 'renowned' cleric that outlines the issues they should consider in electing the next pope. In 1958 this pre-conclave homily, delivered inside the Sistine, was given by Monsignor Francesco Bracci (78), Secretary of the Sacred Congregation for the Discipline of the Sacraments, a curialist since 1935. Bracci urged the cardinals to consider a caretaker pope, ideally one not associated with the curia. Some have suggested that Bracci, in general, couched his homily to favor Roncalli's chances.

7) Who were the *papabili* leading up to the 1958 conclave?

In marked contrast to the last time around, when Cardinal Pacelli, the *Camerlengo* as well as the Secretary of State, had been a clear favorite, there was no front-runner *per se* at the start of this *sede vacante*. So much so that the usually highly decorous *L'Osservatore Romano* [The Roman Observer], the 'semi-official' newspaper of the Holy See, normally expected to have the 'inside track', while advocating against unrestrained speculation, ended up publishing the profiles of *twenty-five* cardinals – all considered to be *papabili*.

Confoundingly, the one who would have been the shoe-in, **Giovanni Battista Montini** [the future Paul VI (#263)] having declined a cardinalate in 1952 had been sent to Milan, Italy's largest archdiocese, as its Archbishop, after thirty-two years as a distinguished and much respected 'moderate' curialist. Now, 580 years of tradition, during which only cardinals had been elected popes, stood in his way. The option of electing Montini despite him being a non-cardinal was indeed supposed to have been raised at one or more of the pre-conclave general congregations. The 'traditionalists', led by 52-year old Italian **Cardinal Giuseppe Siri**, an arch-conservative, were vehemently opposed to this – purely on the grounds that it violated 'sacred' Church tradition. As the story goes, Siri, to emphasize the finality of his feelings, slammed his hand down so hard on the table in front of him, during one of these discussuions, that his cardinal's ring shattered. Nonetheless, it is claimed (in what was apparently a rather porous conclave in terms of secrecy) that Montini did, however, receive at least two votes in one or more of the ballots on the first day of voting.

At the time of this 1958 conclave the context of the terms 'conservative' and 'liberal' were not restricted just to matters doctrinal. 'Conservatives' were vehemently anti-communist and pro-curial. 'Liberals,' on the other hand, were not as intransigent on these or any other issues.

With Montini side-lined, Italian **Cardinal Giacomo Lercaro** (67), Archbishop of Bologna, was considered the most likely of the 'liberals'. Known for his piety, empathy and resourcefulness, he among other things had created an orphanage inside his bishop's palace. He had also advocated a simplified liturgy in local vernaculars – a cause célèbre later adopted by John XXIII's Vatican II. But, his detractors tried to portray him as unpredictable and quixotic.

The Armenian, Oriental Rites cardinal, **Grégoire-Pierre XV Agagianian** (63), Patriarch of Cilicia of the Armenians and *Pro*-Prefect of the Congregation for Propagation of the Faith, who had lived in Rome for many years, was seen as a popular, doctrinally-conservative 'moderate' pick. His chances, however, were handicapped by his non-Italianity (though considered very-Roman given his long tenure in the city), but even more so by his Oriental Rites affiliation. [There has yet to be an Oriental Rites pope.] Nonetheless, with broad backing from a cross-section of the College, he was one of the original favorites with odds of 3 to 1.

French Cardinal Bishop, bearded and imposing, **Eugène Tisserant** (74), the Dean of the College of Cardinals, the *Camerlengo* of the College of Cardinals, Secretary of the Sacred Congregation for the Oriental Churches, Librarian & Archivist of the Holy Roman Church, was also thought to be a 'moderate', if not 'liberal', contender. He was well known, popular and respected within the College. Poland's **Stefan Wyszyński** (57), Archbishop of Gniezno and Warsaw, persecuted by both the Nazis and the communists, was another top-tier 'liberal' contender who had at one time commanded odds of 4 to 1. The U.S. Cardinal Francis Joseph Spellman (69), Archbishop of New York, was only a *papbile* per the U.S. media.

On the 'conservative' side, two Italians, **Cardinal Giuseppe Siri** (52), Archbishop of Genova, and **Cardinal Alfredo Ottaviani** (68), *Pro*-Secretary of the Supreme Sacred Congregation of the Holy Office [today's Congregation for the Doctrine of the Faith], were the most discussed. Both were extremely conservative.

The newly elected *Camerlengo*, Italian **Cardinal Bishop Aloisi Masella** (79), yet another curialist, the prefect of the Sacred Congregation for the Discipline of the Sacraments was also sometimes mentioned. *[q.v. #2 above]* Italian **Cardinal Ernesto Ruffini** (70), Archbishop of Palermo, was another who was touted as a possible 'conservative' candidate.

Siri's 'youth,' particularly in light of Pius' lengthy reign, was a concern; Siri, if elected, was young enough to be pope for upwards of twenty-five years.

However, as the start of the conclave grew nearer, **Cardinal Roncalli's** name started to be mentioned with increasing frequency. The U.S. Time Magazine mentioned him in their October 20th issue (five days ahead of the conclave) as: '... *is popular, devoted to charitable works, nonpolitical, lives up to his cardinal's motto:* "Obedientia et Pax"'. It is said that when the conclave started, Roncalli was the bookmakers' favorite with odds of **2:1**, the odds having been 7:1 just a couple of days earlier. Agagianian and Wyszyński were the joint second favorites. Roncalli, however, had left Venice with a return train ticket.

8) What was the 'cell' assigned to Cardinal Roncalli for the conclave?

Accommodating the cardinal electors attending the conclave, in the [at least] '3-star', five-story guest house, the *Domus Sanctæ Marthæ* (St. Martha House), located inside the Vatican, with 106 suites, 22 single rooms and one apartment, only came to be as of the **2005** conclave. This innovation to let the cardinal electors have some comfort and privacy during a conclave was made **by John Paul II** (#265), in his 1996 Apostolic Constitution *Universi Dominici Gregis* (the Lord's whole flock) that spelled out the latest *sede vacante* and conclave norms; he having participated in two 'old school' conclaves in 1978.

Prior to that, when it came to Vatican conclaves, the prior five conclaves [1878 to 1939] indeed having been at the Vatican, the cardinals would be housed in temporary, spartan, makeshift 'cells' in the Apostolic Palace; the voting taking place in the Sistine Chapel. All of the available office space in the lower floor of the Palace is co-opted to serve as cells for the cardinals. If the office space alone is not sufficient, halls or even large corridors are partitioned off, with inexpensive wood paneling, to create more cells. The conclavists were squeezed in wherever, sometimes in kitchens and even storage rooms. Space, however, was not an issue at the 1958 conclave. It was to be the smallest conclave of the 20th century, 18% smaller than the prior one in 1939.

To ensure unbiased equitability the cells are assigned to the cardinals by lot – typically with the one exception being that the *Camerlengo* is given one of the larger cells in case he has to hold any private meetings with other cardinals to deal with possible eventualities, logistical, medical or otherwise, that may occur during the conclave.

In the case of this conclave the lots for the cells were drawn on Tuesday, October 21st, four days ahead of the start. Cell **number 15**, the office of the commandant of the Noble Guard, was to be Cardinal Roncalli's. A plaque on the door stated '*Il Commandante*'. The Noble Guard, not to be confused with the Swiss Guard, was a household guard unit that had been created in 1801, by **Pius VII** (#252), as a heavy cavalry unit. Cardinal Roncalli's twenty-seven year old factotum, Guido Gusso, one of his two conclavists, was assigned a space, nearby, in a small kitchen used by the Noble Guard to make coffee. Gusso, who had arrived earlier than most, spotted a small room beyond that kitchen and had the presence of mind to quickly commandeer that room through the simple expediency of swapping around the temporarily affixed 'room numbers' attached to the two doors. A conclavist to Italian Cardinal Ernesto Ruffini who had been assigned that room ended up sleeping in the kitchen. Cardinal Roncalli's neighbor in cell number 16 was the Archbishop of Torino [Italy], Cardinal Maurilio Fossati, O.Ss.C.G.N.

9) What was the seating arrangement for the cardinal electors at this 1958 conclave – a tradition that was to soon end since this was to be the last conclave where the number of cardinals met what long held criteria?

The 1958 conclave was the penultimate where the cardinal electors sat on imposing, ornate, *canopied thrones* arrayed against the side walls of the Sistine Chapel. The canopies, as they do on all *sede vacante* insignia, signified that the Church, in the absence of a pope, was being governed, temporarily, on a collegiate basis by the College of Cardinals under the stewardship of the *Camerlengo*.

Prior to the 1939 conclave, cardinals who were created by the recently-deceased pope would have violet canopies with matching upholstery on their thrones. Cardinals who were created by prior popes would sit under a green canopy on green upholstered thrones. As of the 1939 conclave, all the canopies and upholstery were violet, independent of the seniority of the cardinals. This would have been so in 1958. Once a pope was elected the other cardinals pulled a chord to lower their canopies, so that the only open canopy was that above the pope-elect.

With John XXIII's papacy, starting at his very first consistory in December 1958, the size of the College started to increase, dramatically – the pope opting, as was his prerogative, to override **Sixtus V's** (#228) 1586 *Postquam verus* constitution that decreed that the size of the College should not exceed 70.

Consequently this was the last conclave where the number of cardinal electors was less than 70.

The next conclave, in June 1963, had 80 cardinal electors. The two 1978 conclaves each had 111 participating, though, not obviously, the same 111. The 2005 and the 2013 conclaves both had 115 electors – though this was also but a coincidence, and the participants were indeed different.

Space constraints within the Sistine precluded the possibility of having thrones once the number of cardinals participating in conclaves started to shoot beyond 80. Hence, after 1963 cardinal electors had to sit in simple, straight-backed chairs placed behind long tables.

The eighty-year age limit for cardinal electors only came to be with **Paul VI** (#263), as of January 1, 1971. So, the 1958 conclave was not the last that did not have an age limit. The last not to have had an age limit was that of 1963. Nonetheless, despite Paul VI's prohibition, 1963 was not the last conclave attended by an over eighty cardinal. German Walter Kasper, who turned eighty a week before on March 5, attended the conclave of 2013 which elected **Pope Francis** (#267). That conclave started on March 13, 2013. Whereas Paul had deemed that the 80-year cut-off would occur at the start of the conclave, John Paul II (#265), in 1996, had changed it so that it was as of the day prior to the start of the *sede vacante*. This means that cardinals who turn eighty during the *sede vacante*, ahead of the conclave, as had Kasper, are not precluded from attending.

The 1939 conclave had been the last at which Italy had more than 50% of the electors.

10) How many cardinals attended the 1958 conclave and what where the demographics?

Fifty one cardinals participated in the 1958 conclave. Two, viz. Hungarian **József Mindszenty** (66), Archbishop of Esztergom and Yugoslavian **Alojzije Stepinac** (60), Archbishop of Zagreb, were precluded from attending by Communist regimes. Two other cardinals, Italian **Celso Costantini** (82), Chancellor of the Apostolic Chancery, and **Edward Aloysius Mooney** (76), Archbishop of Detroit, died during the *sede vacante*; the former on October 17th, and the latter, unexpectedly, of a heart attack, on October 25, 1958, three hours prior to the start of the conclave. [Cardinal Roncalli paid a visit to Celso Costantini, who was recovering from prostate surgery in Rome, shortly prior to his demise. He attended his funeral on Tuesday, October 21.]

There had been fifty five cardinals on **October 9, 1958**, at the time of **Pius XII's** (#261) death. As with appointing a Secretary of State or a *Camerlengo*, Pius XII, known to be insular, had been reticent about creating cardinals. He only held two cardinal creating consistories during his long pontificate; the distraction of WW II, alone, not an adequate explanation. The table on page 15summarizes the demographics of the College at the start and end of Pius XII's papacy.

The cardinal designated in that table as being from the Soviet Union is Grégoire-Pierre XV Agagianian, the *papabile* talked about in #8 above, who was born in the Caucasus region of Russia [now Georgia]. The numbers in that table shown against Italy, Hungary, Yugoslavia & U.S.A., in the October 9th column, are highlighted and italicized to indicate the cardinals, mentioned above, who did not make it to the October 25th conclave.

So the demographics of the 51 cardinals who participated in the conclave only differ from those stated for October 9th above in that there were *four less* cardinals. Thus, there were: seventeen cardinals from Italy, two from the U.S.A. and none from Yugoslavia and Hungary. *This was the least representation from Italy, numerically, at a 20th century conclave.* No cardinals from the U.S.A. had been able to attend the 1922 conclave. Hence only having two was not a total setback.

This conclave, with 51 electors, was the smallest since the June **1846** conclave which elected **Pius IX** (#256) with but 50 cardinals in attendance.

Country	Number	Region	Count		Country	Number	Region	Count
When Pius XII Elected - 2 March 1939				19.6 years, 7,161 days	When Pius XII Died - 9 October 1958			
1 Italy	35	Europe			1 Italy	18	Europe	
2 France	6	Europe		1st Consistory	2 France	6	Europe	
3 Germany	3	Europe		18 Feb. 1946	3 Spain	3	Europe	
4 Spain	3	Europe		6.9 years since	4 Germany	2	Europe	
5 Austria	1	Europe		elected	5 Belgium	1	Europe	
6 Belgium	1	Europe		8.2 years since	6 Ireland	1	Europe	
7 Czechoslovakia	1	Europe		prior	7 Poland	1	Europe	
8 England	1	Europe			8 Portugal	1	Europe	
9 Hungary	1	Europe		32 created	9 *Hungary*	*1*	Europe	
10 Ireland	1	Europe		Av. Age = 62.9	10 *Yugoslavia*	*1*	Europe	
11 Poland	1	Europe			11 Soviet Union	1	Europe	36
12 Portugal	1	Europe	55	2nd Consistory 12 Jan. 1953				
13 U.S.A.	3	Americas		6.8 years since first	12 Brazil	3	Americas	
14 Argentina	1	Americas		5.7 years before	13 U.S.A.	*3*	Americas	
15 Brazil	1	Americas		death	14 Argentina	2	Americas	
16 Canada	1	Americas	6		15 Canada	2	Americas	
				24 created	16 Chile	1	Americas	
				Av. Age = 64.6	17 Colombia	1	Americas	
					18 Cuba	1	Americas	
					19 Ecuador	1	Americas	14
17 Syria	1	Asia	1		20 China	1	Asia	
					21 India	1	Asia	
					22 Syria	1	Asia	3
				Created 56				
				Av. Age = 63.6	23 Mozambique	1	Africa	1
				63 Died	Australia	1	Ocenia	1
	62			Net = -7	Down 7 cardinals	55		
	Average Age = 67.1 years				Average Age Up 6.3 years	Average Age = 73.4 years		

This conclave would be the first to be attended by cardinals from China, India and 'Oceania' [in this instance Australia]. The two cardinals from China and India also happened to be the firsts created for those countries; viz. Thomas Tien-ken-sin, S.V.D. (60), Archbishop of Peking and Valerian Gracias (58), Archbishop of Bombay. The Australian, Norman Thomas Gilroy (62), Archbishop of Sydney, was the first native-born cardinal of that country.

Teódosio Clemente de Gouveia (69), Archbishop of Lourenço Marques, was Mozambique's first cardinal. He would be the first African cardinal to attend a 20th century conclave. There is a possibility, however, that cardinals from North Africa may have attended some of the early conclaves. Agagianian is considered Armenian though classified as being from the 'Soviet Union', per the norms, per his place of birth. As in the case of African cardinals there is a possibility that Armenian cardinals may have attended earlier conclaves.

The average age of the 51 cardinals that attended the 1958 conclave was 73.5 years.

11) How many rounds of balloting were *supposed* to have taken place in the 1958 conclave and when did these ballots take place?

Given the mandated sacrosanct secrecy, what exactly transpires inside the Sistine Chapel during a conclave is always a mystery; supposed 'leaks' by cardinals present providing the only, hard to verify and invariably incomplete, glimpses into what is said to have happened. That the cardinals are expected to burn all of their notes at the end of each balloting 'session', along with all the ballots, in the *sfumata* (smoke) ritual, exacerbates the uncertainty (albeit with cardinals noted for their ingenuity in this matter, writing notes on their sleeves or discreetly pocketing the odd scraps of paper to augment their memory). This said, there appears to have been a fair amount of 'leaks', *bona fide* or otherwise, after the 1958 conclave – part of this probably attributable to what was unmistakably a sense of atypical euphoria (in the main) at the election of John XXIII, and a desire by the cardinals present to share the vicissitudes that they had experienced in what was a short but dynamic conclave.

Per the general consensus there were *eleven ballots* at this *four-day* conclave. Prior to the **2005** conclave, the first under **John Paul II's** 1996 *Universi Dominici Gregis* which sanctioned this option, there used to be no balloting on the first half-day of a conclave – the cardinals typically entering the Sistine in late-afternoon at the start of the conclave. In 1958 cardinals arrived at the Apostolic Palace during the afternoon of Saturday, October 25th. Cardinal Roncalli, said to have been among the vanguard, is said to have arrived around 3 p.m.

Once all the cardinals have arrived, prior to a pre-specified time, they would proceed, attired in red choir dress and chanting an invocation, to the Sistine Chapel in solemn procession, in reverse-order of precedence. Once in the Chapel, typically following a short prayer, they would take the group and individuals oaths. Then would come the famous *Extra omnes* (All out) by the Master of Papal Liturgical Ceremonies. In 1958 the 'Master' was Italian **Enrico Dante** [1884 – 1967] who held this post from 1947 to 1965. [He having joined the Office for the Liturgical Ceremonies in 1914, participating, most likely unprecedentedly, in five conclaves: viz. 1914, 1922, 1939, 1958 & 1963.] The official sequestered conclave begins at this juncture.

The pre-conclave homily, on the *'issues to be considered in the election of the pope'*, by a renowned cleric, is the first order of business. As mentioned in #6 above, in 1958 this homily was delivered by Monsignor Francesco Bracci who essentially painted a backdrop extremely favorable to the 76-year old Roncalli, albeit only as a stop-gap 'caretaker' pope. In 1958 the cardinals adjourned back to their cells in the Apostolic Palace following this homily. Later in the evening they gathered for dinner in a makeshift refractory on the first floor of the Palace. The refractory was in the Borgia Apartments – a suite of rooms used by the controversial **Alexander VI** (#215) in the late 15th century. These rooms had been lavishly frescoed by *il Pinturicchio* (Bernardino di Betto), an early 'great' of the Italian Renaissance.

Voting in 1958 thus started on Sunday, October 26. The balloting schedule, per the four-a-day norm, would have been as follows:

Sunday, October 26:

2 in the morning. Black *sfumata*. 2 in the afternoon. Black *sfumata*. [4 ballots]

Monday, October 27:

2 in the morning. Black *sfumata*. 2 in the afternoon. Black *sfumata*. [4 ballots]

Tuesday, October 28:

2 in the morning. Black *sfumata*. 1 in the afternoon. **White *sfumata*.** [3 ballots]

On the last day of the conclave black smoke, undeniably, was seen starting at 11:10 a.m., Rome time. This would have been from the burning of the papers from rounds nine and ten. At **5:08 p.m.**, that afternoon, white smoke was spotted. The official *Habemus Papam* announcement, by Italian Cardinal Nicola Canali (84), the Grand Penitentiary and the protodeacon (as of 1946), was heard exactly one hour later. The new pope appeared on the balcony twelve minutes after that.

[Per some accounts, often bandied by advocates of the so called *'Siri Thesis'*, i.e., that *papabile* Cardinal Giuseppe Siri gained the necessary majority and as such should have been the new pope, the *sfumata* on Sunday evening and Monday 'morning' was white; that on Sunday night supposedly lasting for upwards of twenty minutes – so much so that at 6 p.m. Vatican Radio, obviously in error, claimed that a new pope has been elected. Others contend that in each instance, as was also the case on Sunday 'morning', there was indeed some white smoke that quickly turned to black. *Sfumata* that changes color (even with the use of modern chemicals to ensure better consistency) is not uncommon and is part-and-parcel of the conclave mystique. This author has not been able to find any credible proof that the Sunday night white smoke lasted for over twenty minutes and that Radio Vatican claimed that a new pope had been elected. Film footage of the Monday morning event, now available on YouTube, does show that the initial puff of smoke was white but turned to black as the next puff came out.]

12) What is the conjecture as to the supposed voting at the 1958 conclave?

The same caveat as that in #11 above applies in that any and all accounts of what happened inside a 'modern' conclave has to be based upon supposed 'leaks' whose true veracity can never be satisfactorily established. However, in the case of the 1958 conclave there is at least one revealing data point by an impeachable source, viz. the new pope himself. He made it three months later while visiting the Armenian College of Rome: *'... names of Roncalli and Agagianian ... went up and down like two ceci (chickpeas) in boiling water'*. This at least confirms that Grégoire-Pierre XV Agagianian, one of the original pre-conclave favorites, was indeed a contender during the conclave – albeit, per the leaks, only during the ballots on Sunday afternoon and Monday morning.

The supposed voting, as best as can be deciphered through the sifting and rationalization of multiple, sometimes inconsistent sources, was as follows. The backgrounds of the names mentioned were discussed in #7 above. Bear in mind that the *'Siri Thesis'*, *if* credible, is said to have happened during the first two days of balloting, i.e., Sunday and Monday.

Per Pius XII's new formula the necessary majority for election, for the first time in history, was to be two-thirds plus one (rounded up). With 51 cardinals participating this meant that a candidate needed a minimum of **35 votes** to be pope-elect.

1st Day of Voting: Sunday, October 26 [Feast of Christ the King]:

Voting on this first day, as is often the case, was scattered and unthematic. The first round, if not also the second, per a custom that had gained traction over the last century and a half, appears to have been devoted to felicitation – with the electors choosing to initially honor distinguished, but not strictly *papable*, colleagues. The French contingent, at a minimum, honored Tisserant, the Dean. The Italians showed their appreciation for Ruffini, while the Americans did so for Spellman. Wyszyński, who had prevailed through much, was also duly acknowledged. Roncalli is said to have voted for Italian Cardinal **Valerio Valeri**, his predecessor as nuncio to France. In 1944 he had to be recalled because the liberated French, under Charles de Gaulle, objected to his supposed cooperation with the *'Vichy France'*, the German mandated (nominal) rule of France during 1940 to 1944. *[q.v. #56.]* Roncalli is said to have been expressing his opinion that Valeri had been unjustly tarred. Roncalli's was apparently the only vote cast for Valeri in this round (though, obviously, this is all hypothetical in that there was no mechanism at this conclave to identify who voted for whom).

During the afternoon session there had also been some votes for Agagianian, Roncalli, Ottaviani, Ruffini and Lecaro. It is widely believed that Montini, true to expectations, received at least two votes in one or more of the rounds that day – despite him not being a cardinal. There is a claim, at odds with other reports, that on the fourth ballot Agagianian had got eighteen votes and Roncalli 20. Others maintain that Roncalli did not receive this level of support until the next day.

What is fairly conclusive, however, is that Siri, though he probably did get a few scattered votes, certainly did not receive 35 (or more) votes during round three or four that Sunday to make him pope-elect – as claimed in the *'Siri Thesis'*.

2nd Day of Voting: Monday, October 27:

This appears to have been the pivotal day of this conclave. Ottaviani, the 68-year old, the initial candidate backed by the 'traditionalists' and curialists, had run out of steam. So had Ruffini and Lecaro. The curialists, most of them also conservatives, now threw their lot behind the newly elected *Camerlengo*, a fellow curialist, Cardinal Masella. He is said to have garnered nearly half of the votes, i.e., ~25, on the second round of balloting that morning. His prospects looked promising at that stage.

Those opposed to curial control of the Church then started to vote for Roncalli, in earnest. They were led by the six-strong French contingent – Roncalli having been an immensely popular nuncio to France from 1944 to 1953. The Dean, Tisserant, though a curialist of longstanding, was a patriot at heart, and one, moreover, very disillusioned with the how the curia, under Pius, had set out to oppressively control the Church. It is said that starting on this second day, he, masterfully, started to forge together a coalition, aided by **Cardinal Maurice Feltin** (75), Archbishop of Paris, around the nucleus of French votes, to back Roncalli as a counter to the curial favorites. Feltin and Roncalli were firm friends from their days in Paris; as was Roncalli and Tisserant.

Agagianian, after going *'up and down like a chickpea'*, peaked in the afternoon, after enjoying some early support in the prior rounds. Masella also faltered after lunch; possibly due to canvassing by the Tisserant coalition during the break. The conservatives then countered, yet again, by switching their votes to the youthful Siri. But his age, 52, was a definite impediment. The votes cast for him peaked below the necessary majority, contrary to what his many fans like to claim. It is also noteworthy that Siri peaked on Monday, rather than on Sunday – the night of the supposed twenty minutes of white *sfumata*.

On the eighth round of balloting, at the end of this second day, Roncalli, had between *twelve to fifteen votes*. This was, of course, well short of the thirty-five required. However, unlike with the others, Roncalli's tally had not tapered during the day. Instead, thanks to the efforts of the French, he had gained momentum. So, to his supposed amazement, he left the Sistine that evening the apparent favorite – though he, himself, had never during the course of the conclave tried to promote his claim to the papacy.

The French led coalition must have been busy during dinner. Nearly all the accounts agree that during the night Roncalli was visited in his cell, No. 15, by quite a few electors. These visitors who were all pledging their support for him included a few staunch 'conservatives' such as Ruffini and Ottaviani. It appears that some of the 'conservatives' now believed that Roncalli (given his age) would be an ideal, 'short-term,' transitional pope. There are even claims that a number of these cardinals, Ottaviani, for one claiming credit, suggested that Roncalli, when pope, should convene a new Church council.

The bottom line here is that Roncalli, before he retired for the night, knew that he would most likely be pope the next day.

Hence, he had some time to think about the name by which he wished to be known, and to even write some notes to explain his selection. It is said, furthermore, that he borrowed an *Annuario Pontifico* (Pontifical Yearbook) to research the usage of that name.

3rd Day of Voting: Tuesday, October 28

The nocturnal bonhomie notwithstanding, it took another three rounds of balloting before Roncalli finally got the necessary majority – and even then with over a dozen dissenters. During the first two rounds on Tuesday the notion of an affable, non-curial, ex-diplomat, 'caretaker' pope -- well-liked across Europe -- had gained currency; Roncalli by then having the votes of all of the moderates and even some curialists. At lunch he was in the lead, but short of the majority.

The first ballot after lunch gave Cardinal Roncalli the requisite majority. His final tally is thought to have been in the region of **38**, with ten or so 'conservatives' continuing, doggedly, to back Siri.

38 votes represent 74.5% of the electors; the majority for election having been 68.6%. The pope is said to have stated that he again cast his vote for Valeri in these last rounds. If the Roncalli vote is discounted, the new popes enjoyed 76% of the votes. John XXIII was the first pope, ever, to be elected per a two-thirds plus one majority requirement.

John XXIII, at **76 years, 11 months** & 3 days [28,095 days], was the ***fifth oldest*** pope to be elected since 1400 [with no reliable birth dates available for popes prior to that]. He was the oldest pope to be elected since **Clement XII** (#247), on July 12, **1730**, *228 years* previously; Clement having been older by sixteen months.

13) Upon accepting his canonical election, the new pope was asked by the Dean of the College of Cardinals, Cardinal Tisserant, as to what name he wished to be known by. He replied ***'Vocabor Johannes'*** (I will be called John).

This name had not been used by a pope since the time of the opportunistic, schematic, onetime *bona fide* buccaneer, antipope John (XXIII) [1410 to 1415]. He had been an antipope during the latter stages of the Great Western Schism that, in the end, had three competing claimants for the papacy.

Media reports the next day stated that the new pope at this stage took out some notes from within his vestments and made a statement explaining his choice of name. The English translation of this statement, now widely available, starts as follows: *'I choose John ... a name sweet to us because it is the name of our father, dear to me because it is the name of the humble parish church where I was baptized, the solemn name of numberless cathedrals scattered throughout the world, including our own Basilica [St. John Lateran]. Twenty-two Johns of indisputable legitimacy have [been Pope], and almost all had a brief pontificate. We have preferred to hide the smallness of our name behind this magnificent succession of Roman Popes'*. There are *three incongruities* in this statement. What are they?

The 'easiest' of these has to do with the 'twenty-two Johns' statement. Though he would indeed correctly be '**XXIII**' there had not been, per official Vatican records, twenty-two legitimate Johns. There had only been twenty *prior* to that 1958 conclave. There had never been a *John XX* – pope or antipope. *XVI* was an antipope in 997 - 998 and the next John, remissly, chose to be John XVII (#141) rather than reclaiming the discredited ordinal, as would have been proper.

The eminently scholarly, polymathic, Portuguese medical doctor, Pedro Julião, personal physician to **Gregory** *'father of modern conclaves'* **X** (#185), was elected pope in September 1276, in Viterbo [once a favorite papal summer respite cum refuge]. His election followed the 38-day papacy of **Hadrian V** (#187) which had come on the heels of the five month papacy of **Innocent V** (#186). So the Portuguese doctor, the respected author of a textbook on Aristotelian logic, was the third pope elected in 1276, Gregory having died, on his way back from the landmark Second Council of Lyon [France], in January of that year. In 1273, ahead of the Council, which he attended, Pedro Julião had been created, by Gregory, the Cardinal Bishop of Frascati. This bishopric, particularly so in those days, was associated with the ancient Roman suburb of Tusculum and its ruling family. **John XIX** (#145) was from Tusculum and, moreover, had been from the ruling family. Most likely due to this Tusculum connection Pedro Julião opted to be a 'John'. He was aware that the numbering of the 'Johns' had gone awry at some point – if nothing else with XVII. Thus, in effect, to reset the numbering, he decided to skip 'XX' and be 'XXI'.

So John XXIII's claim of *'twenty-two Johns of indisputable legitimacy'* is a bit of a stretch. He would have been on firmer ground if he had omitted the part about legitimacy.

The assertion that *'almost all had a brief pontificate'* also has an element of some poetic license. **John XXII** (#197) was pope for 18.3 years; **John III** (#61) for 13 years; **John VII** (#108) & **John XV** (#138) for at least 10 years; **John XIX** (#145) for 8.5 years; **John XII** (#131) for 8.4 years and **John XIII** (#134) for 6.9 years. The average length of the papacies of the twenty 'Johns' that preceded Roncalli was **5.87 years**. The average length of the 261 papacies before him was **7.13 years**. So, in that respect he was indeed correct; though 30% of Johns surpassed the average. 'Johns', in this context, were nonetheless definitely below average. But, the sixteen 'Benedicts' at 5.27 years, the eight 'Bonifaces' at 5.33 years and the ten 'Stephens' at 2.56 years had done worse.

The most puzzling statement is: *'it is the name of the humble parish church where I was baptized ...'.* Two of his biographers and other sources maintain, unequivocally, that he was baptized in the small parish church of **Santa Maria di Brusicco,** not far from his parent's house in **Sotto il Monte** [10 miles southwest of Bergamo]. His parent's house was in the locality of 'Brusicco' adding further credence as to where he was indeed baptized. The future pope was born on a cold, rainy day in November 25, 1881 and was baptized later on that very day by the parish priest Francesco Rebuzzini; his great-uncle, his grandfather's brother, Zaverio Roncalli was the godfather. *[q.v. Chapter II.]* Nearly twenty-three years later, on August 15, 1904, on the Feast of the Assumption, he celebrated Mass, at this very church; his first Mass in his home town.

There is indeed an older *San Giovanni Battista* parish church on a nearby hillside. That was most likely where his father 'Giovanni Battista' was baptized. With much on his mind, Cardinal Roncalli most likely mixed up the two local churches.

14) What was the long cherished conclave tradition, inexplicably overlooked by his two predecessors, viz. **Pius XI** (#260) & **Pius XII** (#261), that was joyfully reinstated by the newly elected **John XXIII**?

The tradition was that of placing the new pope's no longer required red cardinal's *zucchetto* on the head of the Secretary of the Conclave, when he kneels in front of the pope to present him with his new, white silk papal *zucchetto*. This is supposed to symbolize that the new pope will reward the Secretary, at a later date, with a cardinalate.

The white zucchetto ritual takes place soon after the new pope has stated the name by which he wants to be known. This happens ahead of the pope retiring to the small sacristy, decorated in red, on the left side of the Sistine, colloquially known as the *sala delle lacrime* (room of tears) to be vested in his new, albeit temporary, white ('ivory') papal vestments, topped with a red cape.

The 'Secretary of the Conclave' is one of the non-cardinal officials that must be present at a conclave -- though not in the Sistine during voting. The Secretary of the *College of Cardinals* is by default the Secretary of a *Conclave*. Traditionally the Secretary of the *Congregation for Bishops*, a curialist appointed by the pope, is the Secretary of the College of Cardinals and thus the conclave. [In other words, the Congregation for Bishops, the College of Cardinals and conclaves share the same person as their Secretary.]

In 1958 the Secretary was Italian Monsignor Alberto di Jorio (74).

On December 15, 1958, at his very first cardinal creating consistory, John created Jorio (who was not a bishop at that point) a cardinal deacon. Jorio was the twentieth named out of the twenty-three created at that consistory.

15) Is it at all conceivable that Cardinal Giuseppe Siri, per the *'Siri Thesis'*, received thirty-five or more votes at some point during the 1958 conclave and was elected pope only for that election to be overruled and overturned?

The 'Siri Thesis' does not 'compute' at multiple levels. Per the thesis, not only was he elected, but he assumed the name Gregory XVII. Given conclave protocol this claim, by itself, provides a very definitive clue as to how far things had supposedly progressed. As discussed above a new pope does not assume a name until he has formally and irrevocably accepted the papacy. So if Siri had already assumed a name, he was pope – the coronations but a symbolic formality. Once pope that person, at once, is very much on a different plane to the cardinals that elected him. That is fact. At that juncture it would be very difficult for the cardinals to apply any pressure on the pope. So, that is one aspect that is troubling. It would have been easier to formulate a more credible retraction scenario if it was said to have taken place before the pope-elect, Siri, accepted his election; i.e., before the magical word *'Accepto'* (I accept) was uttered.

Then there is always the thorny issue of how and when Cardinal Siri got the thirty-five votes. None of the 'leaked' accounts show him getting anywhere close to that, at anytime, nor scenarios where he was picking up momentum to sweep the field. Moreover, in the thesis, Siri got the votes at the end of the first day of voting or at the latest by lunch the next. But, by all accounts Siri did not even get sufficient votes to reach a tipping point. And this makes sense. He was fifty-two years old. If elected he had the potential to have been pope for even longer than Pius XII. To compound matters this was a notably elderly electorate with an average age of 73.5 years. It just does not sound credible that the traditionalists would have favored such a youngster when they had alternatives such as Masella, Ruffini or even Ottaviani.

The thesis has also vacillated as to what caused the cardinals to 'demand' Gregory XVII's immediate abdication so soon after they had elected him. To begin with it was presented as a case of the cardinals suffering an acute attack of buyer's remorse. Then some journalistic sensationalism got injected. The Soviets supposedly threatened the cardinals and the Vatican with a nuclear attack! A kind of imperial veto on steroids. But, again the timing is a problem. 'Gregory XVII' had yet to appear on the St. Peter's balcony. So the outside world had yet to be told of Siri's election. In order for the Soviets to make that threat they would require two-way communication, via radio, telephone or semaphores, with those still in conclave. While there has been plenty of intrigue about radio devices smuggled into 20th century conclaves, one has to ask why the Soviets would wait until after the election to make such a threat. Would it not have been much simpler and more effective to make their supposed objection to Siri be known to the cardinals prior to the conclave? So, all in all, the thesis just does not ring true.

16) John XXIII, in what would become a practice emulated by **John Paul I** (#264), **John Paul II** (#265), **Benedict XVI** (#266) and **Francis** (#267), asked the cardinal electors to spend another night with him 'in conclave' so that he could seek counsel from them over dinner in a family atmosphere. The pope seeking this extension caused some unexpected disruptions to the proceedings. This necessitated the new pope having to make two early pronouncements. What transpired and what did the pope have to say?

Now that he was pope he realized that he would not be going back to the *Domus Mariae*. He would also be spending that night in the Apostolic Palace – though he did move out of the *Il Commandate's* office to the long vacant first floor apartment suite of the Secretary of State. So, ahead of appearing on the balcony to greet the public, he requested Guido Gusso to return to the *Domus Mariae* and retrieve his belongings; he was particularly anxious for a pair of comfortable shoes. The *Camerlengo* (and possibly the Dean) would not let Guido leave since the *Habemus Papam* (We have a pope) announcement had yet to be made. When Guido went back to the pope to say that he had been prevented from leaving, the new pope, in what would become his trademark warm and humorous manner, instructed Guido to inform the *Camerlengo* that the new pope, in need of his shoes, had given him a special dispensation to leave the conclave. The pope had already determined the vast powers now at his disposal!

When the doors of the Sistine Chapel were opened to let Guido out, a number of curial prelates who had been standing outside rushed into see who had been elected. This was a breach of conclave etiquette, if not protocol. The standard punishment for any such breach was excommunication and these prelates were supposedly excommunicated, on the spot, by either the *Camerlengo* or the Dean. Sometime later the new pope heard about the unfortunates that had been excommunicated for their enthusiasm. Now adding aplomb to his characteristic good nature he sent the excommunicated a message, using the royal 'we', that the pope would soon be using his new influence to absolve them of their punishment.

Figure 4: John XXIII (#262), the pope, October 4, 1962.

II.
THE YOUTH

Angelo Giuseppe Roncalli was born at around 10:15 on the morning of Friday, November 25, 1881. He was born in a 300-year old, four-family farmhouse at 42 Via Brusicco in **Sotto il Monte** in the Lombard diocese of **Bergamo** in north-central Italy. Sotto il Monte (beneath the mountain), now called **Sotto il Monte Giovanni XXIII** (after its most famous son), lying twenty miles northeast of Milan and eight miles due west of Bergamo.

Angelo Giuseppe Roncalli's parents were **Giovanni Battista Roncalli** [1854 – 1935] and **Marianna Giulia** (Mazzolla) [1854 – 1939]. Both his parents would have then been '27' when he was born. Giovanni Battista was a tenant farmer (*mezzadro*) who at that time worked ~8 acres of land belonging to the Counts Morlani of Bergamo [Ottavio Morlani in particular]. They, in addition, had the rights to the milk produced by four to six cows that they kept in stalls on the ground floor of their farmhouse. The rest of the tenancy was paid mainly in the form of veal and silkworm byproducts.

The farmhouse where Angelo was born was a patriarchal household headed by his great-uncle (and godfather) **Zaverio Roncalli**, a lifelong bachelor [referred to as *Barba* (the beard), not only for his appearance but in part to also denote his status as the head of the household]. The family of one of Angelo's paternal uncles shared that residence.

17) What is considered to be the origins of the name 'Roncalli' and how far back can their lineage be traced?

As soon as he became the unlikely pope there was a tremendous amount of curiosity on the part of the public, as was to be expected, as to the antecedents of this rotund, robust and gregarious newcomer, supposedly from farming stock. This further accentuated by the fact that he had succeeded a lean, delicate and reserved Roman aristocrat from the *'Black Nobility'*. Suffice to say that extensive research was therein conducted by journalists and academics to establish the pope's heritage.

The name 'Roncalli' is thought to originate from the Italian *'ronchi'*: a terrace cut into the side of a hill to permit the plantation of grapevines – a feature not uncommon in the winegrowing but hilly region of Lombard. If so, then 'Roncalli' was either a place or vocational name, a family that in some way was associated with a *'ronchi'*.

Figure 5: The heavily restored *Camaitino* as it is today, serving as a museum.

source: PIME

The earliest 'Roncalli' that can be traced to the Sotto il Monte region is a Martino Roncalli who settled in the area c. 1430 having come across from the *Valle Imagna* area on the foothills of the Alps of Bergamo, ~75 miles directly north of Sotto il Monte. *Valle Imagna*, noted for its scenic beauty, now a year round resort area, was a hotbed, from the late 13th century to the mid 15th century, in the often vicious *Guelphs* and *Ghibellines* [i.e., pope vs. Holy Roman Emperor] conflicts. A particularly nasty rebellion started in 1407 and lasted until 1443. It is thus possible that this primo-Roncalli decided to find safer pastures during this uprising. This Martin, credited as 'landed gentry', built himself a substantial dwelling called *Camaitino* or *Ca' Maitino* [i.e., Casa Martino] when he got to Sotto il Monte. It, heavily restored, is now a John XXIII museum; the exhibits including some of the gifts given to the pope by Heads of State.

The 'Roncallis' somehow managed over the ensuing centuries, albeit well before the time of Angelo's grandparents, to lose possession of *Camaitino* and the land it stood on. In **1925**, while spending some time in Sotto il Monte, awaiting his episcopal consecration prior to his posting to Bulgaria, Fr. Roncalli, well aware of its provenance, took out a long-term lease on *Camaitino*. He wanted it to be his new base, a retreat, on his future visits home; but, moreover, he wanted it to be a comfortable residence for two of his sisters Ancilla and Maria Elisa. He continued to rent this house until he became pope in 1958. By then both those sisters had passed away. At one stage Archbishop Roncalli had considered buying it and making it an orphanage, but this never came to pass.

18) How many brothers and sisters did Angelo Giuseppe Roncalli have?

A total of *twelve*, he the *fourth* of thirteen – the *oldest* of the *boys*.

	Name	Born	Died	~ lifespan (years)
1	*Maria Caterina*	1877	1883	6
2	*Teresa*	1879	1954	75
3	*Ancilla*	1880	1953	73
4	**Angelo Giuseppe**	**1881**	**1963**	**82**
5	Francesco Zaverio	1883	1976	93
6	*Maria Elisa*	1884	1955	71
7	*Assunta Casilda*	1886	1980	94
8	Domenico Giuseppe	1888	1888	0
9	Alfredo	1889	1972	83
10	Giovanni Francesco	1891	1956	65
11	*Enrica*	1893	1918	25
12	Giuseppe Luigi	1894	*post 1963*	69 -->
13	Luigi	1896	1898	2

Three of his siblings died young. Though the date of his passing remains elusive, Giuseppe Luigi was alive in 1963. The eighth child, Domenico Giuseppe, only lived for twenty-one days. Angelo would have been six at the time.

'Giuseppe' [Joseph], possibly the name of a grandfather, was shared by three of the siblings.

Three of his brothers, Francesco Zaverio, Alfredo and Giuseppe Luigi, as well as his sister Assunta, attended John XXIII's (#262) coronation on Tuesday, **November 4, 1958**, feast day of the celebrated Counter-Reformation reformer Charles Borromeo (one of the pope's favorite saints). They were also at his deathbed in **June 1963**.

Eight predeceased Angelo (as shown highlighted in the table above). One sister and one brother lived to be over ninety, while another brother exceeded the pope's lifespan by a year. Three of his sisters lived to be over seventy, though Enrica, the youngest, died at twenty-five of cancer as WW I was coming to an end.

As a youngster the would be pope was affectionately referred to as *'Angelino'* by his family.

19) Who were those influential in young Angelo's exposure to socially-responsible Catholicism and the virtues of conscientious study?

His mother, very devout, instilled in him, very early on, a sense of awe and wonder in Christianity, especially a devotion to the Virgin Mary. But, she had her hands full. Francesco Zaverio was born within eighteen months of Angelo while her oldest, Maria Caterina, was to die around the same time. A procession of eight other kids arrived on a regular basis, each within two years of the other.

Angelo's godfather, Zaverio 'the beard', was in his late fifties, probably fifty-seven or fifty-eight, when Angelo was born; Angelo the first boy of his generation in that household. Zaverio, though entirely self-educated, was the intellectual in the family; a patriarch not only committed to the spiritual and civic wellbeing of his household but one also determined to ensure that they, despite their arduous labors, were aware of what was happening in the world outside of their hillside commune. Most evenings, radios a thing of the future, he would either read aloud from the Bible or from one of the many Catholic periodicals he subscribed to (probably his only luxury and indulgence).

One of these publications was the *Salesian Bulletin* published by (now Saint) Don Bosco [1815 – 1888] of nearby Turin, the founder of the *Salesians* and a tireless crusader for the betterment of children's lives, in particular for those from poor or disadvantaged families. Zaverio was also very involved in *Azione Cattolica* (Catholic Action) a non-political lay organization under the direct control of bishops, which originated in Bergamo in 1878. Its goal was to promote social wellbeing of common people through a pervading Catholic influence over society. Zaverio made sure that the rest of the family appreciated the goals and values of this pioneering movement (at a time when the papacy, in Rome, bitter over the loss of the Papal States in 1870, chose to isolate itself from the Italian citizenry). So to Zaverio, with his commitment to the *Salesian* and *Azione Cattolica* beliefs, Catholicism was not just piety, sacraments and doctrine, it was an all-encompassing ethical way of life embodying compassion, selflessness and obligations.

As his younger siblings started to appear, Angelo started spending increasingly more time with his great-uncle. Zaverio would provide him with his initial inspiration, guidance and instruction on all matters spiritual and educational. Angelo would grow up greatly influenced by his great-uncle's brand of all encompassing Catholicism for the good of the soul and society.

In 1888 Zaverio, on his own, by rail, made a pilgrimage to Rome to attend the fiftieth anniversary celebrations of **Leo XIII's** (#257) priestly ordination; the only one from Sotto il Monte to do so. Angelo, not even eight years old as yet, desperately wanted to go but was, rightly, deemed too young.

Another early mentor, who was a guarding and guiding spirit during the first decades of his life, was the local parish priest that had baptized him on the very day of his birth, the pastor of Santa Maria of Brusicco, **Don Francesco Rebuzzini**. He was Angelo's first teacher, in grades 1 to 3 in Sotto il Monte's only school, a one-room affair with a single bench for each grade. He got Angelo started in Latin and ensured that he was Confirmed, at the age of seven years and one month, in the neighboring parish of Carvico, on February 13, **1889**, by Bishop Gaetano Guindani [1834 – 1904] of Bergamo. [Though it would be another twenty-one years till **Pius X** (#258) with his *Quam Singulari* would change the 'age of discretion' from twelve to seven, it was common practice in the late 19th century for bishops to have local discretion to perform early Confirmations.] Angelo received his first Communion forty-six days later on March 31st.

It was also Don Francesco that determined which schools the young Angelo should attend and, moreover, made sure that he was accepted by those schools. It has been widely claimed that Angelo Roncalli had admitted that he could not remember a time when he did not want to be a priest. It is also known that Fr. Rebuzzini had once joked with the young Angelo as to the sartorial difficulties of being a priest during hot Italian summers (well ahead of the days of air conditioning). Nonetheless, it has to be assumed that this local parish priest was the impetus for steering the future-pope towards a life in the Church.

Both Zaverio Roncalli and Don Francesco Rebuzzini now have roads named after them in the Brusicco area of Sotto il Monte Giovanni XXIII. There is also a road named *Camaitino*.

20) Around the time he was six (possibly a bit older), Angelo's extended family moved from Via Brusicco to a well preserved, substantial farmhouse, built in the 17th century, on twenty-seven acres of land. Angelo Roncalli would consider this farmstead 'home' for the remainder of his life. What was this farm?

The **Colombra Farm** (*La Colombera*). His father, Giovanni Battista, obtained it, initially on a lease, from the predominant property owners of the area the Counts Morlani of Bergamo. In 1921, using money he had saved as a down payment and a mortgage from a bank in Bergamo, Giovanni Battista was able to buy the property, along with the twenty-seven acres of land, from the Morlanis. Over the next nineteen years, Angelo, off and on, but with increasingly larger contributions over time, helped pay off this mortgage.

The two-story, red tile roofed farmhouse, with a porch, that spanned two sides of a red brick courtyard had eighteen rooms. It had faded yellow stucco walls built of local stone. Sheds for animals occupied another side of the courtyard. In time Cardinal Roncalli's coat of arms would be painted on the wall below the porch. Later still an earthenware 'lion of San Marco', the symbol of Venice, was hung on the opposite wall.

Following Giovanni Battista's demise, in 1935, aged 81, the ownership of this farm went, jointly, to Angelo's three surviving brothers, Francesco Zaverio, Alfredo and Giuseppe Luigi. Around 1944, using his own savings and a special 'gift' from the pope, Pius XII, [probably a 'bonus' for his sterling efforts in Greece and his soon to be promotion to nuncio], Archbishop Roncalli purchased another farm, of about ten acres, **Le Gerole**, not far from La Colombra, with joint ownership across *Fraterna Roncalli* – i.e., he and all of his surviving siblings, irrespective of gender. At that time there were twenty-four Roncallis, across multiple families and generations, living together at La Colombra.

Both farms, well maintained and productive, were in Roncalli hands long after the pope's death.

21) In **1890**, following three years at the one-room school in Sotto il Monte, Angelo's teacher and early mentor Fr. Rebuzzini along with his grand-uncle Zaverio arranged for him to attend another school. Where was this, and what was drilled into him, quite painfully it appears, at this school?

It was another one-room parish school, this one in neighboring Carvico (where he was Confirmed), just to the west of Sotto il Monte, taught by the local priest, Don Pietro Bolis. Don Bolis was a locally renowned Latin scholar and a strict disciplinarian. Though he did not need it, Angelo's father gave the priest *carte blanche* permission *'not to spare the rod'* if Angelo fell short of expectations. Consequently, Angelo would later reminisce that at Carvico he translated aloud Book I of Julius Caesar's *Commentarii de Bello Gallico* (Commentaries on the Gallic War) at a rate of one page per clout on the head. Maybe this was what got him thinking about the benefits of having liturgy and the Mass in the local vernacular as opposed to Latin! [He actually started with Turkish. *q.v. #52.*]

22) Luckily Angelo's tenure at Carvico with the frequent physical admonishments was to be short. In **October 1891** again at the instigation of Fr. Rebuzzini he would move on, as day scholar, a few weeks short of his tenth birthday, to a faculty-based, multi-classroom secondary school – actually a Catholic pre-junior seminary. What was this Catholic 'College', what would be its significance in the future-pope's life and how well did he do, academically, while there?

This pre-junior seminary was the ***Collegio Convitto Maschile Celana*** (Celana Male Boarding School), in **Celena**, in the Valley of San Marino. It was sprawling and large, imposing and somewhat monasterial [with a cloistered look]. Though it was only about *5 miles* directly north of Sotto il Monte, Monte San Giovanni (Mount St. John), however, intervened. So to get to Celana from Sotto il Monte, one had to take a circuitous route, to the west of San Giovanni, through the village of Villa D'adda. This increased the distance by a couple of miles.

The College had been founded in 1579 by **Carlo (Charles) Borromeo**, Cardinal Archbishop of Milan from 1564 to 1584 [who was beatified in 1602 and canonized in November 1610]. Charles Borromeo, noted for his zeal to see a well-educated cadre of clerics to spearhead the Counter-Reformation, created this seminary, which was in his diocese, to cater for families that were at that time under the political rule of the Republic of Venice but were dependent on Milan for their ecclesiastic needs. Two hundred years later the College was taken over by the local authorities and put under the control of the Bishop of Bergamo to serve as a secondary school for children of that region.

Though Angelo was most likely well aware of St. Charles Borromeo before he started attending Celna, attending this College gave him a tangible affinity with this storied, much venerated, pillar of the Church. Over the next two decades St. Charles Borromeo would be a constant leitmotif in Angelo's life – with the future pope often stating that St. Charles Borromeo was one of his favorite saints. One of the reasons he brought forward the date of his papal coronation to Tuesday November 4th, 1958 (rather than having it on Sunday, November 9th) was because that was the feast day of this saint. [The other reason was to permit the overseas cardinals who had been in Rome for nearly three weeks to get back home as quickly as possible.]

It would appear that the possibility of Angelo staying at Celana as a border was never considered – most likely due to financial considerations. Most of the other students at the College, in addition to being older, were 'better-heeled' than the tenant farmer's son. To avoid the long trip back and forth from the Colombra farm, Angelo during that first winter in 1891 stayed with some distant relatives in the village of Pontida roughly halfway in-between – going home at weekends. But, in the early spring of 1892 the lady of the house was embroiled in some minor scandal and Angelo's mother not wanting her angelic son to be in any way sullied immediately brought him home.

For the next few months Angelo walked to school and back again, daily, leaving early in the morning around 6 a.m. and returning late in the evening when it was getting dark – sometimes stopping for refreshments at the homes of relatives on the way back. Often during parts of his arduous journey, some of it across rugged terrain, he would have the company of other boys who were attending various schools in that area. But usually, especially in the mornings, Angelo tried to read some of his school books while walking because he was too tired to do any reading when he got home at night. Many a time during the summer months he would walk barefoot, his shoes slung over his shoulders, to avoid wearing them out too quickly.

Angelo, at best, was a mediocre 'C' student at Celana – his youth and, even more so, the physical toil of his daily trek proving to be impediments. As was always the case in those days Don Francesco Rebuzzini was, luckily, at hand to take care of Angelo. He tutored Angelo during that summer of **1892** and made sure that he got accepted in **November** to the **junior seminary in Bergamo** (also founded by St. Charles Borromeo), located in the *Città Alta* (ancient city) section, this time, albeit, as a border – though the future-pope, about to turn eleven, had yet to categorically state that he wanted to be a priest.

23) Who financed Angelo's board & tuition at the junior seminary in Bergamo as of the fall of 1892?

It would appear that Don Francesco Rebuzzini, devoted to the young Roncalli and having realized early on that this was indeed an atypical talent, contributed in someway, though it is not clear whether as the pastor of a rural farming community he had much income (or resources) at his disposal. What he also did do, however, was to find a benefactor for Angelo who too appreciated his potential. This benefactor was a member of the Counts Morlani of Bergamo, the Roncalli's landlords – **Fr. Giovanni Morlani** [1870 – 1939], at the time a canon at the Cathedral of Bergamo. He would go onto be a canon at St. Peter's at the Vatican [albeit well before the time of the ascendancy of his protégé].

24) The early 1890s, when Angelo enrolled in the junior seminary in Bergamo [about eight miles directly east of Sotto il Monte], were still tumultuous days in the *'unified since 1870'* Italy; rampant Italian nationalism defying what had for so long been earthly rule by the Church. The popes, by choice, but in high dudgeon, were prisoners of the Vatican, and forbade Catholics from participating in Italian politics. Within this climate of sociopolitical discord, Bergamo, already the focal point of *Azione Cattolica*, and now under the stewardship of an inspired and inspiring bishop, Camillo Guindani, began to emerge as the center for a new brand of socially-conscious Catholicism. The Vatican's semi-official newspaper, *L'Osservatore Romano*, started to refer to Bergamo as the *Catholicissima Città* (most Catholic of cities). Angelo, at an impressionable age, away from home, already in the thralls of fascinated admiration for St. Charles Borromeo, was in the thick of this Bergamo Catholic renaissance. In **1895**, three years into his stay in that most Catholic of cities, what did the teenage Angelo Roncalli start doing – something which would be a profound guiding influence for much of his adult life?

Pope John XXIII's canonization on **April 27, 2014**, is, quite remarkably, the absolute fulfillment of lofty (one could in most other cases even say improbable) goal envisaged by the pre-teen Angelo during his first year at Bergamo. Now wearing a cassock most of the time (as required by the seminary), readily conforming to the rigid discipline expected of him (though still not excelling in his studies) and immersed in the pervading piety of his surrounds, young Angelo conceived of the notion that he wanted to make every effort possible in order to become a saint. In 1895, pursuant of this objective Angelo started to maintain a *spiritual diary* – an undertaking he persevered, diligently, for at least the next fifty years of his life and sporadically even after that.

He started this diary on a standard school notebook of that time; sixty-four sheets of square-ruled paper bound between two stiff black covers. His first entry in this notebook, written on the inside cover to serve as a kind of leitmotif, was a Latin motto: *Fuge quae in ore saealarium nugae sunt in ore sacerdotum blasphemiae* (Faults which are trifles in the mouths of lay people are blasphemies in the mouth of priests).

The first entry in this diary, following the Latin motto, was the transcription of a narrative of the ideal attributes of a 'model priest'. These were based upon guidelines that had been approved by the **Council of Trent** [Trento, Italy], the nineteenth ecumenical council, which had lasted off and on from 1545 to 1563 – the latter part of which was masterfully orchestrated by Angelo's hero, Charles Borromeo.

This council, which lasted 6,565 days, was convened during the time of the *Reformation* to validate doctrine and enact reform. Its overarching *raison d'être* was to formally refute and condemn what the Catholic Church perceived as the *Protestant heresies*. It is considered as being the vital impetus for spawning the *Counter-Reformation*. At the instigation of Charles Borromeo the council paid particular attention to the need for a new cadre of well educated, dedicated and 'professional' Catholic clerics to ably counter the Protestant threat. This followed the realization that much of the discontent that had led to the Reformation could be traced back to poorly-trained, ill-disciplined clerics.

This, the longest of the councils, consisted of twenty-five sessions. Many of these sessions included a section on *reform* to deal with a multitude of topics deemed worthy of reevaluation. These included: Holy Scripture, sacred tradition, original sin, righteous Justification, indulgences, the sacraments, the Eucharist of the Holy Mass, and the veneration of icons and Saints. The reform portion of session twenty-two set out to tackle the *'life and conduct of clerics'*. The beliefs of the council on this topic, within the framework of their overall *decretum de reformatione* (decrees of reformation), where published in the proceedings for *that* session under the heading: *'Chapter 1: The Canons relative to the life, and propriety of conduct of Clerics are renewed'*. This relatively short chapter contained statements such as: *'There is nothing that continually instructs others unto piety, and the service of God, more than the life and example of those who have dedicated themselves to the divine ministry. ... Wherefore clerics called to have the Lord for their portion, ought by all means so to regulate their whole life and conversation, as that in their dress, comportment, gait, discourse, and all things else, nothing appear but what is grave, regulated, and replete with religiousness; avoiding even slight faults, which in them would be most grievous; that so their actions may impress all with veneration. ...'* [Note that Angelo's opening Latin motto in his journal appears to be a paraphrasing of the latter part of the second statement.]

It was this 'Chapter 1' from session twenty-two of the Council of Trent that Angelo had transcribed as his first entry. It is unclear whether he had found it himself or whether it had been brought to his attention by one of his teachers. Using the Trent decree as inspiration, the young seminarian then started to iterate his own set of prescripts that he intended to follow such as that of devoting at least a quarter of an hour to mental prayer, first thing in the morning, before getting out of bed.

What becomes clear from these early entries is that by 1895, after two full years at Bergamo, the young Angelo was preparing himself for a lifetime in the priesthood. Later on in life he would claim that he could never remember a time in his life when he did not want to be a priest.

In 1961, at the urging of his personal secretary, Monsignor Loris Capovilla, the pope, after considerable reflection, agreed that this spiritual diary, which by then stretched across upwards of thirty-eight notebooks, should be published, given its potential to help and inspire others contemplating priesthood. Monsignor Capovilla had them published as a book, *Il giornale dell'anima* (*Journal of a Soul*), in 1964, a year after the pope's death. Translated into many languages it remains a best seller to this day.

25) In June of 1895, the same year that he started his spiritual diary, at age thirteen years and seven months, he received his first tonsure. The next year, 1896, he was admitted to his very first 'order'. What was that order?

He was admitted to the Secular Franciscan Order, i.e., **Franciscan 'Third Order'** [also referred to as 'tertiary']. It is a means by which *lay* Catholics, married or single, can live a life devoted to Christ per the edicts of St. Francis of Assisi without having to join the Order and take the necessary vows *per se*. Popes **Pius IX** (#256) and **Leo XIII** (#257), the two popes of his time, had both been Franciscan 'Third Order' members. So, Angelo was following in the footsteps of his current pope. He was admitted by Fr. Luigi Isacchi, the spiritual director of the Bergamo seminary – one of Angelo's new mentors. In May 23, **1897**, following the necessary training he made the profession of its Rule of life.

26) When and where did Angelo Roncalli first get to see a pope in person?

In **September 1900**, from the 12th to the 19th, Angelo, then a young man of eighteen years and nine months, got to visit **Rome**, for the first time. He was doing so as a *Holy Year Pilgrim*; Pope **Leo XIII** (#257) having in May 1899 declared that December 24, 1899, to December 24, 1900, would be a Jubilee Holy Year. While in Rome he got to see the Pope, then 90.5 years old; he having been pope for the previous 22.5 years. So Leo had been pope for the entirety of Angelo's life to that point. Angelo, in the grip of his unfaltering reverence to the Church, considered Leo an exceptional and inspiring pope.

On Sunday, September 25, 1898, Don Francesco Rebuzzini who had been such a towering influence in Angelo's life died, unexpectedly. Angelo happened to be in Sotto il Monte at the time. His brother, Giovanni Francesco, had been ill. On Saturday, September 24, his brother appeared to be recovering. So, that evening Angelo spent some time with Fr. Rebuzzini. When he took his leave, he promised to meet the priest again the next morning, at church, to help him get ready for Mass. When Angelo arrived at the church on Sunday morning he found Don Rebuzzini dead, at the foot of the altar. He appeared to have fallen and hit his head on the altar while preparing for Mass.

As Angelo approached adulthood, and furthermore was becoming increasingly more clerical, he was experiencing, as was probably to be expected, some occasional contretemps with his family, mostly to do with 'attitudes' and 'outlook'. Some of this familial 'disunity', however minor, would deeply distress the future pope. The new pastor assigned to Santa Maria of Brusicco was Don Ignazio Valsecchi. He happened to encounter Angelo after one of these incidents and noted his obvious anguish. It would appear that Fr. Valsecchi somehow came up with the funds to send Angelo to Rome, on pilgrimage, to assuage his soul and provide him with broader perspectives on life.

On his way back from Rome he extended his pilgrimage by visiting the shrines at Assisi and Loreto. On October 4, **1962**, exactly a week ahead of the opening of Vatican II, the pope retracted his pilgrimage to Assisi and Loreto. [q.v. #88.] He traveled by train, the Italian presidential train lent to the pope for the day, and departed from the Vatican City railway station; the first time a Pontiff, while Pontiff, had travelled by train since the time of Pius IX (#256) some 99 years earlier. [Incidentally Pius IX had also been the last pope to have visited Loreto, the shrine of the holy Virgin.]

27) How long would it be before Angelo returned to Rome – albeit this time for a much longer stay?

Angelo Roncalli, then just over nineteen years of age, was back in Rome early in the morning of January 4, **1901**. He had won a scholarship to attend the **Pontificio Collegio Romano**, the diocesan seminary of Rome then located (as of 1824) in Palazzo di Sant'Apollinare (and as such often referred to as *Seminario Romano dell'Apollinare*).

The Council of Trent in its 23rd session (the one after the session that formulated the 'model priest' guidelines that appeared at the start of Angelo's spiritual diary) had decreed the need for establishing diocesan seminaries to produce a new cadre of well-educated clerics. Two years later, in early 1565, **Pius IV** (#225) decided to get the ball rolling by establishing this Roman Seminary – initially with just 60 students. The charter for the seminary was drawn up by the General of the Society of Jesus (the Jesuits), and Pius IV entrusted the running of it to that order – Jesuits noted for their commitment to academic and intellectual excellence.

It had taken the prepubescent Angelo a couple of years to get into the swing of things at the junior seminary in Bergamo. He also had to learn to curb his innate good-natured humor – witticism, however apropos, not well tolerated by seminarian teachers. By 1895 his grades had improved significantly, though he would never reach the topmost tier of his class. With this upswing in academic performance he also started to gain leadership roles. He was made a 'prefect' – i.e., a student charged with monitoring and enforcing discipline on his peers. On May 21, 1899, he preached his first formal sermon – albeit just to his classmates in the form of a 'practice run'. It was the eve of Pentecost for that year. The theme he chose, accordingly, was *'Mary in the Ceneacle'* – i.e., the basis for the Pentecost, the descent of the Holy Spirit into the 'Upper Room' (Ceneacle), where Jesus' apostles and disciples were gathered together in prayer, with his Mother Mary. [Sixty years later the pope would often refer to

Figure 6: Angelo Roncalli (middle) in 1901, most likely taken at the College in Rome.

the Pentecost, or to be precise 'a new Pentecost', in his speeches and prayers when talking about the forthcoming Council.] In early 1900 he was assigned responsibility for the school's Gregorian chant program (he maintaining an abiding love for 'plainchant' (as it is also called) for the rest of his life). By then the faculty at the seminary, as had Don Rebuzzini and Fr. Giovanni Morlani much earlier, were beginning to appreciate the promise inherent in the young Roncalli.

In 1640 a Bergamascan canon had established a small college in Rome, with an attendant scholarship program, for the most promising students at the Bergamo seminary. In time this small Bergamo-specific school had merged with the *Pontificio Collegio Romano* – with the scholarship program still intact. Thus, each year, a select number of Bergamascan seminarian scholars had the opportunity to study in the Eternal City, the epicenter of Catholicism. The capture of Rome in September 1870, to bring about Italian unification, resulted in the interruption of this scholarship program. But, it had been agreed by all parties that the program would be resumed as of 1901. Angelo, upon his return from his pilgrimage to Rome, Assisi and Loreto in September 1900, was invited by the Bishop of Bergamo, Camillo Guindani, to sit for the scholarship examination. He did, and passed. He was selected as one of three that would be sent to Rome in 1901.

Prior alumni of the College that he was to attend included: **Gregory XV** (#235), **Clement IX** (#239), **Innocent XIII** (#245) and **Clement XII** (#247). When he became pope he would be #262. Exactly 30 days after his election Pope John XXIII visited his old College to demonstrate his esteem, appreciation and solidarity – and no doubt also to reminisce and relive, if but briefly, what had proved to be a very happy and illuminating period of his life.

28) It was not to be all plain sailing once he got to Rome. What event rudely interrupted his path towards priesthood a few days after he turned twenty – though it was not as traumatic as it could have been?

On November 30, 1901, five days after his birthday, per the prevailing Italian government laws of the time, which provided no dispensation for priests or seminarians, Angelo Roncalli was conscripted for his mandatory one-year of military service. The one concession, often pivotal, afforded to seminarians was that they could pick the 'unit' in which they wished to serve.

The future pope, astutely, had picked the 73rd Infantry Regiment of the Lombardy Brigade which had a garrison in Bergamo. [This regiment's motto was *Accerrimus Hostibus*, which was meant to signify 'strong against enemies'.] So 330 days after leaving Bergamo he was back again, this time to the *Caserma Umberto I di Bergamo* barracks, as Soldato Roncalli. Angello was recruit number 11331/42 of the Italian army.

Many of those in the barracks were, like him, from the local area; he even knew some of them. He had opportunities to visit Sotto il Monte and his old seminary. The food was good, there was even a wine ration and the officers were gentlemanly (and, moreover, looked favorably on the young, would-be-priest). It, nonetheless, was a major departure from his prior nine years of cloistered life. He at first also found military discipline wearing and fretted about not being able to maintain his religious obligations. But, his year in the army, as he would later admit, was not that onerous. Growing up on a poor farm, trudging across hills to go to school and then entering a seminary very young, Roncalli, who was fit and rugged, who had learnt by necessity to be adaptable, was no stranger to strict, demanding regimes.

During his time in the military he grew a moustache for the first time in his life; but not the last. As had been the case in his last years at the seminary his leadership skills were soon recognized and he was promoted to *caporale* (corporal) and then, shortly prior to the end of his tour of duty in November 1902, to *sergente* (sergeant).

He, after a short visit home, returned to the *Pontificio Collegio Romano* to resume his path towards priesthood.

Figure 7: *Sergente* Roncalli, with the mustache, c. 1902.

29) In 1903 the twenty-one year old Roncalli, who had yet to travel beyond the bounds of Italy, got his first exposure to two Protestant Heads of State. Who were they and what was the occasion?

On February 20, 1903, **Leo XIII** (#257), two weeks shy of his 93rd birthday, reached the twenty-fifth anniversary of his papacy. He was only the second pope (*after* **St. Peter** (#1)) to have reached the once mystical *"Peter's Years"*. The other was his immediate predecessor, **Pius IX** (#256), who had been pope for a remarkable 31.6 years. World leaders, irrespective of their religious stripes, were quick to pay homage to the elderly (and ailing) pope who had managed to usher the Catholic Church, hesitatingly though it was, into the increasingly-democratic, 'modern' industrial world.

On April 29, 1903, **Edward VII**, King, by the Grace of God, of the United Kingdom of Great Britain and Ireland and of the British Dominions beyond the Seas, Defender of the Faith, and Emperor of India from 1901 to 1910, visited the pope at the Vatican. A few weeks later Wilhelm II, German Kaiser (Emperor) and King of Prussia from 1888 to 1918, also paid a visit. [This was the Kaiser's second trip to the Vatican, he also having paid a visit on October 12, 1888, four months after his coronation, while in Rome to meet with the Italian king].

The future pope was impressed. He thought it providential that Edward and Wilhelm, both Protestants, the former Anglican and the later Lutheran, had come to show their respect to a pope – despite the fact that the pope had become increasingly more conservative and intransigent as he got older. He wrote about the visits, gleefully, in his diary – though it is not clear whether he actually got to see either of royals parading through Rome.

30) The conclave that started July 31, 1903, following **Leo XIII's** (#257) demise on July 20th, after a 25.4 year reign, was the future pope's very first conclave; Leo having been pope his entire life. Suffice to say, given that he was in Rome, in the thick of things, Angelo Roncalli, though saddened, was fascinated by all that took place over the *sede vacante*. Once the conclave started he would, whenever he could, walk to St. Peter's Square to wait for the *sfumata*. This was a conclave noted for its porosity; reports from supposed knowledgeable insiders were in circulation around Rome on a daily basis. So, the future pope when at the Square would often hear alleged tales of the intrigue taking place within the Sistine. An event that happened at this conclave, and the reason for it, troubled Angelo, greatly. It got him thinking about the 'politics' that affected the Church in a whole new light. What was this incident and why did it come about?

The incident, of course, was the infamous *Jus Exclusivæ* (right of exclusion) veto of leading *papabile*, Sicilian Cardinal Mariano Rampolla del Tindaro, Leo XIII's fourth and last Secretary of State, by Franz Joseph I, Emperor of Austria and King of Hungary. This veto, delivered by Cardinal Jan Maurycy Paweł Puzyna de Kosielsko, Prince-Bishop of Kraków [southern Poland – then under Austrian rule], took place at the start of the second day of balloting, i.e., August 2.

This veto power, claimed by the sovereigns of France, Spain and Austria [then on a one per country, per conclave basis], was the last remaining vestige of the imperial interventions that had plagued papal elections for so long in earlier days. *Jus Exclusivæ* was a practice that was never sanctioned either by canon law or papal edict. Instead, it had become an accepted, *de facto* privilege honored by the College of Cardinals. Its origins date back to the end of the 16th century when Spain's King Phillip II submitted to the College a long list of cardinals that were deemed unacceptable as the next pope. The last time, prior to 1903, that a veto had been successfully used was in the December 1830 to February 1831 conclave that elected **Gregory XVI** (#255). At that conclave

Spain's Ferdinand VII had Cardinal Giacomo Giustiniani, once a nuncio to Spain, vetoed.

Cardinal di Santo Stefano, Camerlengo and Dean of the 1903 conclave, instructed the cardinals to ignore the veto, citing that a round of balloting had already begun and that conclave procedures dictated that it needed to be completed. At this point, Rampolla, though claiming indifference to being elected, nonetheless objected forcefully to this external interference. To defy the veto, Spanish Cardinal José de Calasanz Félix Santiago Vives y Tutó proposed that Rampolla be elected, forthwith, by acclamation. Di Santo Stefano, who was not a fan of Rampolla, overturned this motion – again on the grounds that a ballot was already underway. The voting then proceeded with Rampolla's tally supposedly staying the same as it had the night before at twenty-nine. By the end of that day, however, Rampolla started losing votes – possibly as a delayed reaction to the veto.

The news of the veto was known in Rome well before the end of the conclave. This was Angelo's first exposure to overt secular impingement on Church matters. He was shocked. His worldview at that stage was rather limited. Not only was he very young, but having been a seminarian for over a decade, during which time his access to newspapers and other publications was strictly controlled and curtailed, he had lived a secluded existence with hardly any regular exposure to world politics. The reason for the imperial veto bothered him even further. A few months earlier two Protestant Heads of State had paid homage to Leo. Now a Catholic emperor was objecting to Leo's protégé, the *papabile* expected to continue Leo's agenda. He had to come to terms with the fact that Leo's papacy was not as universally accepted and respected as he had imagined for so long. The veto incident and the realization that it had all to do with Rampolla's 'values' got the future pope thinking – along lines he had never done before. Some of the principles in the mindset that would make him an extremely effective Vatican diplomat -- and a pope – are believed to have originated from the lessons he perceived from the 1903 veto.

III.
THE PRIEST

On April 10, 1903, Angelo Giuseppe Roncalli was installed as a subdeacon at St. John Lateran, the cathedral church of the Diocese of Rome and the official ecclesiastical seat of the Bishop of Rome, i.e., the pope. On June 18, 1904, he was ordained a deacon and then, per the *'three degrees of ordination'* tradition, formally requested elevation to the ministry [the formal request referred to as 'entreating']. Around that time he also earned his doctorate in theology from the *'Apollinare'*, i.e., the *Pontificio Collegio Romano*.

On August 1, 1904, he went into seclusion at a retreat house atop Rome's Caelian Hill, run by the (Saint Paul of the Cross) Passionist Congregation, along with ten other seminarians who were also awaiting priestly ordination. On the evening of August 9 he went to the Lateran to pray – his last visit to the cathedral prior to priesthood.

Early in the morning of Wednesday, **August 10, 1904**, Angelo Giuseppe Roncalli, was ordained a priest, in *Santa Maria al Montesanto*. It was one of the two baroque twin churches, built in 1675, on the Piazza del Popplo. The ordination was performed by Giuseppe Ceppetelli, titular Patriarch of Constantinople and Vicegerent of Rome. Fr. Roncalli was 22 years, 8 months, 2 weeks and 2 days old. He was 3.5 months ahead of the twenty-three years which was then the canonical norm for priesthood.

31) Shortly after becoming a priest, Fr. Roncalli got to *meet* with a pope for the first time. What were the circumstances that led to this meeting?

Fr. Domenico Spolverini, the vice-rector of the *'Apollinare'*, was in charge of his ordination. He had accompanied the future pope to *Santa Maria al Montesanto*. He had also arranged for Fr. Roncalli to celebrate his first Mass, the next day, August 11, to a group of invited friends. It was to be at St. Peter's Basilica. This votive Mass, that of Saints Peter & Paul, was held in the crypt at an altar above the tomb of St. Peter (#1).

Fr. Spolverini, had also made arrangements, unbeknownst to his charge, for a brief audience with the pope, **Pius X** (#258) – the new pope who had been elected a year earlier. It was not a private audience and took place in a hall crowded with pilgrims. The new priest, nonetheless, still got to be introduced to the pope with the descriptive that he was: *'from Bergamo'*. Fr. Roncalli was given the opportunity to kneel in front of the pope and repeat his priestly vows. The pope blessed him, promised to ask the Lord for additional special blessings for his impending priestly endeavors and wanted to know when he planned to get back home. Fr. Roncalli replied that he would be back home for the Feast of the Assumption.

That was the future pope's first face-to-face interaction with a pope.

32) In November 1904, having spent a few months back home in Sotto il Monte, Fr. Roncalli returned to the *Pontificio Collegio Romano* to pursue a doctorate in canon law. But these plans were interrupted, forever, within five months when he was chosen, serendipitously, in **March 1905**, to be the *secretary* to the newly appointed *Bishop of Bergamo*, **Giacomo Maria Radini-Tedeschi** [12 July 1857 to 22 August 1914]. Though it was not an influencing factor in him been chosen, their paths had crossed twice before – the first in 1899. What were these two occasions?

Angelo Roncalli first met, casually and by chance, blue-blooded (once a Count) Giacomo Radini-Tedeschi in September 1899 in Ghiaie (di Bonate Sopra), a village situated between Sotto il Monte and Bergamo, about five miles from each. The parish priest at Ghiaie at the time was Fr. Alessandro Locatelli. He knew Radini-Tedeschi, they having taught together at Bergamo at one time. When Don Francesco Rebuzzini had died, a year previously, Fr. Locatelli appreciating the loss had reached out to Angelo. *[q.v. #26.]* So, Angelo when he had time had got into the habit of visiting Ghiaie to meet with Fr. Locatelli. He was visiting that day, September 17th, because it was the feast day of 'Our Lady of Sorrows'. Radini-Tedeschi also happened to be visiting.

Radini-Tedeschi, forty-two at the time, had been working at the Vatican for over a decade, often directly for **Leo XIII** (#257), as a liaison, facilitator and diplomat. He had been heavily involved for the prior six years in the *Opera dei Congressi* (Work of the Congress). It was a Catholic organization formed after the fall of the Papal States (and the popes becoming prisoners of the Vatican) to promote Catholic values, beliefs and culture – at a time when the Vatican was instructing Italians to avoid all political involvement. It was a precursor to *Azione Cattolica*. Radini-Tedeschi was thus in the vanguard of the socially-responsible Catholicism that was so dear to Zaverio Roncalli. *[q.v. #19.]* As such, Angelo and Radini-Tedeschi would have had much in common to talk about. It is said that they, spurred by Fr. Locatelli, explored of the possibility of Angelo moving to Rome to get involved in the new social programs that were beginning to be implemented. Suffice to say that this, for whatever reasons, did not come to pass. It is, however, possible that Fr. Locatelli, at the behest of the new pastor at Santa Maria of Brusicco, *may have* contacted Radini-Tedeschi for help funding Angelo's Holy Year pilgrimage. *[q.v. #26.]* One of Radini-Tedeschi's facilitator roles at the Vatican was that of organizing the

1900 Holy Year – in particular the mass pilgrimages. So he was indeed in a position to help.

But, it is clear that Radini-Tedeschi did not stay in contact with Angelo after that meeting in Ghiaie. When given his bishopric Radini-Tedeschi did not seek out Angelo Roncalli to come work for him. Instead he was recommended by Fr. Domenico Spolverini, the vice-rector of the *'Apollinare'* (who oversaw Roncalli's ordination), when the new bishop contacted the College looking for a young priest from the Bergamo district to serve as his secretary.

What is ironic here is that Fr. Roncalli, as a Bergamascan, had been chosen to assist in the new bishop's consecration just a few months earlier!

Following the papal transition of 1903, British-born, Spanish blue-blood, Rafael María José Pedro Francisco Borja Domingo Gerardo de la Santíssima Trinidad Merry del Val y Zulueta [October 1865 to February 1930], became the Secretary of State. He was an arch-conservative. Though the new pope, **Pius X** (#258), was not as conservative, he, considering himself to be better equipped with dealing with the spiritual needs of his flock rather than with matters of Church 'governance'. So he relied heavily on Merry del Val on all matters to do with 'state' and politics. Given his ingrained conservatism Merry del Val was opposed to the increasing interest in socially-responsible Catholicism – or to put it in other terms, 'democratic Catholicism'. He equated efforts such as *Opera dei Congressi*, with its emphasis on social justice, with **'modernism'** – i.e., the influence of any contemporary ideas, whether it be related to political democracy, scientific thought or social justice, on traditional age-old Catholic teachings. He thus prevailed upon Pius X to dissolve *Opera dei Congressi*. This was a major blow to Radini-Tedeschi.

Irrespective of his involvement in *Opera dei Congressi*, Pius, personally, liked and respected Radini-Tedeschi, considerably, and fully appreciated his past contributions to the Church. He also saw a yet unfulfilled potential for greatness. So, to an extent to make up for dissolving his favorite 'public cause', Pius decided, as consolation, to make him, at forty-eight years of age, a bishop. The curia, glad to get rid of one they saw as a trenchant 'progressive', suggested, unsuccessfully, the vacant bishoprics of Palermo [Sicily] and Ravenna. Bergamo was the next option, Gaetano Camillo Guindani (who had Confirmed Angelo in 1889 and to whom Fr. Roncalli had written the very day he received his ordination) having died in October 1904. Pius stating, cryptically, that Bergamo was *"Italy's first diocese"* thought it was an ideal fit. Why the pope thought so is a bit curious. Bergamo, the birthplace of *Azione Cattolica*, was the hotbed of Italian Catholic-based social action. It is very possible that the pope was not totally averse to Radini-Tedeschi's 'progressiveness' and wished to give him a diocese that not only would be very receptive to his presence but would also readily embrace his views and intentions.

The pope, again showing his fondness for Radini-Tedeschi, let it be known that he would, personally, perform the requisite episcopal consecration.

The consecration, with Pius X presiding, took place at the Sistine Chapel on January 29, 1905. Fr. Roncalli and another young priest from Bergamo assisted; Fr. Roncalli holding the bible during the actual hands-on consecration. It is not known whether he and the new bishop got a chance, that day, to renew their acquaintance from Ghiaie. It would appear that Bishop Radini-Tedeschi did not take stock of Fr. Roncalli at the time – since he did not have him in mind when he asked the *'Apollinare'* for recommendations.

This had to have been the first time that Fr. Roncalli had officiated at the Sistine. It probably was also the only time he likely officiated at the Sistine prior to the conclave of 1958 which elected him pope. That was the only conclave he ever attended; he only having been made a cardinal five years earlier during what had been **Pius XII's** (#261) 19.6 year papacy.

Figure 8: With Bishop Giacomo Maria Radini Tedeschi (seated, second left) and his secretary, Fr. Roncalli (standing, third right).

33) Shortly after moving back to Bergamo with Bishop Giacomo Radini-Tedeschi Fr. Roncalli set off on his first trip outside of Italy. Where did he go and what was the significance of this trip?

The bishop and his new secretary, Fr. Angelo Roncalli, arrived in Bergamo on April 9, 1905. Many of Bergamo's church holdings including the cathedral, seminary and bishop's palace were in disrepair and the new bishop ordered an immediate program of repair and restoration. In the meantime, around the third week of April the bishop and his secretary set off on the first of many extensive pilgrimages that they would undertake together over the next eight years. They first visited the crypt of Saint Charles Borromeo in the basement of the *Duomo di Milano* (Milan Cathedral).

Then on April 29, they departed Genoa by ship headed to France. They landed in Marseilles. Their eventual destination was the Sanctuary of Our Lady of **Lourdes**. But they also visited Paray-le-Monial (with its famous Cluny-affiliated Basilica), Montepellier and Lyons. Over the next eight years they would revisit Lourdes four more times. Following the 1905 visit they returned to Italy via Rome meeting with the pope while there.

Four decades after his last visit with the bishop, Cardinal Angelo Roncalli, Patriarch of Venice, would once again be visiting Lourdes, this time on a much grander scale as the pope's special envoy. In 1957 the massive 627' long Basilica of St. Pius X (a.k.a. the Underground Basilica), which can accommodate 25,000 worshippers, was completed at Lourdes (at a then cost of $5.6 million). **Pius XII** (#261) chose Roncalli, who had been an extremely popular nuncio to France, as his representative to consecrate the new Basilica – the consecration taking place on March 25, 1958, seven months ahead of the fateful conclave.

In 1906 the bishop and his secretary visited the Holy Land – Fr. Roncalli sending back dispatches of that visit to a local newspaper in Bergamo. During their time together they also visited: Spain, Germany, Austria, Hungary, Poland and Switzerland.

34) During his time in Bergamo, which in 1914 was tragically cut short by cancer, Bishop Radini-Tedeschi (fifty-seven at the time) in addition to providing spiritual inspiration, worked tirelessly to better the social and economic wellbeing of his flock. Fr. Roncalli was his veritable shadow, though at the bishop's urging he had started teaching some classes at his old seminary. In 1909 there was a labor strike at a local iron works over work hours and pay. To the chagrin of the 'upper classes' and 'conservatives' the bishop and his secretary were regularly seen in the locality of the strike providing both spiritual and material succor. Some thought this very overt support of social-action very progressive or even 'modernistic'. Many decades later, when pope, John XXIII would discover some observations that had been made about him – the *roots* of which went back to his time in Bergamo with the socially-conscientious bishop. What had been said and how did the pope react?

Once in office, Pope John XXIII, probably having a hunch as to what might have been said about him during prior papacies, requested to see his own Vatican personnel file – most likely the one maintained by the Holy Office. In the file he found, to his dismay and vexation, that he had indeed been suspected of modernism. Asking for a pen, the pope is said to have, famously, written underneath the accusation that he, Pope John XXIII, was never a modernist. Later on, his good natured humor always near at hand, the pope while urging a group of seminarians never to shy away from what they believed was right, pointed out that he was a living example that a priest suspected of 'unorthodoxy' by the Holy Office could still become pope.

35) Thanks to Bishop Radini-Tedeschi's wide circle of friends in high places, Fr. Roncalli, in 1906, got to meet a future pope and to form a working relationship with him -- on a project that would be very dear to Fr. Roncalli's heart. What was this project and who was the future pope?

Bishop Radini-Tedeschi was good friends with Cardinal Andrea Carlo Ferrari, Archbishop of Milan – another suspected modernist. In late 1906 the bishop accompanied by his secretary visited the Cardinal. While the two prelates talked Fr. Roncalli took the opportunity to browse through the Archbishop's extensive library. There he discovered, serendipitously, buried among long-neglected books and documents, thirty-nine volumes of parchment chronicling Charles Borromeo's visitations to the diocese of Bergamo in 1575 – Charles Borromeo having been the Archbishop of Milan from 1564 to 1584. Fr. Roncalli immediately saw this as manifest destiny, the intersection of his favorite Saint with his adopted city. He knew that he had to do something to make sure that these narratives would not remain unknown and unappreciated. The manuscripts provided a unique insight into Renaissance era central Italy, especially the emergence of the Counter-Reformation initiatives – related by an architect of that movement as it applied to one of the most Catholic of cities.

Fr. Roncalli, as was to be expected, sought advice from his bishop as to how he should proceed. Radini-Tedeschi arranged for Fr. Roncalli to meet with yet another of his influential friends – this time the Prefect of Milan's historic and eminent *Biblioteca Ambrosiana* (named after the patron Saint of Milan). This Prefect happened to be **Msgr. Achille Ratti** [b. May 1857] who sixteen years later was to be become **Pius XI** (#260).

Msgr. Ratti immediately saw the full merits of Fr. Roncalli's intent and started at once to provide him with the necessary advice, support and help. Though the bishop, noted for his organizational zeal, established two committees in Bergamo to help his secretary with his publication project, in the end the only genuine help he received was that from the kindly and studious Msgr. Ratti.

It has been claimed that the twenty-four year difference in their ages, and their respective stations in life precluded them from becoming true friends *per se* at that time. While this may be true what cannot also be denied is that Fr. Roncalli was no stranger to Pope Pius XI – and that is patently clear. Pius XI plied him with responsibility: got him involved in the organization of the 1925 Holy Year, made him a titular archbishop and sent him off on his first overseas diplomatic mission. The meeting in Milan in 1906, orchestrated by Radini-Tedeschi, definitely was fortuitous, if not providential.

Given his other commitments it took Fr. Roncalli quite a longtime to complete his publishing project, but by 1958 he had published a five-volume set of *'Records of the Apostolic Visit of Saint Charles Boromeo to Bergamo'*.

36) What happened to Fr. Angelo Roncalli when on May 23, **1915**, Italy (siding with the Allies despite original posturing to the contrary) declared war on Austria and Germany within the context of World War I which had begun in July 1914?

Per the prevailing Italian government laws of the time, thirty-three year old Fr. Roncalli, irrespective of his priestly status, was an active military reservist – who had already received his mandatory one-year training and had reached the rank of sergeant thirteen years earlier. *[q.v. #28.]* On May 24, 1915, he reported for duty in Milan per his orders. He was all at sea as to what would be expected of him. He thought that there was a chance that he would be dispatched, forthwith, to 'the front' – at the time just 200 miles to the north. Though there were some pockets of anti-clerical sentiment among the commanding officers, in general common sense prevailed when it came to the deployment of clerics. Consequently, *Sergente* Roncalli was assigned to the army medical corps, at his current rank, and sent back to Bergamo – a key medical care center for the wounded. Sergente Roncalli, who decided yet again to grow a very dashing mustache, acted as both a medical orderly taking care of patients as well as an 'at large' priest fulfilling the spiritual needs of any and all he encountered. As a sergeant he was also in charge of a small number of junior orderlies; being a disciplinarian, however, not his forte. He faced some anti-clerical resentment at the hospital, but was able to overcome it with his force of personality.

Whenever he had any free time he would try to celebrate Mass in Bergamo for the troops or visit Sotto il Monte; all four of his brothers also conscripted by then. In early 1916 all enlisted priests serving in the Italian army were made chaplains and promoted to *tenente* (lieutenant). Upon his elevation *Tenente* Roncalli promptly shaved off his mustache. He was now responsible for the spiritual wellbeing of a number of military hospitals, as well as some parochial schools in and around Bergamo. He, given his background, also paid heed to the oft overlooked 'social' aspects of the community – arranging for convalescent facilities and organizing support groups for bereaved families. Remarkably he also managed to get permission and find time to teach some classes at the seminary – as well as to publish a biography on his beloved bishop, Radini-Tedeschi. The bishop had passed away in August 1914, dreading the war, and imploring for peace even as he lay dying. *Tenente* Roncalli was granted leave to visit Rome to present a copy of his book to the new pope – **Benedict XV** (#259). The pope like so many other prelates of the time had been very close to the popular, bestriding bishop. This was Fr. Roncalli's first meeting with this pope; the *first pope* that would *directly* influence the trajectory of his life.

His youngest sister Enrica, at the age of twenty-five, was to die of cancer on October 15, 1918. Roncalli was able to attend the funeral. Just under a month later, on November 11, 1918, at 11:11 a.m., the War finally ended.

In 1918, as an adjunct of his ongoing 'social' agenda, the new bishop of Bergamo, Luigi Maria Marelli, asked *Tenente* Roncalli to establish a new *Casa dello Studente* (a youth hostel) in the Palazzo Marenzi, located on the Via San Salvatore in Bergamo's old city quarter. After the war he was to become the permanent resident warden of this hostel – and have the opportunity to have his two sisters, Ancilla and Maria, also living there. Given that the bishop had not been forthcoming with all of the necessary funds, Roncalli used his own funds, even borrowing a small sum from his father, as well as all of his 'demob' pay, to furnish and repair the long-neglected palazzo.

In November 1918 upon being discharged he moved to the palazzo and opened the hostel which was meant to house lay students.

37) *Casa dello Studente* prospered. Bishop Marelli, appreciating Fr. Roncalli's immense capacity and competence, kept on giving him more responsibility. One of his new responsibilities was in essence to provide spiritual guidance to all of the Catholic women's organizations in Bergamo – in particular the women's arm of *Azione Cattolica*. *[q.v. #1.]* In early 1919 he became the spiritual director of the seminary (the one that he had once attended). He was as such responsible for ensuring the smooth, or at least the smooth as possible, reintegration of the seminarians returning from the War -- many traumatized, conflicted and disillusioned. He was asked to help with the organization of the September 1920 **sixth National Eucharistic Congress** in Bergamo. He even delivered an address at this Congress. On top of all this he continued to teach at the seminary (though he was not awarded a 'professorship' possibly because he was suspected of being 'progressive'). But, he still found time, at least once a month, to visit Sotto il Monte and spend time with his family. Fr. Roncalli was content and grateful. He was doing what he had 'always' wanted to do. He had a perfect mix of pastoral, social, organizational and academic responsibilities.

But, his happy stay in Bergamo would come to a permanent end in early 1921. What happened?

Six years into his papacy and a year after the end of the War (that he had worked so hard to end), **Benedict XV** was eager to revitalize some of the inner workings of the Church. One of his key priorities was to rejuvenate and bolster Catholic missionary activity. Since 1622 there had been a *Sacra Congregatio de Propaganda Fide* (Sacred Congregation for the Propagation of the Faith) at the Vatican to organize, oversee and coordinate missionary work, as well as to provide aid to the 'mission lands' [i.e., developing nations], around the world. *Propaganda Fide* relied on a network of national societies, under local jurisdiction, in the major Catholic countries, to raise most of the money they needed. This decentralized feeder-network was proving to be disorderly and inefficient – especially after the disruptions caused by the War.

The pope wanted the management of these dispersed societies to be more centralized and be allied with the curial administration of *Propaganda Fide*. To this end the pope needed a capable, energetic, personable and young cleric, with proven organizational credentials, to subtly persuade the national societies to accept more 'coordination' from Rome. He asked for a list of potential candidates. By now Roncalli, particularly so after the recent Eucharistic Congress, was no stranger to those in the upper echelons of the Church. His name was included in the list. The pope immediately spotted it and asked for him by name. The pope knew him. Roncalli had already had two audiences with this pope in addition to their interactions when he worked for Radini-Tedeschi.

In late 1920, the Prefect of *Propaganda Fide*, the very influential Dutch Cardinal Willem Marinus van ('Red Pope') Rossum, C.SS.R., wrote to Fr. Roncalli offering him the job as the head of the Italian Society for *Propaganda Fide*. Fr. Roncalli was torn. He appreciated the honor that was being granted but it was not the kind of limelight he was seeking. He was happy with his work in Bergamo, close to home. So he sought counsel from Cardinal Andrea Carlo Ferrari, Archbishop of Milan (i.e., Bishop Radini-Tedeschi's friend). The cardinal, wisely, advised him to accept. Father Roncalli, thus, reported to the sprawling, palatial offices of *Propaganda Fide* in Rome's Piazza di Spagna on **January 18, 1921**.

38) Within four months of starting work at the *Propaganda Fide* headquarters in Rome the future pope was to receive his first ecclesiastical title beyond that of 'priest'. What was it and what did it mean in terms of added responsibility?

In March 21, 1921, two months into his new job, Fr. Roncalli was given the grandiose title of *Presidente per l'Italia del Consiglio centrale delle Pontificia Opera della Propagazione della Fede* (President of the Central Council for Italy of the Pontifical Missionary Works) – which essentially meant that he was the Director of

Figure 9: *Propaganda Fide* offices in Rome's Piazza di Spagna.

the Italian Society for *Propaganda Fide*. He started a program of visiting missionary centers in Italy to familiarize himself of their workings – well aware that the pope's intent was for him to convince the centers abroad, especially in France, Germany and Belgium, of the need for a new operational regime. He was inspired by the work that was being done by the *Pontifical Institute for Foreign Missions*, a society founded in Milan in 1850 by pastoral priests and laity. Its motto was: *'All the Church for all the world'*. Fr. Roncalli could relate to that.

On May 7, 1921, Fr. Roncalli, now approaching his 40th birthday, was named a **Domestic Prelate of His Holiness** – a non-exclusive, honorific title granted by the pope to recognize services granted to the Church. As some who have held the title have wryly noted, it is a 'political' title that means very little other than the likelihood that the holder may have, at some point in time, worked a bit harder than others in the interest of the Church.

Irrespective, a 'Domestic Prelate' (called 'Honorary Prelate' as of 1968) automatically becomes a **'Monsignor'** (basically 'my lord') – entitled to wear some 'purple', though they are not bishops, and as such are not permitted to wear a pectoral cross or a skull cap. Shortly after becoming 'Msgr. Roncalli' he visited Sotto il Monte in June 1921 for the Feast of St. John wearing a purple cape and purple sash. This caused quite a bit of excitement and some confusion with people thinking that their 'little Angelo' had been made a bishop – while a few thought that he was wearing unentitled vestments!

The bishopric, of course, would follow soon enough.

39) In 1921, about to turn forty, Don Roncalli, finally got his first, very own, personal residence. When and where was this and who came to live with him?

Come 1921 Don Roncalli had yet to live in a place that he had been able to call his very own. He had always lived with others; whether it be with his parents, a seminary, a college, military barracks, a bishop's palace, a youth hostel or with friends. Now in Rome as a curialist he, at last, felt that he could afford a place of his own, though his funds were still quite limited. In reality he did not have much of a choice in this matter any longer. He needed a place to stay on a permanent basis while in Rome -- working in the offices at Piazza di Spagna. This was the first job he had held that did not come with free board and lodging. He had not been offered any accommodation in or around the Vatican. His limited budget restricted his options. Eventually, in between his work related travels, he found a 'roof-top', seven-room apartment (a crow's nest as he called it), on Via Lata, above the church of Santa Maria. It was close to his place of work. Once settled in, he took a train to Sotto il Monte and brought back his two maiden sisters, Ancilla and Maria, to live with him and be his housekeepers.

Figure 10: *Santa Maria* on *Via Lata* where Fr. Roncalli had his "crow's nest".

On the very day that he had arrived in Rome to start work for *Propaganda Fide, viz.* January 18, 1921, Fr. Roncalli, serendipitously, on the street, in front of the Piazza di Spagna, had run into Msgr. Vincenzo Bugarini, once the rector at the *'Apollinare'*. Upon learning that Roncalli had yet to make any arrangements as to where he was going to be staying this time around in Rome, Msgr. Bugarini had insisted that Roncalli share his room until he got better settled. Msgr. Bugarini was old, ailing and in need of care. Now that Msgr. Roncalli not only had a 'spacious' flat of his own, but also the fulltime assistance of his two sisters, he wished to return the favor. He persuaded Msgr. Bugarini to move in with the Roncallis. He accepted and enjoyed Ancilla's country cooking. Msgr. Bugarini was to die on February 14, 1924 (bequeathing his former student his old typewriter). Though he was not with them for long, their time together proved to be mutually rewarding. Many important prelates around the world, had like Roncalli, been Msgr. Burgarini's students at the *'Apollinare'*. That their old rector was now living with this upcoming 'Bergamascan' curialist did Roncalli's 'stock' no harm. Msgr. Roncalli, still new to Roman intrigue, also had the benefit of having an 'old hand' at home with whom he could discuss 'shop', in detail, over a leisurely meal.

40) Eight months into being a 'Monsignor' there was to be another papal transition, this the third in Roncalli's life. How long did it take this time around before Msgr. Roncalli got to meet the new pope?

Benedict XV (#259) died on January 22, 1922, unexpectedly, at the age of 67, from influenza that progressed into pneumonia, after a papacy of 7.3 years. Again, as had been the case in 1903, the future pope was in Rome, except this time around rather than being a twenty-one year old seminarian with no real Vatican contacts, he was now a forty-year old prelate, a Vatican-insider, a curialist no less. **Pope Pius XI** (#260) elected on February 6, 1922, after a five-day, fourteen ballot conclave was none other than Ambrogio Damiano Achille Ratti who he had first met, with great success, at Milan's *Biblioteca Ambrosiana* sixteen years earlier.

Though the status of the Vatican following the fall of the Papal States [i.e., the 'Roman Question'] had yet to be resolved, Pius XI, the contemplative academic, opted to deliver the traditional *urbi et orbi* (to the city (of Rome) and the world) public blessing, per the norm, from the outside balcony of St. Peter's, to the crowds gathered below. His three predecessors in righteous high dudgeon over their self-imposed 'Prisoner of the Vatican' situation had insisted on performing the blessing inside the Basilica just to a select audience.

Following the *urbi et orbi* the pope returned to the Sistine Chapel for a final round of homage from the cardinals. The conclave was now concluded and as such some prelates, curalists and lay dignitaries that had gathered outside of the Chapel were permitted inside to witness the post-conclave ceremonies. Msgr. Roncalli was one of those that was permitted to enter the Chapel. So, he got to see the new pope very soon after he was elected – probably within the first two hours.

As the new pope and his entourage of cardinals were leaving the Sistine, heading to the Apostolic Palace, Roncalli stood to a side to let them pass. The pope, most likely recognizing him, stopped in front of him. Msgr. Roncalli knelt down for a papal blessing. Cardinal 'Red Pope' Rossum, the head of *Propaganda Fide* and as such Roncali's boss, was immediately at the pope's shoulder to make sure that the pope knew exactly who the monsignor was and what he was working on. Then, somewhat self-servingly, he went onto add that during the *sede vacante* the monsignor had been very anxious that the new pope would not falter on the prior pope's urgency as to the realignment of the national *Propaganda Fide* societies. Astute and undemonstrative, the new pope made no comment.

Within three months, however, on May 3, 1922, the new pope issued a *motu proprio, Romanorum Pontificum,* that centralized the national societies within the purview of a new pontifical institute in Rome, run by a superior council. Msgr. Roncalli helped write the *motu proprio* and was, as to be expected, a member of the executive superior council. He had managed to achieve, within fifteen months, the key objective he had been tasked with by **Benedict XV**. He, nonetheless, continued to work tirelessly on *Propaganda Fide* related tasks, establishing a magazine along the way, and travelling extensively as a peace-maker to smooth over any and all slights to nationalistic egos caused by the realignment.

Figure 11: Pope Pius XI (#260), c. 1930.

IV.
THE ARCHBISHOP

This chapter in the life of the future John XXIII, as would again be true thirty-three years later, came to be thanks to the charismatic, larger-than-life Eugène-Gabriel-Gervais-Laurent Tisserant of France. At the 1958 conclave, as the Dean of the College of Cardinals, Tisserant, from all accounts (as mentioned in chapter I), masterfully marshaled the necessary votes to have Roncalli elected pope. Polylingual Tisserant, an academic very familiar with the Oriental church, had been associated with the Vatican Library since 1908. But, just as with Roncalli, Eugène Tisserant [1884 to 1972] despite being an ordained priest had served in the military during WW I– in his case in the French army's intelligence division. After the war he came back to the Vatican. In early **1925**, given his Oriental expertise, he had been sent on a mission to **Bulgaria**. On his return he

Figure 12: Eugène-Gabriel-Gervais-Laurent Tisserant.

suggested to the pope, **Pius XI** (#260), that it would advantageous for the Holy See to have an *Apostolic Visitor* in Bulgaria.

Most Bulgarians at the time belonged to the Bulgarian Orthodox Church, the oldest of the Slavic Orthodox Churches; formed in 870 under the jurisdiction of Constantinople. Though there is mutual, bilateral recognition of the validity of their respective sacraments, the Bulgarian Orthodox Church is schismatic in that it does not recognize the authority of the pope. Rome, however, has always harbored some hope of reconciliation.

The acceptance of the sacraments had meant that Bulgaria was willing to accept aid for schools and hospitals from Rome, particularly so after the devastation of the War. But, Catholic evangelization was taboo, though there were around 50,000 Catholics in Bulgaria in the 1920s, 90% of whom were of were around 50,000 Catholics in Bulgaria in the 1920s, 90% of whom were of the Latin Rite, the others Eastern Rite. Following the War Bulgaria also had about 20,000 Macedonian Catholic refugees -- living in camps.

Given the lack of recognition of 'Rome' by the country's prevailing church, the Holy See did not have official diplomatic relations with Bulgaria – which had only been an independent state as of 1908. That precluded the sending of a nuncio *per se* to Sofia, the capital. Hence, the notion of an Apostolic Visitor.

There are two widely divergent interpretations as to why Pius XI chose Msgr. Roncalli for this quasi-diplomatic post – given that the monsignor had no diplomatic training, did not speak Bulgarian and was not an expert in the politics of this region. The prevalent, preferred, 'mainline' interpretation is that it was meant to be a papal 'thank you'. Per that theory, the pope having been impressed with Msgr. Roncalli's 'Midas-touch' success in everything that had been asked of him so far wanted to honor him with a larger role. The other theory, that merits credibility given what John XXIII found in his personnel file for this period *(q.v. #34)*, is that he was conveniently shunted off to remote Bulgaria because there were those in the Vatican that worried that he was a simmering Modernist. Either way the pope opted to make him a titular archbishop to ensure that he carried the appropriate authority when in Bulgaria. The title chosen was that of the ancient Palestinian see of '**Areopolis**' [now in Jordan], known to have been active at least between 449 to 536 before it was swept up by the Arabic Islamic Empire c. 637.

He was named titular Archbishop of Areopolis on March 3, 1925.

He was consecrated on Thursday, **March 19, 1925**, Saint Joseph's Day, at the Roman basilica church of *Sant'Ambrogio e Carlo al Corso* (a.k.a. San Carlo al Corso) – a church dedicated to St. Ambrose and St. Charles (Carlo) Borromeo [with the 'Corso' referencing the street it is located on]. So, this was to be another St. Charles Borromeo connection in the life of Pope John XXIII.

The future pope was consecrated by Cardinal Giovanni Tacci (Porcelli) [1863 to 1928], Secretary of the Sacred Congregation of the Oriental Church, assisted by Francesco Marchetti Selvaggiani, titular Archbishop of Seleucia di Isauria, Secretary of the Sacred Congregation for Propagation of Faith, and by Giuseppe Palica, titular Archbishop of Filippi, Vicegerent of Rome.

For his consecration Angelo Roncalli wore a cassock bequeathed to him by his revered former bishop, Radini-Tedeschi – the one that he had worn when he had been consecrated in 1905.

His parents and all his siblings attended the consecration, as did a delegation from Bergamo led by Bishop Marelli. The next day he celebrated Mass at the same St. Peter's altar as he had done the day after his priestly ordination twenty-one years earlier. Then Archbishop Roncalli took his parents to the

Papal Apartments to meet the pope and to receive his blessing as an archbishop.

41) When did 'Areopolis' become a titular bishopric; who was its first titular bishop; when was it promoted to an titular archiepiscopal see; who was the first titular archbishop of this see and prior to Archbishop Roncalli who was the most distinguished prelate to have held this title?

Areopolis (Areopoli) was designated a titular episcopal see in **1728** when Italian Maurice di Santa Teresa Baistrocchi, O.C.D. [1662 to 1726], Vicar Apostolic of Great Mogul (India) was appointed titular bishop on January 28, 1728. It was promoted to a titular archiepiscopal see on April 27, **1903**, when U.S. Henry Moeller [1849 to 1925], recently appointed Coadjutor Archbishop of Cincinnati [U.S.A.] was appointed titular Archbishop of Areopolis.

Prior to the appointment of the future pope, the only other Areopolis title holder to be created a cardinal (let alone be elected pope) was Spanish Ciriaco María Sancha y Hervás [1833 to 1909], who was given the titular bishopric in 1876. He was created in 1894 and *beatified* in 2009. He and John XXIII are the only two associated with Areopolis to be beatified to date, John the only one, of course, to be canonized.

Areopolis was demoted back to a titular episcopal see in September 1935, Archbishop Roncalli having transferred out of that title in **November 30, 1934**.

42) What did Archbishop Roncalli choose as his episcopal motto, what was the inspiration for this motto and what was the key symbol that graced his coat of arms?

The motto he chose, which became his guiding principle for the remainder of his life was ***Obedientia et Pax*** (Obedience and Peace).

In his then daily journal he acknowledged that he was borrowing it from Cardinal Cesare Baronio (Baronius) [1538 to 1607], considered *papabile* in the two conclaves of 1605, but best known as the ecclesiastical historian who penned the twelve-volume *Annales Ecclesiastici* (Ecclesiastical Annals). The cardinal is said to have uttered *Obedientia et Pax* every time he kissed the foot of the ancient bronze statue of the seated **St. Peter** (#1) in the Vatican Basilica – he supposedly setting out to do so on a near daily basis.

Archbishop Roncalli's coat of arms featured a round, 'waisted', crenellated tower, on a red base, against a white background. This tower is said to have also appeared in the coat of arms of Martino Roncalli, the first Roncalli to have settled in the Sotto il Monte region. *[q.v. #17.]* This same 'waisted' crenellated tower, albeit topped by the lion of St. Mark to signify his Venice Patriarchy, would also grace the papal coat of arms of Pope John XXIII.

43) Archbishop Roncalli, Apostolic Visitor to Bulgaria, arrived in Sofia on **April 25, 1925**, accompanied by his newly appointed secretary, Belgian Benedictine, Fr. Constantine Bosschaerts. The Vatican at the time had no real infrastructure, let alone a nunciature, in Bulgaria. So where did the Archbishop and his secretary stay when they got to Sofia?

They stayed in a small cottage on the grounds of the Catholic *Eastern Rites* church, the Svate Bogoroditza, as the guests of the resident priest, Msgr. Stefan Kurteff. This had been a shrewdly calculated move thought out by the Vatican. The first Apostolic Visitor to the country would be seen as being hosted by a Catholic community that accepted, without equivocation, the pope -- though preferring to practice the Byzantine liturgy.

44) When he left for Bulgaria, nobody, especially the future-pope, had any real idea as to how long he would be staying there. In the end how long did Archbishop Roncalli end up staying in Bulgaria as the (hugely popular and mainly efficacious) Apostolic Visitor?

Archbishop Roncalli ended up staying in Bulgaria for a total of 3,541 days, i.e., 9 years, 8 months and 10 days. He arrived in Sofia on April 25, 1925 and left Sofia, on a bitterly cold, snowy day on **January 4, 1935**.

He had received intimation from the Vatican that his mission to Bulgaria was coming to an end in August 1934. That he was being transferred from Bulgaria appeared as a curt, one-sentence note in the **November 21, 1934** edition of *L'Osservatore Romano*. The future pope is said to have received his written communiqué from the Vatican three days later.

Archbishop Roncalli had become very attached to Bulgaria and its people, irrespective of religious differences, during his long stay there – and them to him. He wanted to celebrate Christmas with them, one last time, before he left – and, moreover, have plenty of time to say his many goodbyes.

He delivered his Christmas sermon (cum public goodbye), in Bulgarian, at the Roman Catholic Cathedral of Saint Joseph, in Sofia, on Christmas day; the event broadcast across the country by the national radio station. This was a profound, unmistakable testament to the high esteem that had been earned by the charming, humble and avuncular ***Apostolic Delegate*** (who was now 53 years of age) in what was still a non-Catholic country. His title, with the concurrence of the Bulgarian government, had been changed on September 26, **1931**. It was upgraded from 'Visitor' to 'Delegate'. It still did not amount to diplomatic recognition, and he definitely was not a nuncio, but this upgrade did indeed signify an elevation in status that had been agreed by the host country - - in part to ameliorate embarrassments caused to the Archbishop, the Vatican and the pope by the ruler of Bulgaria. *[q.v. #45.]* As an Apostolic Delegate he was entitled to a larger, better furnished residence – one in which his two sisters, Ancilla and Maria, could come and visit for extended periods of time. He, around that time, also got a new secretary; twenty-three old, newly ordained Bergamascan Fr. Giacomo Testa [who under Pope John XXIII would be the President of the Pontifical Ecclesiastical Academy].

45) Though overall his nine-year mission to Bulgaria was quite a success, and did much to bolster the standing and stature of the Vatican, Archbishop Roncalli suffered two high-profile, very public, interrelated setbacks, with all of Europe, intrigued, watching on. What were these setbacks and how did the Archbishop react?

Both rebuffs suffered by the future pope had to do with **Boris III of Bulgaria** [b. January 1894], the Tsar of Bulgaria as of October 3, 1918. He had become Tsar in the midst of WW I when his father, **Ferdinand I** [1861 to 1948], abdicated in the face of mounting reversals during the War. Ferdinand and his wife, Prince Marie-Louise, were both Catholics. However, very cognizant that his son was heir to a country that was predominantly Orthodox (and to facilitate further reconciliation with Russia), Ferdinand, to the intense chagrin of his wife, family and the Vatican, had Boris baptized in the Bulgarian Orthodox Church. The Catholic Church excommunicated Ferdinand for this flagrantly political expediency. Somewhat chastened he christened his subsequent children as Eastern Rites Catholics. Ferdinand had tried to vindicate his position to the aging **Leo XIII** (#257) in a visit to the Vatican. This proved to be a stormy meeting which ended with the pope ordering the Tsar to leave the room.

Boris III was thirty-one years of age, a bachelor and six years into his reign as Tsar when the Apostolic Visitor arrived in Sofia. Despite his lack of diplomatic standing Boris invited the Archbishop to visit with him, at his palace, just four days after his arrival. They talked for three hours. This was a start of what would be a close relationship, the ever kindly Roncalli only ever seeing good in the Tsar.

In early 1930 the prospect of a marriage between Orthodox Boris III and Catholic Princess Giovanna of Italy, the daughter of King Victor Emmanuel III of Italy, came to the fore. Her mother, Queen Elena, was Slavic, originally from Montenegro and had been born Orthodox. This pleased the Bulgarians. Though there were obvious political motives on both sides, with even the Prime Minister of Italy, Benito Mussolini, expressing favor, it was not a marriage-of-convenience *per se*. The two knew each other and there was genuine mutual attraction.

But, in order for a Catholic princess, Italian no less, to marry an Orthodox Tsar, the Vatican needed to provide a dispensation. The Vatican, per the norms for such dispensations, was adamant that the marriage had to be performed per Catholic Rites and that any and all ensuing children had to be raised Catholic. The Archbishop was tasked with making sure that the Tsar fully understood and truly acquiesced to these terms. He spent a lot of time with the Tsar going over the issues, though he appreciated that these Vatican terms put the Tsar in a rather invidious position. The Vatican terms notwithstanding, the Tsar, baptized Orthodox, was the ruler of a mainly Orthodox nation. Boris III, however, agreed and even signed a 'consent'. Irrespective, Archbishop Roncalli, tacitly, harbored some doubts as to the Tsar's genuineness.

The marriage took place, per Catholic Rites, in Assisi, on October 25, 1930. It was a lavish royal wedding. Archbishop Roncalli attended, as did Benito Mussolini. Six days later, back in Sofia, Boris insisted on an Eastern Orthodox ceremony, what he referred to as a 'nuptial blessing', at the imposingly grand Orthodox Cathedral of St. Alexander Nevsky in Sofia. Despite the pretext of the 'blessing' the marriage sacrament was repeated. So they had got married again, this time per the Orthodox Rites. It received much publicity in Orthodox circles. There was even mutterings, possibly unjustly given what would transpire later, that the Tsaritsa, in order to please her husband, had been a part of this double-cross.

The Catholic Church and the pope had been embarrassed. The Apostolic Visitor had been blatantly deceived. Even some Orthodox Bulgarians felt bad for the Archbishop. He was summoned to Rome and chastised by the pope, forced to kneel, throughout, while the pope had his say! The Vatican felt that Roncalli should have foreseen this. The pope even made an oblique reference to the sorry affair in his Christmas speech of 1930! There were rumors that the Archbishop would be 'expulsed' from Bulgaria in the New Year. Roncalli basically held his peace. Suffice to say worse was to come, though at least his title was upgraded to 'delegate' in the lull that followed -- the Tsar wishing to make some amends.

On January 13, 1933, Tsaritsa Ioanna (Bulgarian for 'Giovanna') gave birth to her first child, Princess Maria Louise of Bulgaria. The very next day, while the mother was still recovering in bed, the Tsar took the baby and had her baptized by the Orthodox Metropolitan, in the palace chapel, with considerable fanfare. The mother had not consented and was very distressed. It was a repetition of what had happened with Boris himself when his father had him baptized Orthdox against the wishes of his mother. Another uproar erupted in Catholic circlés, the Apostolic Delegate again in the epicenter. He went to the palace to lodge his protest. The Tsar would not receive him – and would continue to shun him for a year. The pope was yet again upset and made his feelings clear at a consistory a couple of months later – though he made a point of exonerating the mother based on Roncalli's assessment of what had happened.

In time the pope came to realize that he had been unduly harsh in his treatment of Archbishop Roncalli over the Tsar's duplicity. He summoned Roncalli to Rome and made amends – though it would take another year before he was finally given a posting away from Bulgaria.

46) Archbishop Roncalli's 9.6 year tenure in Bulgaria was incontrovertibly a personal triumph overall. He, unpretentious and genial, did much to foster better relationships with the Orthodox and Eastern Rites churches. In the process he was to become revered by the citizenry. The Vatican, nonetheless, even outside of the unfortunate Boris III betrayals, did not often see it that way. What were the 'issues' as the Vatican saw it, what was a key project that they thwarted and what were some marked successes that Roncalli still managed to secure?

In essence the Vatican wanted Archbishop Roncalli to be more 'imperious' in his dealing with the Orthodox church – a *modus operandi* that was alien to the Archbishop. In what was a predominantly Orthodox country the Archbishop tried not to stand on ceremony or to take offense at perceived slights. Soon after arriving in Sofia the Diplomatic Visitor paid a courtesy visit to the patriarch of the Bulgarian Church, Metropolitan Stefan Gheorgiev. This was unprecedented and, furthermore, he had done so without seeking approval from the Vatican. He just knew that it was the right and proper thing to do. The Metropolitan, probably not as easy going as the Italian, may have been perturbed by this groundbreaking visit by a papal envoy. He did not return the compliment as was the expected norm. Instead the return visit was made by one of the Metropolitan's secretaries. The Vatican was horrified and felt demeaned. The pope, in person, asked Roncalli for an explanation. Roncalli, placid as ever, tried to downplay the event by pointing that the Metropolitan tended to be rather busy.

Whenever he could Archbishop Roncalli tried to attend Orthodox services. He would even visit Orthodox monasteries and be seen praying at their altars.

He urged greater local autonomy for both the Latin Rite and Eastern Rite Catholic churches in Bulgaria. He wanted to see Bulgarian clergy nurtured and promoted to positions of responsibility rather than have the Catholic schools and hospitals run by priests and nuns from Italy and France. He wanted to open a seminary for would be priests, irrespective of their 'Rite'. He once sent a typewritten twenty-page report of his suggested Catholicity-related reforms for Bulgaria to the Vatican. Some in the curia, understandably, were discomfited by such perceived 'radical' thinking when it came to ecumenism – coming, moreover, from a suspected 'modernist'.

A project dear to the Archbishop's heart, one on which he expended much time and energy, even negotiating a possible land deal, was that of building a Bulgarian Catholic seminary for both Latin Rite and Eastern Rite aspirants. Though the Vatican at various times led him to believe that funds for this worthy project would be forthcoming shortly, in the end they never materialized.

But, there were also notable achievements. Fairly early on he managed to have Msgr. Stefan Kurteff, his initial host in Sofia, elevated to Exarch Apostolic of the Bulgarian Catholics of the Byzantine Rite. Roncalli, who had formed a close and lasting friendship with Kurteff, was very happy about this deserved promotion. Unfortunately Kurteff's elevation reduced the amount of pastoral duties that the Archbishop had been performing in Bulgaria with undisguised pleasure; pastoral work always dear to him, particularly so given the long periods when other commitments precluded him from administering to a flock.

One of the Archbishop's high-profile humanitarian achievements, realized with prompt help from the Vatican, was that of providing comfort and proactive, tangible aid during the earthquakes that wracked central Bulgaria in the spring of 1928. Roncalli who as an intrepid traveler had visited many remote parts of Bulgaria by that time, hurried to the scene as soon as he heard the news of the first series of quakes. Aftershocks and heavy rains persisted. Thousands were homeless. Roncalli directed and helped with the distribution of the meager relief supplies at hand. He cabled the Vatican for emergency aid funds. Despite the consternations he had sometimes caused he still had many influential friends and supporters in Rome. The funds arrived quickly and the Archbishop, who for a while was actually sleeping with the refugees in a tent, was able to establish much appreciated food dispensaries, which came to be referred to as *"the Pope's soup kitchens"*. It was an unintended, but nonetheless a significant, public-relations coup in what was an Orthodox country. It is, therefore, not surprising that the Bulgarians continued to follow the career of their rotund papal emissary, with great interest and undisguised affection, long after he left Sofia – and doing so even when Bulgaria was under communist rule.

47) While in Bulgaria he tried, as much as he could, to help his large and growing family, which now included in-laws as well as nieces and nephews, with counsel, moral support and most of all with funds. To this end, for a while, particularly prior to 1932, he was the recipient of some unexpected, but much appreciated, largess from the U.S.A. Who in the U.S. provided Archbishop Roncalli with some regular sums of money while he was in Bulgaria?

The U.S. benefactor was Francis Joseph Spellman [1889 to 1967], then the auxiliary bishop of Boston, Massachusetts (ahead of becoming the Archbishop of New York in 1939, a cardinal in 1946 and a very marginal *papabile* in 1958). Spellman had met Archbishop Roncalli in Bulgaria when he was on a tour of Eastern Europe. Bulgarians in fairly large numbers had started immigrating to the U.S. during the second half of the 19th century. Some of the Catholic American Bulgarians wished to have special Masses celebrated for them in Bulgaria. That was where Archbishop Roncalli came in. Bishop Spellman on a regular basis would send him a list of names and an accompanying check for these expatriate Masses. It has been said that the Archbishop was very fastidious in carrying out these requests — never sending the monies to Italy until he had celebrated the desired Masses.

Despite this amiable association when they were both bishops, it appears that Spellman was not impressed at the election of John XXIII — possibly because he had been an unrealistic, distant contender himself. It is recorded that he, after the conclave, stated: *'he is no pope, he should be selling bananas'*! A year later, when sent as a papal delegate to the Eucharistic Congress in Guatemala, he openly defied the pope's instructions and stopped in Nicaragua to meet with the ruling dictator. He, to begin with, was also critical of Vatican II.

48) As the Archbishop turned forty-five he, not that atypically for that era, started experiencing various health-related concerns. In 1926 he underwent, by today's standards, a fairly major and no doubt somewhat painful procedure — though, to be fair, it was not that unusual at the time. What did the Archbishop have done?

In 1926 he had *all* of his teeth extracted and resorted to wearing a full set of dentures. He did wryly admit to his family, in writing, that while his dentist was quite skilled he still did not manage to escape this ordeal without some suffering. It is doubtful given the strides made in dental care in the interim whether an Italian archbishop would have undergone such a drastic procedure even twenty-five years later [i.e., in the 1950s].

The future pope had been prone to weight gain since he was in his early twenties. Now heading towards his fifties he was increasingly concerned about his obvious rotundness — though it is very unlikely that vanity played a role. The Archbishop was probably concerned about the impact to his health and the perception it conveyed of possible 'excesses' on his part. In reality he had been dieting for decades. He was noted for having a light breakfast and trying to abstain from snacking. But, true to his farming stock heritage, he did enjoy one hearty Italian country style meal a day — trying, though, to eschew delicacies and expensive trimmings. It is, however, possible that this hearty, family-style meal-a-day was, per the norms of that time, was heavy in carbohydrates, pasta in particular. That would explain the weight gain despite his efforts to watch what he ate. Yet again, as with the teeth, this appears to have been a *'sign of the times'*.

It is also known that by this stage of his life the Archbishop was known to suffer from frequent bouts of stomach ailments and 'the cold'. It is possible that he had some undiagnosed gastronomic issues that contributed to his weight gain. In 1927 he had a spate of kidney problems that necessitated treatment in Italy.

At times, discouraged by these ailments, the Archbishop is said to have confided to his family that he did not expect, despite the inescapable evidence of his family's propensity for longevity, to live to see 60. He turned sixty in 1941. Obviously he lived to be much older; only getting elected pope in 1958.

49) That the pope, John XXIII, had a nephew, Giovanni Battista Roncalli, who was a priest -- one that he had ordained himself in July 1955, in Venice, while the Patriarch, is well known. *[q.v. Chapter 1.]* Battista Roncalli, however, was not the first nephew who wanted to follow the uncle's footsteps into the clergy. Who was that first nephew who wanted to enter a seminary and what happened to him?

The first in the next generation of Roncallis who wanted to 'heed the call' was brother Giovanni Francesco's eldest son, another 'Angelo' [undoubtedly named after the uncle], who was born in 1923. In April 1934, eleven years old, he wrote to his uncle in Sofia that he wanted to become a priest. Archbishop Roncalli suffice to say was overjoyed and eager to help. He immediately wrote back with words of encouragement, advice and 'caution' along with an unconditional offer to help *'along the road to the altar'*.

It was arranged that he would start attending the seminary in Bergamo the next year – following the very same footsteps of his already distinguished uncle. Then in November 1934, on a wet day, he caught a 'cold'. Within a week, November 30, 1934, he was dead! He was twelve at the time.

Archbishop Roncalli happened to be visiting Rome when he got the devastating news. He immediately set off to Sotto il Monte for the funeral and took care of all the funeral expenses.

Giovanni Battista was this Angelo's younger brother – the fifth of Giovanni Francesco's nine children. He was born on March 7, 1927. He indicated his desire to try and emulate his older brother in 1940, when he was thirteen.

50) Where was the Archbishop transferred to in November 1934 and what appears to have been the motives behind this transfer?

A pithy but bland one sentence announcement in the November 21, 1934 *L'Osservatore Roman* stated that the Holy Father had appointed his Excellency Angelo Giuseppe Roncalli, Apostolic Delegate, to Apostolic Delegate for **Turkey and Greece**. The repeated 'Apostolic Delegate', whether intentional or not, alas, highlighted that this was not a promotion.

Upon learning of his transfer, the Archbishop asked the pope whether his titular archbishopric could be changed to that of '*Mesembria*'. It was an ancient Greek city (now Nesebar) on the Black Sea coast of Bulgaria. It was a city that he had visited; its congeniality striking a chord. So much so that he had established an aid program therein to feed 250 needy children.

The titular archbishopric had been established in March 1930 to be assigned to a previous Apostolic Delegate to Turkey, Italian Carlo Margotti. In July 1935 he had been appointed the Metropolitan Archbishop of Gorizia e Gradisca [Italy]. So the title was vacant. The pope agreed and on November 30, 1934 Angelo Giuseppe Roncalli became the titular **Archbishop of Mesembria**.

In his nationally broadcast, farewell Christmas sermon in Sofia, delivered in *Bulgarian*, on Christmas day 1934, at the Cathedral of St. Joseph, he, proudly conveyed the news of his new title to the citizenry, pointing out how it would remind him, each day, of his affection for Bulgaria.

It was also this Christmas address that included the first of the two '*windows-related*' statements indelibly associated with him; though the provenance of the second is now under some scrutiny. He made a promise that day, borrowing a Christmas tradition from Catholic Ireland where a lit candle is placed in the window to show 'Joseph and Mary' that they are welcome inside. This promise was: '*... if any Bulgarian away from home passes by my house, he will always find the **candle of welcome burning in my window**. ...*". This came to be known as the pope's '*candle in the window*' saying.

The second '*windows*' statement, of course, is the oft repeated one that he as pope wanted to '*open the windows*' of the Church. Though the pope may very well have said this in conversation, research efforts in the last few years to find documentation of this quote have so far proved to be futile. The pope's secretary, Archbishop Loris Capovilla, when asked about this quote, is said to have claimed that the pope never made it! Apocryphal or not '*open the windows*' will always be associated with the Good Pope though in terms of poignancy the '*candle in the window*' is hard to beat.

[The future pope relinquished the Archbishopric of Mesembria when he became the Patriarch of Venice on January 15, 1953. Six months later it was given to Silvio Anggelo Pio Oddi, the Apostolic Delegate to Jerusalem and Palestine. The title again fell vacant in April 1969 when Oddi became a curial 'president' (as a cardinal). The title remained vacant for 2.3 years. Then on September 25, 1971, **Paul VI** (#263) in an inspired perspicacious gesture granted it to no other than Loris Capovilla. As of February 2014 Archbishop Loris Capovilla, 98 years of age, was still alive. He was created a cardinal deacon on February 22, 2014. Hence only four clerics have held the title Archbishop of Mesembria up to early 2014. It is interesting that the last three holders of this title all became cardinals.]

Archbishop Roncalli's transfer was at best a marginal promotion. It was yet again not a nunciature. Given its Byzantine antecedents, its strategic *'gateway to Asia'* location and the historic significance of Constantinople [by then 'Istanbul', Turkey] as the 'new Rome', it was, nonetheless, a notch above Bulgaria in both diplomatic and ecclesiastical circles. And Greece, in addition to its glittering past, was a *bona fide* top-tier European nation – albeit in the throes of considerable political and social upheaval in the 1930s. So, in terms of civilian stature this was indeed a leg up. Neither country, however, was a major Catholic nation.

As of 1923, the emerging post-Ottoman Turkey, moreover, was zealously committed to being a totally irreligious, absolutely secular 'Western style' republic. In this context a theory that Archbishop Roncalli was actually sent to Turkey primarily because of his by now well proven propensity for equanimity and conciliation has much merit. The Vatican in July of 1934 'replaced' the prior delegate in Turkey, Carlo Margotti, the first Archbishop of Mesembria, because he was having trouble accepting Turkey's restrictions on religious activity with grace. Roncalli was the replacement.

In reality Bulgaria had more Latin Rite Catholics than either Turkey (~20,000) or Greece. Archbishop Roncalli, however, was not been sent to Istanbul just to tend to this loyal congregation. His mission, it would appear, was to repeat what he had done so superbly in Bulgaria, the unseemly Boris III contretemps notwithstanding, i.e., that of establishing rapport with the other churches, establishing goodwill with the ruling powers and in general enhancing the stature of the Holy See within that region.

Archbishop Roncalli arrived, by rail, in Istanbul on January 5, 1935. He was met at the station by the secretary to the Turkish Holy See delegation, the local vicar-general, Angelo Dell'Acqua who was Italian. *[q.v. #73.]* At the time the delegation did not own a car. So other than when he took a taxi, Archbishop Roncalli would get about Istanbul either by bus or on foot.

51) On June 13, 1935, just five months into his stay in Turkey, the Turkish government, led by the ex-revolutionary Mustafa Kemal Atatürk, enacted an odious restriction on all clergy, irrespective of religion and gender. What was this restriction and what was Archbishop Roncalli's reaction to it?

This was the enforcement of a law passed in 1934 banning the clergy from wearing of any type of religious dress in public. They were expected to wear 'western style' dress when in public. Many clerics, as was to be expected, including the Orthodox patriarch, railed against this injunction; the French ambassador, on behalf of the Catholic French religious orders, lodged a formal protest – albeit all to no avail.

Archbishop Roncalli, per his nature and possibly heeding instructions from Rome, opted to comply without demur. Furthermore, he set out to ensure that all Catholics within his purview, despite some misgivings, also complied --sans exception. Business suits replaced cassocks. A skill that Roncalli had mastered during his two stints in the army came in handy, and he gladly shared it with others – this being the knack of tying a necktie. Archbishop Roncalli, when in public, would typically wear a dark business suit with a dark, hard felt bowler (derby) hat. He gave the impression of being a rather prosperous banker – his generous build contributing greatly to this perception.

52) Fairly soon after he arrived in Turkey the Archbishop, per his own volition, embarked on a strategy to provide better assimilation between 'his' Catholics and the nascent aspiring secular nation. A major innovation of the Second Vatican Council, twenty-eight years later, would echo this 1930s initiative undertaken in Turkey. What was this initiative?

Archbishop Roncalli, in an effort to show his and the Holy See's respect for the new Turkey, decided to embrace the Turkish language – not just in terms of his personal proficiency but as a language for the local church. It was an extension of his conscientious efforts in Sofia to learn Bulgarian.

At the time Catholic church services in Turkey, even the sermons and prayers, were not conducted in Turkish. French or Italian was typically used – even for church communiqués. Roncalli believed that this was not appropriate or conducive for inclusiveness. He set about having Turkish translations provided so that the congregation could follow what was being said. Important church documents were made available in Turkish. Finding the appropriate Turkish words to convey the necessary meaning proved sometimes to be a challenge. *'Allah'* for 'God' would not have gone down well either in Turkey or in Rome. So the Archbishop, who was already in the process of taking Turkish lessons and assiduously studying the history of the Oriental Church, following consultations with academics, came up with *'Tanre'* [derived from the name (possibly in Sanskrit) given to the chief deity of a very early 'Turkish' religion].

As would also be the case post-1963 when the Vatican II's *Sacrosanctum Concilium* encouraged greater lay participation in the liturgy, which could now be conducted in the local vernacular, Archbishop Roncalli's promotion of

Turkish did not, at least at first, receive universal approval from his flock. But, the Archbishop was content; he truly believed that he was doing the right thing. It was his way of showing that the Catholic Church respected and welcomed all; language and race not a barrier.

The Turkish authorities, pleasantly surprised, were quietly appreciative of the Archbishop's motives. Roncalli and President Mustafa Kemal Atatürk never met or had any direct communications. However, Roncalli was apprised, indirectly, that the President was suitably impressed with his efforts to foster better unity.

53) Though Istanbul was his primary residence and he spent much of his time in Turkey, Archbishop Roncalli was also the Apostolic Delegate to Greece. How many times did he visit Greece in 1935, his first year in Turkey?

He visited Greece three times in 1935, in May, August and November.

In theory Greece was more tolerant of religion than Turkey. However, the predominant religion in Greece was the Greek Orthodox Church and historically there had been little love lost between them and the Holy See. To exacerbate matters further, Greece, in the 1930s, was in near constant political turmoil. Consequently, within the overall scheme of things, 'playing nice' to Apostolic Delegates was not a high priority for the Greek authorities. Roncalli, to his credit, had no difficulty both understanding and appreciating this.

This, alas, had not been so with his much more 'prickly' predecessor Carlo Margotti. As he had done in Turkey he had managed to antagonize the Greek authorities – this time by insisting on diplomatic 'niceties' even though it was well understood by all that an 'Apostolic Delegate', at best, was 'borderline' in terms of *bona fide* diplomatic stature; indisputable rights only afforded to a 'nuncio'.

At that time the Apostolic Delegate needed a visa in order to enter Greece.

Margotti had even managed, for a time, to have his visa revoked.

Archbishop Roncalli, so masterful in such delicate situations, opted to be very low-key and unpretentious. He, in person, applied for a visa at the Greek consulate in Istanbul. He said it was for a visit to assess the spiritual needs of Greek Catholics. He refrained from even mentioning any diplomatic prerogatives that may have been in order. He was, within a week, granted a visa – albeit a standard tourist visa valid but for eight days. The Archbishop did not complain. Instead he set out to comply.

As was the case in Turkey the Vatican did not own any vehicles in Athens. So as in Istanbul the portly Delegate had to walk or take public transport. He realized quite quickly that he was being constantly tailed (a 'privilege' also enjoyed, though not with the same degree of composure by most of the Catholic bishops in Greece).

His tact and diplomacy on his first visit was such that he was permitted to make two further visits later that year. In 1936 he was given a diplomatic visa that enabled him *carte blanche* access.

During his subsequent visits in 1935 and 1936, he was invited to meet with King George II, King of the Hellenes [1922 to 1924 & 1935 to 1947], General Ioannis Metaxas, Prime Minister of Greece [1936 to 1941], and heads of the Ministry of Foreign Affairs. Paralleling what happened in Bulgaria, Roncalli established a sound rapport with the King – as well as with other 'higher ups'. These personal relationships would, as was to be expected, prove to be very beneficial over time.

Whereas Turkey imposed religious restrictions across the board, sans any bias, Greece, in the 1930s, at the behest of the dominant Orthodox Church which was paranoid of potential defections, tended to target Catholics in the main. A set of regulations imposed early on during Archbishop Roncalli's tenure tried to make it very difficult for Catholics to evangelize, to get married to a non-Catholic in a Catholic church as well as to promote, publish or import Catholic books. The Archbishop, of course, did not try to confront these restrictions head-on. Instead, he opted to calmly discuss the issues, charm in abundance, with the King, the General and his new found contacts in the government. The King, in particular, was receptive. In time these restrictions were modified and relaxed.

54) In addition to all of his bridge-building humanitarian and ecumenical achievements while in Turkey and Greece, the Archbishop also managed to successfully influence the outcome of two landmark cultural initiatives – one in each country. What were these two projects, the end results of which forever changed the cultural landscape of the two cities?

In Turkey the authorities, with their aversion to religion, planned to convert the imposingly magnificent, iconic and historic **Hagia Sophia** (Holy Wisdom) into a secular museum. It was originally a Greek Orthodox patriarchal basilica. Then for a time it was a Catholic Latin Rites cathedral. Later still it became an imperial mosque. The Hagia Sophia stood on the site of a *'Magna Ecclesia'* (Great Church) built in 360 during the reign of Constantius II – the second son of Constantine the Great, the first Christian emperor. The sprawling edifice that now stands was completed during the time of Emperor Justinian I in 537 – it the third Christian church on that strategic site. It was the seat of the Orthodox patriarch of Constantinople and the emperor's favored church – especially for grandiose imperial ceremonies. During the 'Latin occupation of Constantinople' that came to be after the Fourth Crusade, Hagia Sophia, from 1204 to 1261, became a Catholic Latin Rites Cathedral. Following the Ottoman conquest it was a mosque from 1453 to 1935.

The Archbishop quietly persuaded those in charge that the *Hagia Sophia* was a cultural gem, a unique historic relic that should be restored and maintained as a Byzantine shrine – a testament to the glory of Constantinople in its heyday. They quite quickly saw the merits of his suggestion. Rather than trying to convert it into a museum they set about eradicating 480 years worth of embellishments, mainly plaster and paint added by the Ottomans, to expose mosaics, frescoes and paintings from the Byzantine Christian era. Upon painstaking restoration the *Hagia Sophia* emerged as what it is today – a breathtaking, internationally famed monument to the grace and beauty of Byzantine culture. Though this success would appear minor in his huge repertoire of far-reaching achievements one has to believe that there must have been times, later in his life, possibly when walking in the Vatican gardens, that the pope thought back to his role in the revitalization of the *Hagia Sophia* with a wry smile.

In Greece he managed, through a combination of diligence and skill, to get approval from both the local authorities and the Vatican for the building of a new Byzantine Rite Catholic cathedral in Athens. It was, suffice to say, not easy. The very influential Orthodox hierarchy opposed it while Rome was aloofly leery. Concessions were required from both sides and the Archbishop managed to hammer these out. The Vatican agreed to make the Cathedral the seat of the Byzantine bishop of all Greek Catholics, even those living in Turkey along the lines: *'The capital of Greece, Athens, is the capital of all Hellenes'*. This flattered the nationalistic ego of the Greeks. The Greeks wanted the new structure to be built on the exact location and footprint of an ancient Cathedral that predated the Orthodox schism. This permitted the Orthodox to rationalize that they were keeping the Catholic expansion in check – even if it was just in terms of real-estate.

55) In September 1939 World War II broke out. Turkey set out to be strictly neutral during most of it, albeit finally joining forces with the Allies in February 1945 as hostilities were drawing to a close. It, given its strategic geographic location and initial neutrality, became a hotbed for wide scale espionage by all and sundry. The Archbishop, with his ready access to most locals, irrespective of their nationality, was closely monitored by operatives from multiple countries – much to his amusement since he knew he was being followed and could identify his 'tails'. Greece, however, was another story. It was invaded by both Italy and Germany and was occupied, with brutal food depravation, by the Germans. The Archbishop, consistent with, but invariably exceeding, the

Vatican's commitment for humanitarian succor, worked tirelessly in both countries to help as many people as possible, irrespective of nationality – his Catholicity and nationality also dictating that he had to fraternize with German and Italian troops. His overall efforts during this War were far-flung, profound, sometimes covert and multifaceted. They even included some intelligence gathering for his 'friends' and acts of interceding with his old friend Boris III, the Tsar of Bulgaria, who had sided with the Axis powers. He also managed to wield influence in nearby countries, in particular Hungary, Slovakia and Romania. Despite the vast scope of his efforts during these troubled times, he, invariably, is best remembered, with gratitude, for three major initiatives during this period. What were these three initiatives?

Just as they had done very successfully during WW I, the Vatican Information Office, exploiting its unique reach across Europe, became the nerve center and clearing house for those seeking information on missing troops, captured or otherwise, as well as refugees. The Vatican collected all of the incoming requests and then sent them out across Europe by cable, mail or courier to the best located of its emissaries for 'processing'. Turkey with its strategic, geographic cross-roads location, became a crucial coordination point – given its access to Russia, the Balkans, Asian countries to the east and Arab nations to the south. The Archbishop, who remembered trying to get information about his brothers during WW I, became heavily involved in this 'missing soul' program – often relying upon his personal relationships, far and wide, and at all levels of governments and society, to pursue queries or to get messages relayed further down the line. Turkey and the Archbishop became famous for their success, often exceeding that of the Red Cross in locating POWs and refugees – sometimes even those confined to concentration camps.

Greece suffered inordinately during the War. German and Italian troops occupied it, the Allies blockaded it. The Archbishop tried to visit as often as he could, making four visits in 1941 alone. These trips were often arduous, sometimes circuitous. When possible he would try to get there by plane, though he was not thrilled about doing so in winter when bad weather often made flying rather 'adventerous'. The Allied blockade had severely curtailed food supplies; starvation becoming a reality. The Archbishop cajoled his contacts in Turkey, Bulgaria, Hungary and the Vatican for aid. He managed to obtain some food and medical supplies to ease the suffering – thus winning over those that harbored some resentment towards him due to his nationality.

In April of 1941 the King, George II, and much of his government had fled Greece – eventually seeking exile in Britain. The Orthodox Archbishop of Athens, Damaskinos Papandreou, the most senior national figure left in Greece effectively became the *de facto* regent of the country [a scenario once very familiar to popes]. By September 1941 Greeks were dying in the thousands from malnutrition. Without outside aid, brought in through the blockade, much of the population was likely to succumb over the winter months. Damaskinos and the leaders of the occupation forces knew that they had to have an emissary to intercede with the Allies. Damaskinos knew who that had to be, and was prepared to do so despite the centuries of bitter division between the two factions. Archbishop Roncalli, of course, made sure that Damaskinos never felt at a disadvantage, publicly or privately. He assured Damaskinos that the pope himself would, if asked, approach the Allied leaders. Damaskinos, putting aside any and all reservations in the interests of his compatriots, wrote a letter to the pope. Archbishop Roncalli delivered it, in person, to **Pius XII** (#261), in Rome, on October 7, 1941. The Allies honored the request and permitted ships carrying wheat to reach Greece. A terrible disaster had been averted.

The Apostolic Delegate to Greece managed to make four trips to Greece in 1942. Then escalation in military operations in the region made travel near impossible. However, he had managed to have his onetime secretary Giacomo Testa deputize for him in Athens as the representative of the Holy See.

Archbishop Roncalli's greatest and most enduring success during WW II, however, had to do with his manifold enterprises, from neutral Turkey, to protect and save Jews from Nazi persecution. He intervened, at the highest possible levels, far and wide, across borders – most notably in Greece, Slovakia, Bulgaria, Romania and Hungary. His personal relationship with Bulgarian Boris III paid dividend with the Tsar repeatedly delaying German pressure to enact the 'final solution'. He prevailed upon the Turkish authorities to permit safe passage to Jewish refugees arriving in Istanbul to either Palestine or other sympathetic nations.

Then, having heard that the Nazis honored baptismal certificates given to some Jews in Hungary by Catholic nuns, he immediately mounted *'Operation Baptism'*. The Archbishop instructed that as many baptismal certificates as needed should be issued forthwith – with no obligation, whatsoever, on the recipients to convert to Catholicism. Per the Archbishop the recipients were not to even be asked to consider such a move. This was not about proselytizing, it was all about saving lives. Archbishop Roncalli is credited by Jewish organizations of having saved thousands of Jewish lives during WW II.

His personal efforts during the War, notwithstanding, he, when pope, publicly sought forgiveness on behalf of Christians for all the atrocities committed against the Jews over the centuries.

V.
THE NUNCIO

Archbishop Roncalli was to suffer three major bereavements, two of them very personal, during his stay in Turkey. In all three instances the absence of a deputy to take care of his local obligations precluded the Archbishop, to his great distress, from being able to attend the funerals, let alone being at the bedsides. In July 1935 his father died at the age of 81. On February 10, 1939, **Pius XI** (#260) died; he too was in his 81st year. Ten days later his mother, who had been ill for a while, would die. She was close to 84. The nine days of official mourning afforded to a pope, the so called *novendiali*, is what prevented the Archbishop from making it to Sotto il Monte to be with his mother – he having to be in Istanbul for a high-profile requiem Mass for the pope.

On March 2, 1939, Eugenio Maria Giuseppe Giovanni Pacelli, was elected as **Pius XII** (#261) on what was his 63rd birthday: the only known instance of a pope getting elected on his birthday. As had been the case with Pius XI, Roncalli had known this pope for a long time, actually a very long time; Pacelli having been one of his canon law lecturers at the *'Apollinare'* over thirty years ago. This time, moreover, unlike with Pius XI, the two had worked together. Pacelli, Secretary of State since February 1930, had been Archbishop Roncalli's official point-of-contact at the Vatican for the last nine years. He had also been a much-needed admirer and a supporter back in 'HQ' of the Archbishop's selfless endeavors 'out in the east'. Suffice to say that the Archbishop was very pleased with the election and clearly saw the Lord's hand at work.

In the early evening of Wednesday, December 6, 1944, Archbishop Roncalli while working in his study in Istanbul received a telegram, in code, from the Vatican. His secretary at the time, Irish Father Thomas Ryan, who normally deciphered the coded messages was out on an errand. So the Archbishop retrieved the code book and started to tediously unscramble the words from Rome. He deciphered two words early on, 'nuncio' and 'France'. He thought he had made a mistake with the code or that the telegram had been mistakenly sent to Istanbul rather than Paris. When Fr. Ryan returned, shortly, he immediately set about deciphering the telegram. There was no mistake. The pope had nominated Archbishop Roncalli as the nuncio to France – at that time the top diplomatic posting for a Holy See ambassador. The Archbishop had gone from being a quasi-diplomat, for nineteen years, to the top spot in the Vatican's diplomatic hierarchy in one giant leap.

The Archbishop, not surprisingly, was duly amazed. He was 63 years old. He had been away from the 'mainstream' for so long that he had given up thinking about getting promoted. He, in his unassuming way, had been quite happy doing his unstinted best, with patently marked success, in Turkey, Greece and the surrounding regions.

On December 22nd he received an official letter from Rome stating that he needed to be in Paris by January 1, 1945. On the 27th he left Turkey headed for Rome on a rickety 'old warhorse' B-24 bomber (built in the U.S.) loaned for the occasion by the French.

The next day Archbishop was at the Vatican to be briefed on his new duties. He met with Monsignor Domenico Tardini, the Secretary of the Sacred Congregation for Extraordinary Ecclesiastical Affairs. He along with Monsignor Giovanni Battista Montini [future Paul VI (#263)] helped Pius XII run the Secretariat of State. Tardini was convivial, straightforward and very competent. He was also known to be blunt and caustic. Tardini, unabashedly not to mention tactlessly, informed the Archbishop that the decision as to his nunciature had been made by the pope and the pope alone, without any recommendations, support or endorsement from the curia. It was just as the Archbishop had suspected. He was still a curial 'outsider'.

Figure 13: Monsignor Domenico Tardini.

On December 28th at a private audience with the pope, Pius confirmed Tardini's statement, but did so as a compliment. The pope wished to stress that it was indeed he who had thought of Roncalli for this demanding though prestigious post and had gone through with the decision without seeking any external input. In terms of the Vatican and the Church that is all that mattered: Archbishop Roncalli was the pope's personal choice to be the nuncio to France.

56) What was the significance of Archbishop Roncalli's appointment to this post and why was he, indubitably, the right choice?

Just as it had been in Bulgaria, Turkey and Greece, the Holy See was, at that time, at a disadvantage in France. The marked difference, however, was that France was a Catholic nation. The issue here had to do with the German occupation of France from July 1940 to August 1944, and the role of the Catholic Church and French Catholic clerics during that time – the matter complicated by the fact that many of the German troops were Catholic and attended church.

Many among the liberated French, especially those that were in or supported the *'Resistance'*, felt that there had been too much collaboration and complicity between the Catholic hierarchy and the despised occupiers. General Charles de Gaulle, the President of the Provisional Government, a devout Catholic, seasoned and astute, appreciated the predicament faced by the clerics. Nonetheless, at this delicate stage as his country healed, he was not willing to openly go against the popular hue and cry. Plus, his ego would not permit him to retain a nuncio that had also worked with the puppet Vichy Regime. Though he wanted to maintain diplomatic relations with the Holy See, Charles de Gaulle was adamant that Archbishop Valerio Valeri, the nuncio to France since July 1936 had to be replaced and, moreover, that at least thirty-three French bishops also had to be removed. The Vatican quickly realized that the General was not open to negotiation when it came to Valeri. Valeri had to be replaced. The Vatican sought approval of Archbishop Roncalli. The General immediately agreed – no doubt having heard of the Archbishop's gallant work in Greece and his intercedings on behalf of the Jews. Valeri was recalled to Rome – though ironically, and incongruously, he was awarded the Grand Cross of the *Légion d'Honneur* by Charles de Gaulle prior to his departure!

Archbishop Roncalli, with his proven charm, warmth, empathy and tact was now expected to rebuild and bolster bilateral relationships between the Holy See and the resurgent France, just as he had done so exceptionally well in Bulgaria, Turkey and Greece. He, with his fondness for Lourdes, knew France quite well and spoke fluent French. However, though his prior official dealings with France, while with Propaganda Fide, had not been extensive they had been somewhat contentious; the French hierarchy not happy that the administration had been centralized and moved to Rome. Pius XII, all the same, had chosen wisely. He was the ideal candidate for this tricky posting, where larger egos than his may have faltered. The pope, nonetheless, was also realistic. His parting words to the new nuncio were, in French, the equivalent of: *'do as well as possible'*. The nuncio did quite a bit better than that.

57) Once his appointment had been accepted by General Charles de Gaulle there was an unseemly urgency to have Archbishop Roncalli accredited and installed as nuncio to France prior to January 1, 1945. To this end the French provided a B-24 to fly the Archbishop from Turkey to Rome, and then Charles de Gaulle's personal plane, no less, to get him from Rome to Paris on December 30. Why this rush?

New Year's Day, January 1, had for long been a rather special, celebratory holiday in France. In light of this, per a long cherished tradition, the elite Paris-based *Corps Diplomatique* to France would formally call upon the President of France and officially deliver a New Year's greeting to the President and the nation. This greeting would be orated by the 'dean' of the Corps. Per custom, going back to 1815, given France's Catholicity, the 'dean' of the Corps was always the pope's nuncio to France, irrespective of his length of tenure in France – provided that there was an accredited nuncio in residence.

In the absence of a nuncio, the 'dean' tasked with delivering the New Year's greeting would be the Ambassador who had served in France for the longest time. In December of 1944, the longest serving Ambassador was from the Soviet Union. Charles de Gaulle and his government were not that keen, at this stage of the still bitter War, to have the first New Year's greeting to the newly liberated France delivered by a Soviet.

Hence the rush to get a nuncio properly installed in Paris prior to New Year's Day.

Archbishop Roncalli was scheduled to land in Paris' Le Bourget airport during the afternoon of December 30. Dense fog diverted the plane, the presidential plane, to the other Parisian airport, Orly – in those days primarily a military facility. A fairly large and impressive welcoming committee, from the nunciature and the government, waited in vain at Le Bourget unaware that the plane had diverted. So yet again the unassuming Archbishop arrived at a host country sans any fanfare – this time even without a local priest to accompany him to his residence. The crew of his plane eventually commandeered a jeep to get the Archbishop to nunciature, in central Paris, at No. 10, Avenue du Président Wilson, close to the Seine. The nunciature, a house (some call it a 'palace') once owned by the Prince of Monaco, had been imposing, but was now a tad run down, WW II, in particular, having taken a toll.

Arriving at the nunciature, the Archbishop, with his customary joviality, introduced himself to the confounded priest who answered the door with the greeting that it was likely that they were expecting him. The future pope had arrived in Paris.

The next day, New Year's Eve he presented his credentials to be accredited.

On January 1, 1945, per the plan, he delivered the *Corps Diplomatique's* New Year's greeting, with aplomb – a custom that he maintained, yearly, with increasing flair and affection, during the next eight years of his stay in France. Charles de Gaulle, though courteous and correct, was aloof and a bit frosty, unwilling as yet to let his guard down – and wishing to convey the gravity of his government's displeasure with the Holy See.

58) How did the new nuncio deal with the provisional French government's request to have thirty-three French bishops, including Cardinal Emmanuel Célestin Suhard, the Archbishop of Paris, removed?

Consistent with his behavior in prior postings the nuncio knew better than to openly protest or show disdain or defiance. He appreciated that the French, rightly or wrongly, felt aggrieved. He set about working with the French foreign minister on how to pursue this matter in a pragmatic manner. The immediate removal of such a large number of bishops was not practical. There was a real risk that this could paralyze the Catholic Church in France. The nuncio realized, early on, that some of the allegations against the bishops may be more tenuous than the French realized. So he suggested to the minister that the government should press specific legal charges against each of the bishops. The French were glad to comply; they felt that this was indeed the right way to proceed.

Soon the French had compiled bulging dossiers on each of the accused bishops. The nuncio started going through the dossiers. He quickly realized that much of the alleged accusations were based on newspaper reports and gossip. There was little if any evidence *per se* that would stand up in a court of law. He, respectfully, pointed this out to the French. Legal experts were summoned. They concurred with the nuncio. The government ordered additional investigations on specific allegations. Time marched on. The bishops in questions continued with their ministry. The War in Europe was coming to an end. Life in France was slowly edging towards a new, post-occupation normalcy. Emotions inflamed during the Resistance were beginning to ebb.

Finally, after much negotiations, it was agreed that just three bishops, Cardinal Suhard not among them, would be removed.

It was another major 'feather in the cap' for the future pope. For someone who was never schooled in diplomacy Archbishop Roncalli continued to impress with his knack for getting difficult issues amicably resolved irrespective of the cultures involved.

59) With the matter of the French bishops out of the way the nuncio had the chance to get international recognition -- to the delight of the French, in particular the de Gaulle government -- for a French Archbishop who despite physical frailty boldly resisted, and spoke out against the Nazis and their treatment of the Jews. Who was this Archbishop and how was he recognized?

It was Jules-Géraud Saliège, born February 24, 1870, the Archbishop of Toulouse(-Narbonne) since December 1928. He had served as a military chaplain in WW I and had been gassed. Like the Roncallis he had been an active supporter of *Azione Cattolica* (Catholic Action).

He suffered a stroke in 1932 (at the age of 62) which damaged the lower half of his brainstem leaving him paralyzed below the neck and making it difficult for him to talk.

During the occupation Saliège quickly realized what was happening to the Jews in detention camps in the area around Toulouse, in southwestern France. In November 1941 he sent a letter to the Vichy authorities protesting the way that the Jews were being treated. He was among the first, and few, to publicly take a stand against the Nazi operations in France. He became the leading figure in the Catholic resistance to Nazism in France. He directed his followers to collect as much intelligence as they could of the Nazi operations, particularly what was taking place in the detention and transit camps. By August 1942 his worst fears had been confirmed.

He wrote a scathing, unequivocal denouncement of the Nazi treatment of the Jews, citing it as a violation of the rights afforded to humans by God and laying the blame solely at the feet of the Germans – stating that the French, intrinsically, were too generous and chivalrous to be a party to such horrors. He had copies of this fulmination sent to each of the priests in his diocese and ordered them to read it out aloud, from the pulpit, on Sunday, August 23, 1942. The police heard about it and instructed him to withdraw his order to his priests. He refused.

He had himself carried to his cathedral in Toulouse, on a stretcher, and he too, laboriously, given his speech impediment, delivered his trenchant condemnation to a large, attentive congregation. That same week his blistering words were propagated, with undisguised passion and pride, from various other pulpits in France and reprinted in *L'Osservatore Romano*. They were also broadcast by the BBC and twice on Vatican Radio. The police, incensed, tried to arrest the frail and paralyzed Archbishop a number of times but each time thought the better of it. Jules-Géraud Saliège was a national hero and his brave and gallant deeds were not forgotten after the liberation.

A nuncio has the prerogative to submit names of local 'worthies' to the pope for consideration for a cardinalate. Nuncio Roncalli, appreciating what it would mean to the French, the clear message it would convey to the Germans and the righteousness aspects of it vis-à-vis the Holy See, recommended to the pope, as persuasively as he could, that Jules-Géraud Saliège should be created a cardinal – as soon as possible.

In 1945, six years into his papacy, Pius XII had yet to create any cardinals. The last cardinal creating consistory had been on December 13, 1937. Pius' reticence in creating cardinals cannot be blamed entirely on the War. As discussed in #2 Pius, an intensely private soul not known to be an affable 'people person', also had issues appointing a Secretary of State or a *Camerlengo* – he opting not to have either one of these 'officers' during much of his papacy.

Pius XII held his first cardinal creating consistory on February 18, 1946 – 6.9 years after becoming pope and 8.2 years since the last. He created thirty-two cardinals at that consistory; the average age of those created 62.9 years. Jules-Géraud Saliège, created a cardinal priest, was the seventh named at this consistory; the Archbishops of St. Louis (U.S.), Kraków (Poland) and Detroit (U.S.), two nuncios and Grégoire-Pierre XV Agagianian, Patriarch of Cilicia of the Armenians, were given precedence ahead of him. Saliège, however, was given the title to the very prestigious Santa Pudenziana basilica, recognized as the oldest place of Christian worship in Rome. It was a title held by three popes and one often given to French cardinals in the 13th and 14th century.

Saliège was six days short of his 76th birthday when he became a cardinal. That same day he was awarded the *Croix de la Libération* (Cross of Liberation) a French honor, created by Charles de Gaulle, awarded to heroes of the liberation of France during WW II. Following the consistory the nuncio visited Toulouse to present the new cardinal with his red biretta. This much deserved cardinalate caused much rejoicing in France and among Jewish circles. It was cathartic and seen as a major symbolic honor bestowed by the Holy See to all those in France that fought the tyranny of the Nazis and the complicity of the Vichy regime.

60) The nuncio to France typically did not have any pastoral duties, the national hierarchy in what was a Catholic nation more than capable of taking care of all that was required. But Archbishop Roncalli who enjoyed the interaction with parishioners made himself as available as much as possible, diplomatic obligations permitting, to attend services and gatherings all over France – and even in French North Africa, i.e., Algeria, Morocco and Tunisia. He visited nearly all of the eighty or so Catholic dioceses in France and made at least one pilgrimage, a year, to Lourdes. The nuncio, however, would also gain considerable fame for another accomplishment while in France. What was this accomplishment?

During his tenure in Paris, Archbishop Roncalli and the Paris nunciature became renowned as a center for refined, high-level social soirées and lively, but productive, luncheons – with *haute cuisine* augmented with Bergamascan favorites (e.g., ravioline polenta with game birds, rabbit and tripe) and fine wine. The nuncio hired a top French chef and provided suggestions as to menu items.

A nuncio to a large Catholic country such as France is a fully-fledged, *bona fide* accredited diplomat (though whether they ever have true plenipotentiary rights is open for debate given the absolute, pervading power wielded by the pope). The Paris nuncio, as mentioned earlier, is, moreover, the de facto dean of the French *Corps Diplomatique*. A never ending whirl of cocktail parties, receptions, dinners, national holiday celebrations, lunches, cultural expositions, is part-and-parcel of the elaborate, time-honored protocol of international diplomacy in a metropolis such as Paris. So, the nuncio was doing what was expected of him – though doing so with unexpected flair and aplomb.

For the first time in his life he was in a position where he was expected to entertain high-level dignitaries, in style. He even had an entertainment and upkeep budget from the Vatican; a very far cry from the austere lifestyle he had got accustomed to. Per various records, despite the evidence of his creeping girth, he was supposedly not a big eater, *'eating like a bird'*. During this time he also became an occasional 'non-inhaling' social smoker – it being quite possible that he may have smoked during his two stints in the army. As he approached his sixty-fifth year he started to pay more concern to his health and tried to get to bed by 10 p.m. most nights – so as to dutifully get up, most days, by 4 a.m. to start his work.

The once palatial nunciature at No. 10, Avenue du Président Wilson had been badly neglected during the War and was in need of urgent and extensive refurbishment. Getting the material or the workmen necessary to have all the work finished was not always easy during the nuncios first few months in Paris, though objet d'art for decoration, including paintings and tapestries, were, as somewhat of a consolation, readily available at a discount in the post-occupation turmoil. There were also shortages in food supplies though the nunciature appears to have become quite adept, irrespective, at always laying a good table.

61) During his tenure as nuncio one the divisive issues he was asked to look at by the Vatican was that of the French 'worker-priest' movement. What were the 'worker-priests' and what was the nuncios recommendation as to what should be done with them?

The radical post-War worker-priest initiative which had been supported by Cardinal Emmanuel Suhard, the Archbishop of Paris, and most of the other

French bishops had its roots in a daring program begun during the German occupation.

In September 1942, the puppet Vichy regime acquiescing to the Germans passed a *Service du travail obligatoire* (Compulsory Work Service) law that forcefully enlisted and deported French workers, by the hundreds of thousands, to slave-labor camps in Nazi Germany to aid the German war effort. In theory, the Nazis promised to free one French POW for every three workers sent to Germany. French priests wanted to accompany those being deported as chaplains. When the Germans refused, point blank, to permit French chaplains into the camps, many French priests selflessly volunteered to be deported to these camps as ordinary workers. They, in civilian garb, worked and lived with the deported workers in the labor camps, side-by-side, providing much appreciated ministry and succor. They for, obvious reasons, came to be known and revered as the 'worker-priests'.

During the 1940s, during and after the occupation, French workers had become increasingly alienated from the Catholic Church. They felt that the Church did not truly believe in social democracy; that it identified with and favored the 'ruling classes' at the expense of the plebs. Though France was said to be 80% Catholic at the time, only about 25% of the adult population attended Mass on a regular basis and the baptisms of newborns was way down. Though thousands of parishes throughout France were without a priest there were few, if any, complaints from parishioners – yet another sign of the apathy towards the Church. The French bishops knew that they faced a grave and growing problem. Then a few priests, familiar with the resounding success of the wartime worker-priest program, suggested a resurrection of that concept – but this time within France, with the priests integrated into working class communities, far and wide across the country. With these priests there would be no distinction between the ecclesiastical and secular worlds. The priests, as they had done in the labor camps, would celebrate Mass and perform other religious duties in non-church settings wearing civilian, workingmen's clothes.

Rome, understandably, was uneasy and skeptical about this program. Cardinal Suhard, however, was very adamant and Rome refrained, at first, from trying to stop the initiative. The worker-priest program, as had been hoped, proved to be quite successful – to begin with. Then problems started to surface, mainly to do with the worker-priests, given their personality, education and training, gravitating towards leadership roles. This led to involvements in unions, some affiliated with the communist party, strikes, labor negotiations and political protests. Inevitably some worker-priests ended up getting arrested during periods of labor unrest. Soon the French press was having a heyday covering the activities of the worker-priests – with much innuendo as to how these priests were able to maintain their priestly vows and duties within their secular surroundings. The Vatican's anxiety and unease with the situation, understandably, increased and these were conveyed, in no uncertain terms to the nuncio.

A nuncio, by definition, does not have any jurisdiction over local bishops. Thus, Archbishop Roncalli had not been directly involved in authorizing the worker-priest program though he had, of course, been consulted and briefed on it by Cardinal Suhard and others. Given his background, his empathy with those that struggle to make a living and his past involvement in *Azione Cattolica*, the Archbishop saw the merits of the program. When the agitation from the Vatican started the nuncio decided to personally evaluate how the priests were being perceived by their 'congregations' before making any recommendations. So he visited various regions with active worker-priest presence and talked to the workers and their families. He quickly determined that the worker-priests were very popular and effective and were trusted and respected within their communities. He conveyed his finds to the Vatican; advocating, in essence, to extend the original 'wait-and-see' grace period. Coincidentally or otherwise the worker-priest program continued, unabated, while he was nuncio. It was only terminated once he had left Paris. Vaticanologists believe that this was not a coincidence.

62) In early 1951 the nuncio was given the added responsibility of being appointed as the Vatican's first permanent observer to an international agency. What was this agency and how well did the nuncio manage to deal with this new, added responsibility?

This agency was UNESCO – the United Nations Educational, Scientific and Cultural Organization, formed in 1947, and headquartered in Paris, with a U.N. mandate to further peace, justice, law, freedom and human rights through international collaboration involving education, science and culture.

There had been, not unexpectedly, some consternation among U.N. circles when the Holy See requested a permanent observer at UNESCO. They realized the potential for possible friction given the likelihood of conflicts of interest in the area of science and the perception of overlapping spheres of influence when it came to education and culture. On the other hand, from the standpoint of the Holy See UNESCO might be seen as trying to propagate secular, even materialistic, values at the expense of traditional, Christian spiritual beliefs.

When it came to be known that the Vatican's first permanent observer was going to be Archbishop Roncalli there was an immediate sense of relief within the U.N. community. The Archbishop's reputation preceded him. By then, the

Archbishop's acumen and grace was well known among global diplomats. Moreover, just as in his case, many Ambassadors based in Paris, then (and even now), were often asked to perform double duty, serving both France and UNESCO – and as such quite a few of the other UNESCO diplomats already knew him well. Archbishop Roncalli lived up to his reputation. With him at UNESCO there was not to be any palpable contretemps or even a hint of open conflict. This is not to say that the nuncio did not put forward the perspectives of the Church or refrained from dialog. It was just that he always did so with prudence, tact, inclusiveness and good-nature – once pointing out, to make a point, that he was the representative of the world's largest cultural organization and one that had been around for much longer than UNESCO.

Archbishop Roncalli delivered addresses at UNESCO's sixth and seventh general assemblies, in 1951 and 1952. His tenure at UNESCO, especially his two general assembly addresses, ensured that Archbishop Roncalli's name came to the attention of world leaders and Church prelates, around the globe, ahead of him becoming a cardinal – and eventually pope.

63) At what consistory was Archbishop Roncalli created a cardinal, what was his precedence at that consistory and who else, of note, was created alongside him?

Archbishop Roncalli's eventual cardinalate was essentially preordained as soon as he was named nuncio to France. The previous nineteen nuncios to France, going back to 1641 ended up as cardinals – this tradition that the nuncio to France is a *'would be cardinal'* going back even further to 1530, albeit with three exceptions in that time. So unless Archbishop Roncalli, the once suspected modernist, somehow managed, against the grain, to blot his copybook badly, the odds were indeed that he would one day wear the red hat.

The one danger to this presumed eventuality was **Pius XII's** (already talked about) reticence towards creating cardinals. At the nuncio's urging Jules-Géraud Saliège had been created in Pius XII's first cardinal creating consistory in February 1946.

Six years had passed since that consistory with no word from Rome of another.

On November 25, 1951, he turned 70. He told his household that per his reckoning he was then the oldest nuncio to still have served in France. He must have been glad that he had admonished his family, years earlier, not to even mention the possibility of him becoming a cardinal. But, he could not suppress speculation among diplomats and prelates as to when he would be getting his red biretta – or more to the point, why he had not received one as yet (though they too also knew that there had not been any cardinal creating consistories since 1946).

A year later, on November 10, 1952, as he was approaching his 71st birthday, Archbishop Roncalli, akin to the events eight years earlier in Istanbul, received a coded telegram from the Vatican. This telegram informed the nuncio that Carlo Agostini, Patriarch of Venice since February 1949, though just 64 years of age, was terminally ill and that the pope, Pius XII, had decided that Roncalli will replace him in due course.

Though the 'Patriarchate of Venezia' is purely a formal title held by the ordinary Bishop of Venice (a privilege also enjoyed by the bishops of Lisbon, the East Indies and Jerusalem) it does bestow precedence to the bishop in Church ceremonies. The Patriarch, furthermore, is permitted to wear cardinal red non-liturgical vestments, even when not a cardinal as yet, albeit with the red biretta topped by a tuft to denote that he is a bishop sans a cardinalate. Moreover, by *tradition*, the Patriarch of Venice is invariably created a cardinal at the next cardinal creating consistory following his appointment. Carlo Agostini, however, was yet to be a cardinal since there had been no cardinal creating consistories since his appointment in 1949.

Archbishop Roncalli was now due a cardinalate on two counts: as the departing nuncio to France and the would-be Patriarch of Venice.

In reality, after what until then had been such a long, uncertain, multi-year wait, the news of his creation now came about quite quickly.

Nineteen days after being told that he was destined for Venice the Vatican released the names of those that were due to be created at the next cardinal creating consistory – scheduled for Monday, January 12, 1953. [Monday was the *preferred* day for cardinal creating consistories between 1903 to 1977, with but two exceptions.] Archbishop Roncalli's name was on the list – as were those of Carlo Agostini and Valerio Valeri, the prior nuncio to France.

Carlo Agostini was to die exactly a month later, on December 29, 1952. So he, Patriarch of Venice for 3.9 years, never became a cardinal.

The January 12, 1953 consistory, after 13.8 years in office, was Pius XII's second (and last) cardinal creating consistory. The prior one had been 6.8 years previously.

Twenty-four cardinals were created at this consistory; their average age 64.6 years. If Carlo Agostini had lived there would have been twenty-five. At 71.1 years, Angelo Roncalli was the fifth oldest of those created. Italian Gaetano Cicognani, the nuncio to Spain, who too was created that day, was also 71.1 years of age. But, he was *one day* younger! Cicognani had been born on November 26, 1881 (in Faenza) and Roncalli on November 25, 1881, about 185 miles apart. The oldest of those created, at 80.7 years of age, was Georges-

François-Xavier-Marie Grente, Archbishop of Le Mans (France). The youngest, at 46.6 years, was Giuseppe Siri, Archbishop of Genova (Italy) — who five years later would be the protagonist of the *'Siri Thesis'*. *[q.v. #15.]*

Angelo Roncalli was the *fourth* to be created at this consistory — overall Pius XII's 36th cardinal. He was created a *Cardinal Priest* — as appropriate for a senior nuncio, one, moreover, who was soon to be the Patriarch of Venize.

In a reversal of their chronological seniority, Gaetano Cicognani, as a cardinal, preceded him by one — he being the third created. Though the nuncio to France would typically have commanded precedence, Cicognani had been a nuncio for twenty-eight years, Roncalli but for eight. Both the nuncios were preceded by two 76 year olds: Brazilian Augusto Álvaro da Silva, Archbishop of São Salvador da Bahia (Brazil), and Italian Celso Costantini, the first to be created, the secretary of the Sacred Congregation for the Propagation of the Faith. Having a senior curialist as the first to be created is somewhat of a tradition. Valerio Valeri, at 69, was the fifth created — the pope thus giving Roncalli precedence over his predecessor in France.

Maurice Feltin (66), who became Archbishop of Paris in August 1949 following the death of Emmanuel Suhard in May of that year, was also created that day — eighth in terms of precedence. Siri, the youngest, was the thirteenth to be created, just after the oldest, Grente.

In addition to Siri, three other leading 1958 *papabili* were created at this consistory. *[q.v. #7.]* They were: the 'liberal' favorite Giacomo Lercaro (61), Archbishop of Bologna (Italy); Stefan Wyszyński (51), Archbishop of Gniezno and Warsaw (Poland) who had prevailed against the Nazis and Soviets, and conservative curialist Alfredo Ottaviani (62) who would become a noted gadfly during Vatican II. Lercaro was the sixteenth to be created, Wyszyński the seventeenth, and Ottaviani, given that he was created a Cardinal Deacon, as is typical for most curialists, was the last in line.

Of the twenty-four created, ten, i.e., 42%, were from Italy. There were two each from France and Spain. The other ten, each from a different country, were from: Brazil, Canada, Colombia, Ecuador, Germany, India, Ireland, Poland, U.S.A. and Yugoslavia.

Valerian Gracias, the Archbishop of Bombay, born in 1901 in Karachi (then in British India) to parents from the Portuguese 'enclave' of Goa (India), was to be the *first cardinal from India*. Crisanto Luque Sánchez [b. 1889], Archbishop of Bogotá was the *first cardinal from Colombia*. Carlos Maria de la Torre [b. 1873], Archbishop of Quito, was the *first from Ecuador*. [Valerian Gracias had studied at the Pontifical Seminary in Kandy, Ceylon (now Sri Lanka).]

Of the twenty-four created, seventeen were residential Archbishops — three of Italian dioceses, i.e., Naples, Genoa and Bologna. Four (including Roncalli), all

Italians, were nuncios – to Spain, France, Italy and Portugal. Three, again all Italian, were curialists.

At this consistory Pius XII disclosed that two prelates, whose names he did not divulge, had been his top two choices for cardinalates, but that both had requested that they not be so honored. It was, however, widely known in Rome that the two, who declined the red (at least this time around), were none other than the pope's top two lieutenants, Domenico Tardini and Giovanni Battista Montini (the future Paul VI (#263)) – who helped him run the Secretariat of State in the absence of a Secretary of State. There has never been a real explanation as to why these two, both of whom would later accept the red, refused the pope, quite pointedly, on this matter; Tardini even letting it be known that he told the pope, who questioned their polite refusal: '*yes Holy Father, I thank you for everything you have done for me, but even more, what you have not done for me*'. The implication (and it was always just that) was that both Tardini and Montini wanted to distance themselves from some or all of what had transpired during Pius XII's papacy – which spanned all of WW II.

64) What was the title [i.e., 'property'] in Rome given to Cardinal Roncalli?

Cardinal Roncalli received the title for **Santa Prisca**, a tucked-away, unprepossessing, but ancient, church on the Aventine Hill, built in the 4th or 5th century, dedicated to an obscure 1st century martyr, Saint Prisca (who is not believed to be the same as St. Priscillia, despite 'Prisca' being a diminutive form of that name). It was a titular that had been held by two cardinals who went onto be popes, Jacques Fournier, O. Cist. who became **Benedict XII** (#198) in 1334 and Giovanni Angelo Medici (not directly related to the Florence Medicis) who would become **Pius IV** (#225) in 1559.

The prior holder of this title had been Adeodato Giovanni Piazza, O.C.D. [b. 1884], a former Patriarch of Venice who had also gone onto become the Superior General of the Congregation of the Missionaries of St. Charles Borromeo (i.e., Scalabrinian Fathers). In March 1949 he had opted to be a Cardinal Bishop per the then prevailing *jus optionis* [right of option] promotion mechanism thus vacating this title. So, the title had lain dormant since then. There is no indication whether this title was chosen for Cardinal Roncalli because of the Charles Borromeo or the Patriarch of Venice connection. It is possible that somebody in the curia did spot one or both of these connections and made it possible for Cardinal Roncalli to be given that church.

[On March 10, 1961, John XXIII, with his *Ad suburbicarias dioeceses motu proprio*, rescinded the *jus optionis* privilege, that had stood since 1586, whereby the senior most cardinal priest or deacon could request promotion to a *vacant suburbicarian see* [i.e., to seek promotion to be a Cardinal Bishop]. Thereinafter the pope had the total prerogative of determining who would be elevated to fill a vacant *suburbicarian see*, and thus become a Cardinal Bishop. There are only six suburbicarian sees (not counting Ostia) that can be assigned, and as such there can only be six Cardinal Bishops (as opposed to the Cardinal Patriarchs who do not hold 'Roman' titles). This was an astute decision on the part of John XXIII and it is still the norm.

As will be seen later on in this book, John XXIII, as pope, made more meaningful and insightful changes to the mechanics of the College of Cardinals than any other pope since **Sixtus** 'Iron Pope' **V** (#228) [1585 to 1590]. There was definitely a clear sense that the pope knew exactly what changes he wanted when it came to the College. It was as if in his many years away from Rome he determined much of what he thought needed to be done to 'fix the system'.]

65) When did Cardinal Roncalli get his obligatory scarlet red, watered silk (untufted) cardinal's biretta and who ceremoniously presented it to him?

The heads of state for France, Spain and Portugal had long enjoyed the privilege, and Italy so, since 1929, of being able to confer the red biretta to newly created cardinals from their own country and to the papal nuncio to their country. [Spain had enjoyed this privilege since 1564.]

Hence, in 1953, the French President had the right to request from the Vatican the privilege of bestowing the red biretta, in France, to their beloved nuncio, the soon to be Cardinal Angelo Roncalli. And that is exactly what ensued.

Vincent Jules Auriol [1884 to 1966], a socialist and an atheist, was the President of France from 1947 to 1954. So he had known the nuncio for quite a long time and had, obviously, been the official recipient of the nuncio's much anticipated and always eloquent diplomatic corps' New Year's day greeting for five years. The two liked each other and were good friends.

Auriol, though not a Catholic, did not want to forgo the opportunity of presenting his friend with 'the hat'. Roncalli, recognizing the significance, readily agreed – as did the Vatican. At first it was believed that the bestowing of the biretta would be a small, private affair at the President's official residence, the Élysée Palace in Paris. That was not to be. Too many diplomats and other local dignitaries petitioned the President for the honor of being present at the ceremony. The nuncio too was getting inundated with requests. His three brothers Francesco Zaverio, Alfredo and Giuseppe Lugi wanted to attend, as did the parish priest of Sotto il Monte and the Bishop of Bergamo.

The conferring of the red biretta ceremony was held on Thursday, January 15, 1953, in the armory of the Élysée Palace. It was a gala white-tie affair, with ceremonial guards and the president wearing a tri-color sash. The biretta was conveyed from Rome to Paris by the then apostolic delegate to Turkey, Monsignor Giacomo Testa.

It was a bittersweet occasion for the French contingent and the new cardinal. While they all savored the imbued honor and symbolism of the ceremony, it also signified that the nuncio, now that he was a cardinal, would soon be leaving Paris.

As had been the case when his predecessor, Valerio Valeri, was departing Paris, Cardinal Roncalli is *said* to have been awarded the 'Grand Cross' of the *Légion d'Honneur* by President Auriol for his services to France as well as for his wide-ranging humanitarian efforts during WW II. This would make eminent sense given how highly he was thought of in France – and particularly by the President. However, five decades hence there are frustrating inconsistencies and omissions as to whether the cardinal did indeed receive this honor. Thus, alas, there is now an element of doubt as to this matter.

In reality there are two different red hats associated with a cardinal: the red, peaked, square biretta and the red, broad-brimmed *galero*, with thirty tassels – which is meant to symbolize a crown. The *galero* used to be bestowed upon newly created cardinals by the pope at their first consistory. This had ceased to happen, with a red biretta (and zuchetto) used instead. It is said that cardinals stopped wearing *galeros* as of 1870, as a sign of mourning, at the loss of the Papal States. However, cardinals have the right to have a *galero* made so that it can be displayed in their home cathedral. There is also a tradition that a *galero*, paid for by the congregation, is hung above a late cardinal's tomb. In theory the *galero* remains suspended until it disintegrates and in time falls apart. When it finally falls from its perch, due to decay, it is supposed to indicate that the cardinal's soul has entered heaven.

In 1953, it appears that the pope wanted to present red *galeros* to five of the cardinals he had created to augment the already bestowed birettas. The five cardinals who were to be the recipients of this additional honor were: Angelo Roncalli, Gaetano Cicognani, Pietro Ciriaci (of Portugal), Benjamín de Arriba y Castro (of Spain) and Fernando Quiroga y Palacios (of Spain). The pope was going to do this late February, when Cardinal Roncalli was back in Rome prior to heading off to Venice. The pope, however, had started to suffer from one of his debilitating bouts of hiccups that would plague him, on and off, for the remaining five years of his life. So the ceremony was postponed. On October 29, 1953, a special consistory, that is said to have lasted fifteen minutes, was convened, while the pope was at Castel Gandolfo, to present the galeros to these five cardinals.

On April 15, 1969, **Paul VI** (#263), aware of the rapid internationalization of the College of Cardinals, and not wanting to offend all the countries that were excluded, rescinded the red biretta bestowing privilege that had been enjoyed by France, Spain, Portugal and Italy.

Soon after he learned that he was going to be created Archbishop Roncalli was informed that his elder sister, Ancilla, was terminally ill with stomach cancer. He managed to spend the Christmas of 1952, ahead of the consistory, at home in Sotto il Monte – spending most of the time at his sister's bedside. She died a year later.

Figure 14: Cardinal Angelo Giuseppe Roncalli.

VI.
THE PATRIARCH

Cardinal Roncalli left Paris for Rome on February 23, 1953.

He was, at 71, to finally be a bishop of an Italian see. He had been away from Italy for nearly twenty-eight years.

The sovereign, independent, Vatican City State had been created in 1929 by the 'Lateran Pact' agreement between Italy and the Vatican. Article 20 of this Pact, reflecting the lingering resentment that had persisted in the upper echelons of the Church as to the loss of the Papal States, required that all Italian bishops be Italian subjects. They, moreover, had to speak Italian and take an oath of loyalty to the State.

Cardinal Roncalli now had to take that oath. It was administered in Rome by Luigi Einaudi, the President of the Italian Republic from 1948 to 1955.

Following a few days in Sotto il Monte Cardinal Roncalli set off for Venice, by train, leaving Bergamo on March 10th and making two stops, in Verona and Vicenza, on the way. He arrived in Venice, as planned, on the afternoon of Sunday, **March 15, 1953.**

Venice was agog. They hadn't had a cardinal in five years. Now they were getting one, well known to them all, already, for his piety, humility and good nature. A veritable armada of gondolas, many specially decorated, launches, boats and barges were there to greet him at the railway station to escort him, in a launch provided by the city, along the Grand Canal to the Piazza San Marco. This was the principal public square of Venice off which is the *Basilica Cattedrale Patriarcale di San Marco* (Saint Mark's Basilica), the cathedral church of Venice, and the nearby Patriarchal Palace.

The Cardinal, in time, paraphrasing from Dante's *'Divine Comedy'*, would go onto describe the magnificent *San Marco*, fittingly, as the place where *'heaven and Earth joined hands'*. *San Marco*, whose origins date back to 828, only became the Venetian cathedral in 1807 when the seat of the Patriarch was transferred to Venice. Up until 1797, which is when the Venetian Republic ceased to be, *San Marco* had been but the private chapel of the Dodge of Venice – the civic leader and chief magistrate of the of the *'Most Serene Republic of Venice'*. As such San Marco was next door to the Dodge's Palace (*Palazzo Ducale*) – a museum as of 1923. Between 1451 to 1807 Venice's cathedral was *Basilica di San Pietro di Castello* (St Peter of Castello) – to the west of, and essentially on another island, from *San Marco*. The residence, with its neoclassical exterior, that would be occupied by Cardinal Roncalli was to the north of the Basilica. It was on the eastern edge of the *Piazzetta dei Leoncini* (due to the presence of two marble *lions*) and had been completed in 1850. Though unprepossessing from the outside, especially in contrast to the highly ornate Basilica, the Palace, in reality, was grandiose on the inside. it was a veritable treasure trove of artwork and decoration – much of it placed there for safekeeping when Napoleon Bonaparte conquered Venice in 1797 and proceeded to close down many churches, monasteries and covenants. So Cardinal Roncalli, who grew up in a poor farmhouse and got used to a spartan lifestyle in Bulgaria and Turkey, would now be living in what was very much a lavish, richly appointed, art museum!

The *Piazzetta dei Leoncini* is now known as *Piazzetta Giovanni XXIII* (John XXIII).

Cardinal Roncalli was the 139th Bishop of Venice and the 43rd Patriarch of Venice.

66) Venice, even ahead of the Italian Renaissance, had been a celebrated center for artistic and cultural excellence. *Joie de vivre* is very much part and parcel of Venetian life. Hence, the annual, pre-Lent Carnival, with the elaborate masks, was but a showcase for the festive atmosphere that invariably pervaded the city. Nobody who knew him would ever describe Cardinal Roncalli as being a *'stick in the mud'*. To the contrary; in his own way, within the prescribes of a priestly life, Cardinal Roncalli, cultured, genial and tolerant, lived his life to its fullest, invariably a twinkle in his eyes and a smile not far away. Nonetheless, he was, despite the long ago suspicions of modernism, doctrinally orthodox and a traditionalist. He was, as the Patriarch of Venice, also an elderly man in his early seventies who had, since the age of eleven, lived a very disciplined, orderly and one could even say somewhat 'cloistered' life. Consequently, it should not come as a surprise that Cardinal Roncalli, as Patriarch of Venice, did set out some reasonable guidelines as to how certain cultural and social aspects of the city, over which he had purview, should function henceforth. Three of his actions related to the secular aspects of Venice came to be well known. What were these three actions?

The first of these, and probably the best known, had to do with Venice's world renowned film festival, *Mostra Internazionale d'Arte Cinematografica di Venezia*, held annually, since 1932, towards the end of the summer, on the Island of Lido. Given the importance of the event to the city, it was traditional for the Patriarch to celebrate a special 'Movie Mass', in September each year, at *San Marco*. Roncalli, happy to foster culture and help promote an event of great economic import to the city, never shied away, during his entire time in Venice, from performing the Mass. He even went further by holding a reception at his Palace, each year, for all of the film-makers from around the world, making a point not to exclude any, irrespective of their nationality, politics or reputed morality.

At each reception, as was expected of him, he would address the gathered luminaries -- in French (he never having gained familiarity with English). Each year, in his avuncular manner, he would gently, but unequivocally, remind them, given their power to influence, of their duty and responsibility to uphold and propagate 'positive values'. Echoing a phrase that he supposedly also used when elected pope he regularly asked them to: *'Let fresh air in ...'*. It is hard to determine whether the Patriarch had much demonstrable impact in shaping the rapidly evolving movie culture, but it cannot be denied that he did try, in his own chiding way, each year, while in Venice.

The Venice Film Festival is actually part of a much larger and older cultural event – the *Biennale di Venezia* (Venice Biennial), started in 1895 and taking place every other year [i.e., in odd years]. It is a major international contemporary art exhibition – with several countries, starting in 1907, going as far as installing national pavilions for the exhibition (as they did for World Fairs). Cardinal Giuseppe Melchiorre Sarto (later **Pius X** (#258)), pious, holy, deeply conservative and restrained, was Patriarch of Venice from 1893 to 1903 (when he was elected pope). So the *Biennale* came to be during his time in Venice. He, however, did not approve of it, considering some of the exhibited work to be shocking. He imposed a blanket ban on clerics attending the *Biennale*. Given that he went onto be pope and the overall reverence he continued to command within the Church, subsequent Patriarchs had not dared lift the ban.

Cardinal Roncalli, staying true to the norm, refrained from attending the first *Biennale* held during his term in Venice. It, however, came to his attention that there were exhibits that year that were said to be offensively lewd or blatantly blasphemous. Though he realized that some would argue that he was trying to overreach, he contacted the city officials in charge of the show and expressed his displeasure and urged that they, in future, impose more stringent morality guidelines. Again as with the Film Festival it cannot be established whether the Patriarch was indeed able to make an impact. But, he made a point of attending the next *Biennale* – thus becoming the first Patriarch to do so. It would appear that the Patriarch was happy with what he saw. Emulating his practice for the Film Festival he arranged for a reception at his Palace for the major players involved with the exhibition. At the first reception he announced, to the delight of all, that he was lifting his predecessor's ban on clerics attending the *Biennale*.

Cardinal Roncalli's acceptance of the *Biennale,* and with it his permission for clerics to be able to attend remains the *status quo,* to the relief and appreciation of many. In addition to the *Biennale* and the Film Festival, Venice is also known for many music festivals. The Cardinal embraced these festivals and went about encouraging contemporary music being featured at these festivals to be performed within *San Marco.* Thus, in 1956 and 1958, famed Russian composer, pianist and conductor Igor Stravinsky conducted two of his oratorios within the Basilica. The Cardinal also instituted an annual Mass for journalists, held, apropos, on January 24, the feast day of St. Francis de Sales, the patron Saint of writers and journalists. Some conservatives in the Church 'rolled their eyes' at what they perceived as Roncalli's apparent run away 'liberalism'. However, as was to become apparent, he, as Patriarch of Venice, was only providing a preview of the bigger changes he would seek, later on, when pope. The way he saw it, and had made a point of telling UNESCO audiences when he was in Paris, the Catholic Church had been an active patron of art and culture for centuries.

The 'modern' two-piece bikini came to be in 1946 (named after the Pacific atoll used by the Americans for its post-WW II atomic bomb testing). By the time Cardinal Roncalli arrived in Venice bikinis and scanty clothing had become *de rigueur* on Venetian beaches, especially on the Island of Lido. Though the Cardinal made a point of trying to avoid the Lido during the summer he was well aware of what was going on. Soon it became fashionable for tourists to visit Piazza San Marco in revealing summer wear; short shorts and sleeveless T-shirts in abundance. The cardinal realized that he had to do something, but do so without appearing curmudgeonly or unnecessarily pious. He decided that making a pointed remark to the media, knowing that it would get publicity, was his best option. So he told the media, with a touch of his hallmark humor, that it puzzled him as to why so many ladies resorted to extremes in attire when visiting Venice, when the Venetian climate, in reality, was so temperate at all times to permit the wearing of reasonable clothing.

While he could only, at best, gently chide, through the press, the brazen tourists enjoying the Piazza San Marco, he, however, had absolute jurisdiction over the Basilica that dominated the square. He imposed a dress code for *San Marco* that basically forbade scantily-clad females (and males), showing too much bare flesh, from crossing the threshold.

Around this same time, the city council recognizing the financial benefits, proposed moving a popular casino from the Lido to the throbbing center of Venice, i.e., Piazza San Marco. The Patriarch, as was to be expected, was not in favor. So, per the style he had cultivated so well in Bulgaria, Turkey and Greece, he let his disapproval be known tactfully – though sans ambiguity. In this instance the Patriarch prevailed. There was no casino in the middle of Venice during his tenure.

So, when the cognoscenti talk about Cardinal Roncalli's influence on the secular life of Venice during his time there, the three things that invariably come up are his actions related to the Film Festival, the *Biennale* and tourists exposing too much flesh.

67) Socialism, often bordering towards communism, had gained significant sway in post-War Europe with the working classes in many of the countries severely dissatisfied with their lot. Given his long, long background with 'Catholic Action' and more recently with 'Worker-Priests' Cardinal Roncalli, more than most other prelates, understood the motivations of the workers and appreciated that atheism *per se*, unlike with hard core communism, was not an integral precept of socialism. The Vatican, with **Pius XII** (#261) increasingly sidelined due to illness, and thus at the mercy of entrenched elderly and conservative curialists, was not, however, able or not willing to make this important distinction.

The French President, Vincent Auriol, who given their friendship, had not only presented Roncalli with his red hat but had also visited him in Venice, was a socialist.

Cardinal Roncalli, unsurprisingly, was a supporter of the Catholic-centrist Italian 'Christian Democracy' political party which had been founded in 1943. It was the successor to the "Italian People's Party", which had enjoyed significant popularity after the War – albeit forced in the 1950s to form coalitions with other parties to maintain its clout. The Cardinal's tolerance of 'non-conservative' political views was bound to raise eyebrows at the Vatican – especially given the long ago suspicions that he might be a 'modernist'. What happened in Venice that did indeed cause some traditionalists at the Vatican to roll their eyes and exclaim, in effect: *'there goes Roncalli again'*?

To begin with, the Cardinal who, per his motto of *'obedience and peace'*, always tried to do what was expected of him from Rome, stuck to the Vatican directives when it came to socialism. In mid-1956, a faction from 'Catholic Action' who were involved with the 'Christian Democracy' party tried to forge a coalition with the 'Socialist Party' -- which had communist tendencies. Cardinal Roncalli, echoing the Vatican standpoint, strongly condemned this proposed *'opening to the left'* as a violation of Catholic beliefs and conduct. Archbishop Montini in Milan (the other future pope) said the same thing – given that this was what was expected from the Italian prelates.

Roughly six months later, on February 1, 1957, the 32nd Congress of the Italian Socialist Party (the one with communist tendencies) was due to convene in Venice. As with the Film Festival and the *Biennale* this was an event of import for the City. The Cardinal, as the Patriarch of Venice and an honorary Venetian, felt that it was his duty to welcome and support this Congress – despite its political leanings. So he let it be known, very publicly, that he, per St. Paul's edict to bishops that they should always be *hospitalis et benignus* (hospitable & kind), was in favor of this event and was urging Venetians to appreciate its significance relative to the future of Italy. This last part that suggested that the Socialist Party might be of significance in the nation's future was not widely appreciated by all Italians – particularly so coming from somebody of Cardinal Roncalli's stature.

As was to be expected conservatives in general, and not just those in Rome, were not happy with the Cardinal's graciousness towards the 'Socialists'. The newspapers had a field day. But, as he had done during the Boris III betrayal brouhaha, he kept his peace, albeit with the conviction, that he did share with the media, that someday these Socialists would come back to the Church.

The traditionalist in the curia were obviously not too happy with 'their Roncalli' but there was little that they could do given that he was now a cardinal and the Patriarch of Venice, to boot – as opposed to a 'senior' curialist. The only person that could chastise him, if it was felt warranted, was the pope, and he was preoccupied at the time with his failing health. In time the 32nd Congress flap became just another anecdote in the future pope's eventful life story.

68) Despite the power he wielded when it came to all maters Catholic within the Archdiocese of Venice, Cardinal Roncalli, given his innate humility, was loath to 'force an issue'. There was one well known instance when he graciously backed off, though he had the absolute authority to insist on it, when there was some, probably misguided, public displeasure to a sound and well-intended change he wished to implement. What was this proposed change that did not get done while he was in Venice – but was quickly implemented, albeit not by him, once he became pope?

It had to do with the imposing and magnificent *iconostasis* (rood-screen), which, per the norm for Byzantine churches, separated the nave of *San Marco* from the presbytery. This large eight-columned screen had been made out of red marble during the late 14th century. It was surmounted by fourteen statues of the Apostles, with the Madonna and St. Mark on either side of a huge Crucifix. This indubitable world class work of art, bar the Crucifix, had been the work of two Venetian Gothic sculptors, the brothers Pierpaolo and Jacobello dalle Masegne.

Cardinal Roncalli, a known lover of church art and church architecture, was, naturally, fond of this historic treasure. But, he felt that it served as a very real barrier between the public (in the nave) on one side, and the clergy (at the altar) on the other side. During church services this separation robbed those in the nave from being able to clearly see what was happening in and around the altar. This had not been an issue when *San Marco* was but the private chapel of the Dodge of Venice. The Dodge and his close entourage could get close enough to the 'screen' to see the other side. But now *San Marco* was the popular Cathedral of Venice, regularly attracting large congregations. The intruding screen was depriving those attending services from being able to see what was happening in the presbytery. This did not sit well with the Cardinal.

Cardinal Roncalli, of course, never wanted the *iconostasis* removed. He fully appreciated that it was an integral part of *San Marco's* architecture and ambiance. What he wanted was to have it cleaved and the separate halves mounted on hinges so that they could be swung away to the side when major services were being held. It really it was a win-win solution with no obvious downside – Italy possessing enough master craftsmen, expert in marble, to implement the required changes without ever putting this treasure at risk of harm.

But, there was immediate objections and obfuscation; conservatives in general tending to be rather reluctant when it comes to any change. Some felt that the ancient architectural fabric of the church was being compromised, while others, disingenuously, claimed that the presbytery would be profaned by non-Catholic tourists – despite the fact that altars of most Catholic churches around the world, including that of St. Peter's at the Vatican, were open to the public. Though he had the authority and the right to press ahead, despite the protestations, and have the necessary changes made, he, his humility to the fore yet again, resisted – not wanting to upset anybody. The matter was not raised again while he was in Venice.

However, a few months after he was pope he happened to mention to a Venetian the matter of the *iconostasis* at *San Marco*. It is claimed that the *iconostasis* was hinged, as had been initially proposed, soon after! As some popes have alluded in various ways and at various times: *'it is indeed good to be pope'*.

69) Pope John XXIII will be canonized on **April 27, 2014**. Exactly 61 years earlier, in April 1953, his nephew, Battista, then twenty-six years old, showing quite remarkable prescience explained to his superior, Giuseppe Battaglia, the Bishop of Faenza, when asked as to why his uncle had refused to grant a requested personal favor: *'it is because he is a Saint, nothing less'*. What was this requested favor that Cardinal Roncalli refused to grant that elicited this *'he is a Saint'* explanation?

Though he had the pleasure of personally ordaining him a priest in July 1955, in *San Marco*, Battista's road to priesthood had been a bit circuitous and rocky. In

April 1953, when he turned twenty-six, he had yet to be ordained a subdeacon. Military service in Italy was still obligatory – though seminarians that had attainted at least subdeacon status by the time they were twenty-six were granted an exemption. Since he did not have the requisite ordination Battista received his call-up papers ordering him to report for two-years of military duty. He told his bishop, Giuseppe Battaglia, that he had been summoned and that this would delay his priesthood by another two-years.

The Bishop, who liked Battista, was distressed. He felt that Cardinal Roncalli, given his stature, had to be able to 'pull some strings' to prevent Battista from having to serve. So the bishop wanted Battista to hurry over to Venice to see his uncle. He sent along the 'vicar-general' of Faenza to act as a 'minder'. They got to Venice and met the Cardinal just as he was leaving his Palace for an appointment. Nonetheless, he stopped and wished to know why Battista had arrived, unannounced. Battista showed him his call-up papers. The Cardinal looked them over and handed them back to his nephew and basically told him that he should report for duty as requested – and, moreover, reminded Battista that he himself had served in the military twice. He then calmly left for his appointment.

Battista, who knew his uncle quite well, understood. He really had not held much hope that his uncle would intervene. The vicar-general, on the other hand, was shocked. He was sure that the Cardinal, in his hurry to make his appointment, had misunderstood the situation. He insisted that they remain at the Palace until the Cardinal came back.

When the Cardinal returned Battista again approached him, this time nervously, worried that his uncle might lose his temper, and told him that his bishop had hoped that the Cardinal would intercede. The Cardinal remained serene. He was very fond of his nephew; hopefully the future priest. He took Battista's arm and gently explained to him that what was being asked from him 'was not his to give'. He reminded Battista that he had always given him what was his to give: his love and the little money he had. But, anything that came with the 'office', i.e., that of being a Cardinal and Patriarch, was not his to give. The matter was closed. Battista was not surprised, but the vicar general remained amazed. This was integrity that far exceeded his expectations.

They went back to Faenza and explained to the bishop as to what had transpired. He, like his vicar-general, was perplexed. He had assumed that the Cardinal, whose commitment to his family was well known, would help – especially since military service would further delay Battista's ordination as a priest. This is when Battista explained to the bishop that his uncle had refused to 'pull any strings' because he was a Saint.

There was, however, a happy ending to this story. Bishop Battaglia *'pulled a few strings'* himself, had Battista's ordination as a subdeacon brought forward, and managed to get Battista exempted from military duty. The Cardinal probably smiled, indulgently, when he heard of this.

70) Though Venice was not exactly a poor diocese the Patriarch's staff was often challenged to come up with the funds the Patriarch sought for charity, restoration or new construction initiatives. Often the Patriarch ended up seeking donations from wealthy Venetians, especially so when it came to establishing new churches or church schools – the Patriarch instituting thirty new parishes during his 6.5 year stay. He also managed get funding for a new center to house the Patriarchal archives. Another project, relatively costly, that was dear to his heart was that of building a large new seminary to replace the existing one that had become too small to satisfy the needs of the community. In the end he came up with a creative and somewhat novel way to pay for the seminary – to the surprise and consternation of some. What did he do to get the money to build the new seminary?

He sold the Patriarchal summer residence: the historic Villa Fietta, in Paderno del Grappa, forty-five miles north of Venice, on the mainland, in the Italian Dolomites. The Villa, acquired by the Patriarchate around the start of the 20th century, had also housed a minor seminary. The Patriarch was moving this seminary to Venice and forgoing the comfort of a scenic retreat in the hills. Residents of Paderno del Grappa were amazed. One even inquired from the Patriarch whether he realized what he was giving up, particularly when it came to respite from the heat in the summer. He was told, quite bluntly, that the Patriarch had little trouble sleeping well, year-round, in Venice. He sold the Villa to a female Catholic religious order dedicated to education, the *Maestre Pie Filippini* (Religious Teachers Filippini), who turned it into a boarding school (which is still operational).

71) The cardinal having been a Vatican diplomat for so long, deprived of a diocese of his own, truly relished being a hands-on pastor in Venice. He looked for any and every opportunity to reach out to the Venetians and glorify what the Church had to offer. To this end he made a point of indentifying and commemorating events and anniversaries specific to Venice. In early 1956 he organized an elaborate and grandiose, but sedate, multi-day remembrance event. What was this event and who did it commemorate?

January 8, 1956 was the 500th anniversary of the death of St. Lorenzo Giustiniani, C.S.R.A (i.e., Canon Regulars or Augustinian Canons) [b: July 1, 1381], the *first* Patriarch of Venice, as of 1451 – who was canonized in 1690. Lorenzo, moreover, was a native Venetian from an illustrious family – his brother a senator of Venice and an 'officer' at *San Marco*. The Cardinal felt that the Venetian Saint was not receiving as much reverence as was due and decided to use the milestone anniversary to resurrect awareness by staging a striking, hard to miss, religious spectacular.

Lorenzo Giustiniani had been buried at the *Basilica di San Pietro di Castello* – the original Venetian cathedral. In 1649 following renovations to the cathedral his body was moved to a magnificent new, sumptuously adorned, tomb. The cardinal arranged for Giustiniani's body to be taken in solemn, sacred procession, much of it over water, accompanied by a flotilla of bedecked watercrafts, to seventy-seven parish churches in the diocese – some on the mainland, others on outlying islands. It was billed as a pilgrimage that would culminate with a special service, conducted by the Cardinal, in *San Marco*. The entire event, from start to finish, was momentous, novel, dramatic and obviously memorable. It received much publicity and attention. People came from afar and wide to be a part of this rare and very special occurrence. Cardinal Roncalli, the 43rd Patriarch, had succeeded in achieving his objective – making sure that the Venetians once again remembered and paid due reverence to their first Patriarch, St. Lorenzo Giustiniani, C.S.R.A.

Pope John XXIII will be the third Patriarch of Venice to be canonized. Lorenzo Giustiniani and Giuseppe Melchiorre Sarto, i.e., **Pius X** (#258), being the other two.

72) Exactly four weeks prior to leaving Venice, with a return ticket, on October 11, 1958, to attend **Pius XII's** funeral and participate in the conclave to elect the next pope, Cardinal Roncalli had orchestrated another grand celebratory ceremony to honor another illustrious Venetian. Who did he honor, in what was to be his last celebration in *San Marco*, and what was the occasion?

Cardinal Roncalli was paying homage to the 38th Patriarch of Venice, Cardinal Giuseppe Melchiorre Sarto – who went onto become **Pope Pius X** (#258) in 1903. September 18, 1958, was the centenary of St. Pius X's ordination as a priest. The Cardinal remembered that Pius X had blessed him on August 11, 1904, one day after his own ordination. *[q.v. #31.]*

VII.
THE POPE

Cardinal Roncalli was elected pope in the afternoon of Tuesday, October 28, 1958, probably between 4 and 4:30 p.m., and chose to be known as **John XXIII**.

Per tradition his coronation should have been on November 9, 1958, the second Sunday after his election. The pope, however, decided he would be crowned on Tuesday, **November 4** – the Feast Day of St. Charles Borromeo, his favorite Saint.

His three remaining brothers, Francesco Zaverio, Alfredo and Giuseppe Luigi, his one surviving sister, Assunta Casilda, and close to thirty nieces and nephews attended the coronation. This the first papal coronation to be broadcast live on television lasted the customary five hours. The pope was carried to and from St. Peter's in a *sedia gestatoria* borne by eight stout stewards – the pope taking the time to joke with the stewards that they should get a pay rise since he was considerably heavier than his predecessor. He also noted that it was *'windy up there'*.

He was crowned, per his choice, with the ***'Palatine Tiara'***, the most widely used of the papal tiaras. This was a tiara that had been donated to **Pius IX** (#256) in 1877, a year ahead of his death, by the Vatican's *Guardia Palatina d'Onore* (Palantine Guard), a military unit created by that pope in 1850. It was to commemorate his fiftieth anniversary as a bishop. It was the same tiara used to crown **Pius XII** (#261). Though the city of Bergamo intended to donate a new tiara for *'their pope'* they were not able to get this done prior to the coronation. John XXIII received the Bergamo tiara in 1959. John XXIII would be the last pope to be crowned with the *Palatine Tiara*.

At that time, still harking back to the days pre-1870 when the pope reigned over the Papal States, the pope's brothers were entitled to be elevated to the nobility, assigned titles that denoted them as princes, and move into accommodations within the Vatican. Pope John XXIII would have none of that. He just wanted his brothers to be known, simply and factually, as *'brothers of the pope'*. Very aware that the prior papacy had a reputation for nepotism and was infamous for its 'overbearing' housekeeper, he decided not to have a relative, e.g., one of his nieces, as his housekeeper – or for that matter to employ any relative at all for any posts at the Vatican. He was going to be exemplary when it came to the standards by which his papacy was to be run – and remembered.

Figure 15: The Pope.

73) Though the pope, as discussed in #16 asked for the cardinals who elected him to spend another night with him in their conclave setting, in reality he only had time to have a collegiate dinner with them – supposedly forgoing food and just having a cup of tea while he animatedly chatted with his former colleagues. While the cardinals went back to the cells they had previously occupied the pope requested a larger room, with a desk, since he planned to do some work that night. So the *Camerlengo*, who typically is assigned a larger room since he might have to have logistics-related meetings during the conclave with the three-cardinal 'particular congregation' then in-session, gave the pope his 'room'. This happened to be the (long unused) first-floor apartment of the Secretary of State. He would occupy this apartment till October 30th at which time he moved to the fourth floor papal apartments. That night, aided by an old associate from two decades earlier, the pope set out to start his papacy with a 'bang' knowing that he, right then, had the undivided attention of the world. What did he prepare that first night and who was the prior associate who worked with him that night?

Pope John XXIII (#262) had decided that he wanted to formally start his papacy by broadcasting an earnest message to world leaders appealing for global peace – urging restraint when it came to *'these new monstrous instruments of war … which can annihilate us all'*. It was to be quintessentially Roncalli; diplomatic but unambiguous. The Cold War, with the ensuing proliferation of nuclear arms, was in full swing and the preliminary stages of the war in Vietnam was into its second year. The new pope, who had seen the horrors of WW I at first hand, yet again wanted to advocate peace as he had for so long – but now from a position of international import that he had never enjoyed before.

Monsignor Angelo Dell'Acqua, the vicar-general in Turkey, who had met him at the railway station in Istanbul on January 5, 1935, upon his arrival from Sofia, was now the Substitute for General Affairs of the Secretariat of State. *[q.v. #50.]* He had taken over that post in early 1953 when Msgr. Giovanni Battista Montini (later Paul VI (#263)) left for Milan. The pope wanted Dell'Acqua to help with the proper 'Vatican-speak'. The appeal they crafted was pithy and powerful. The pope repeatedly questioned the need for the *'pernicious instruments of death and destruction'*. He harked back to a theme that had been dear to him for as long as he could recall: improving the welfare of all classes of society, especially the poor.

The pope delivered this incisive appeal for peace during the morning of Wednesday, **October 29, 1958**, the first full day of his papacy – immediately after he had celebrated mass, at the Sistine Chapel, with the cardinals who elected him. The Vatican Radio broadcast the pope's entreaty to the world leaders in thirty-six languages.

Pope John XXIII (#262) had started his papacy with a bang. He had made sure that the world could not be in any doubt as to where he stood when it came to world peace, social justice and nuclear arms. It was an auspicious start – very different to prior papacies, thanks to the pope's acumen to exploit the instantaneous global reach now available to him via television and radio. John would be the first pope to truly appreciate and harness the power of electronic communications.

74) On October 29, 1958, the first full day of his papacy, the pope made his first papal appointment – a long overdue and much needed one at that. Over the next thirty-six hours he normalized an important protocol (or practice) that had lapsed into disuse and sought a significant change in Vatican 'style'. Who was the pope's first appointee, what was the protocol that was reinstated and what was the requested change in 'style'?

Once he had delivered his appeal for global peace, the pope set about rectifying an anomaly that had distorted the workings of the Holy See for 14 years and 2 months – that being the absence of an appointed Secretary of

State to run the all important Holy See Secretariat of State. The Secretariat being responsible for overseeing all the executive, administrative, political and diplomatic functions of the Holy See and the Vatican City State.

As mentioned in #2 **Pius XII** (#261), who had been the Secretary of State prior to his election, had not bothered to appoint a new S.S. once his friend Luigi Maglione, who he had appointed S.S. eight days into his pontificate, died on August 22, 1944. He had instead run the Secretariat himself, initially assisted by Domenico Tardini and Giovanni Battista Montini – and then, as of 1953, with Angelo Dell'Acqua when Montini went to Milan. In November 1952, eight years into this unusual *ad hoc* arrangement, the pope, per his prerogative, created two new titles for his two 'special' assistants: Tardini became Pro-Secretary of State for Extraordinary Ecclesiastical Affairs [i.e., foreign affairs] while Monitini became Pro-Secretary of State for Ordinary Affairs [i.e., Holy See and Vatican City affairs] – where 'Pro' designates 'acting' or temporary. [Dell'Acqua did not inherit Monitini's title. Instead he was given the conventional title *sostituto* (i.e., substitute) for General Affairs of the Secretariat of State, proper for the second in command for that 'domestic' section of the Secretariat.] In the absence of a S.S., Pius XII had basically split the Secretariat into two halves, i.e., Ordinal Affairs and Extraordinary Ecclesiastical Affairs, and put a pro-secretary in charge of each.

Pope John XXIII appointed Roman-born Domenico Tardini, seventy years old at the time and curialist for twenty-nine years, *Pro-Secretary of State. [q.v. #63.]* The Holy See finally had a *bona fide* Secretary of State yet again in charge of the entire Secretariat.

The 'Pro-' in this instance had to do with Tardini not being a cardinal – he having declined a cardinalate in 1953. Vatican protocol dictated that a S.S. who is not a cardinal be deemed 'Pro-' since a cardinalate would be forthcoming. The S.S. is expected to be a cardinal – the title sometimes even referred to as the 'Cardinal Secretary of State'. Tardini, under the new pope, would indeed go onto become a cardinal, quite quickly at that. As it happened the 'Pro-', atypically, was removed from the title, by the pope, ahead of the red hat on November 17, 1958. That was when he let it be known that Tardini was to be created at the next cardinal creating consistory. With the requisite cardinalate now but a formality the pope announced that Domenico Tardini would henceforth be the Secretary of State – sans caveats.

The very competent and effective Tardini, known for his roguish sense of humor, as the Vatican curial head in charge of foreign affairs, had been the new pope's superior for many years. It was Tardini, as mentioned in #55, that had assured Archbishop Roncalli, quite bluntly and cuttingly, that his French nunciature was all the doing of Pius XII without any support from the curia. Now the tables were turned. Tardini would now be working for John XXIII as his second in command. Tardini would prove to be a very loyal, capable and trusted collaborator. He, alas, would die, unexpectedly, of a massive heart attack on July 30, 1961, aged 73. He was in the throes of skillfully maneuvering the manifold preparations for the forthcoming Vatican Council through the umpteen barriers and hurdles thrown in its way by those, especially in the curia, unsettled by the potential prospect of 'change'.

Of the many types of public and private, official and unofficial, audiences that a pope has to grant, a category that is considered official, but rote, are those routinely granted to curial heads. This is to enable them in effect to provide 'status updates' to the pope on a timely basis. These scheduled meetings are known as *tabellla* audiences in that they get printed, published and publicized, in tabular form *[i.e., tabella]*. The *tabella* was in essence a timetable of when the curial heads were supposed to meet with the pope. The curial heads relied on these regular meetings to keep the pope *'in the loop'*. In 1954, at the start of what proved to be a long, debilitating illness, Pius XII, who appears never to have been a 'people person' to begin with, suspended all *tabellla* audiences with the curial heads. This, as was the lack of a S.S., was not tenable, long term, for the Holy See. John XXIII, acutely aware of the need for these regular updates, reinstated the curial *tabellla* audiences within 48 hours of becoming pope.

On his second full day in office, October 30th, he requested a meeting with Giuseppe Dalla Torre, Conte (Count of) di Sanguinetto (b: March 1885), the head of *L'Osservatore Romano* (The Roman Observer), the semi-official newspaper of the Holy See. Dalla Torre, who had held that post since 1920 and as such had served 'under' **Benedict XV** (#259), **Pius XI** (#260) and **Pius XII** (#261), was understandably astonished; he had not had a private audience with a pope since 1946. Now he was been asked to meet with the new pope just two days into his papacy.

He was even more incredulous when he finally fathomed the purpose of the meeting. The new pope wanted him to majorly revise *L'Osservatore's* style of reporting, to reflect the tone of the 20th century, when talking about the pope. He wanted an immediate end to the florid prose always used to describe the pope and his actions. The pope wanted the *L'Osservatore* to basically refer to him just as *'the pope'* and to report his doings sans extraneous devotional hyperbole. The count was shocked. This was indeed a different type of pope. This pope had even forgotten, as he had already done a few times since been elected, to refer to himself using the royal *'We'*. But these were but precursors to the surprises in store.

75) On November 17, 1958, just twenty days into his papacy, the pope announced that he would be holding his first cardinal creating consistory on Monday, **December 15, 1958** and intended to create twenty-three new cardinals. Who was the first cardinal created by John XXIII, what was significant about the timing of this consistory and why was it to be a pivotal consistory in the annals of papal history?

Figure 16: As pope.

The very first cardinal created by John XXIII was the then 61 year old Archbishop of Milan, Giovanni Battista Montini (the future **Paul VI** (#263)) – who five years earlier along with Domenico Tardini had told **Pius XII** that they did not want to be created cardinals. Now under this new pope they were both happy to be prominent front-line cardinals. Montini, as an archbishop, was created a cardinal priest. Tardini, though he was a curialist, was also created a cardinal priest. As the Secretary of State he was entitled to be a cardinal bishop but there were no vacant *suburbicarian sees*.

So rather than make him a cardinal deacon the pope gave him the highest available precedence – though Tardini, incongruously, was the nineteenth created – the last cardinal priest.

What was significant about the timing of this consistory was that no 20th nor 19th century pope had created new cardinals this quickly upon becoming pope. The consistory took place 48 days after the election.

In terms of the ten previous popes the earliest had been 97 days – that with **Pius X** (#258). **Pius XII's** (#261) 2,545 days, as earlier mentioned, was an aberration, but **Pius XI** (#260) had waited 308 days, while **Benedict XV** (#259) took 459 days. It had even taken **Pius VI** (#251), the last of the 18th century popes, 68 days. So, this December 15 consistory was 'ultra-fast' for 'modern' times. But, at the same time, given Pius XII's reticence to hand out red hats no new cardinals had been created in over five years -- the last cardinal creating consistory having been in January 1953 when the current pope was created.

There had been 52 cardinals left in the College when Cardinal Roncalli became pope. This number was still the same on November 17th when the pope announced that he would be creating 23 new cardinals. That meant, barring any deaths, the College of Cardinals following the December 15th consistory would be at **75** – *five above* the maximum of **70** edicted by **Sixtus V** (#228) in his landmark *Postquam verus* constitution of December 3, **1586**.

Sixtus V, a long-term Franciscan, was a noted scholar, an ex-inquisitor general, a renowned preacher and a very able administrator. He had given considerable thought as to what he envisaged for a 'reformed', reinvigorated College when he formulated *Postquam verus*. The 70 limit was to consist of six cardinal bishops, fifty cardinal priests and fourteen cardinal deacons – there being sufficient Roman titles to permit this. [Sixtus, in his follow-on constitution *Religiosa*, of April 13, 1587, made it very clear that the 'churches' assigned to the cardinal priests and the 'deaconries' assigned to the cardinal deacons be kept separate, with no comingling.] The '70', moreover, was not meant to be arbitrary. It was supposed to reflect the seventy elders that shared Moses' burdens (*Numbers 11:16-17*) -- there also having been seventy who assisted Jesus with his ministry (*Luke 10:1*). There was, however, no mandate that the full complement should always be maintained. But, Sixtus was very specific that the upper limit should not be exceeded.

Thirty-three popes, over a span of 372 years, had adhered, without exception, to *Postquam verus*. Many had not found it onerous. During this 372 year period (as far as can be determined) the College was only at its full complement of 70 during periods in: 1660, 1667, 1669, 1670, 1675, 1690 and 1691. This despite the proclivity of some popes as viewing the assignments of cardinalates as an easy and lucrative means of raising quick monies for the papal coffers. Some, Pius XII among them, had no problem with the College being in the fifties. **Pius VI** (#251), who was pope for 24.5 years, during his last year in 1799 even let the number shrink to 45. Now, in 1958, a 77 year old pope, supposedly elected to be a short-term caretaker, was overriding Sixtus V's edict – and doing so matter-of-factly without an edict of his own, or for that matter even an initial acknowledgement that he was bypassing a long-held norm. It would be later that the pope would explain, compellingly, that the scope and reach of the Church in the 1950s was considerably larger than it had been in the days of Sixtus V and as such that the size of the College should be increased to reflect that growth.

On December 4th, eleven days ahead of the consistory, the oldest member of the College, Chilean José María Caro Rodríguez was to die, aged 92. This meant that on December 15th, post consistory the College was at 74 cardinals – as opposed to the more symbolic '75' that Pope John probably had in mind to emphasize his monumental reform to the dynamics of the College of Cardinals.

The '70' limit was never reinstated. Though **Paul VI** (#263) in 1973, two years after he introduced the notion of 'under-80' cardinal electors, limited the number of cardinal electors that may participate in a conclave to 120, he did not impose a maximum size on the College; i.e., the total count of the under-80 cardinal electors and those over 80. Such a limit has yet to be imposed with the College reaching 213, i.e., over three times the Sixtus limit, on February 18, 2012 after **Benedict XVI's** (#266) cardinal creating consistory that day; his fourth.

Though he would go onto make three more significant changes to the norms related to the College, overriding *Postquam verus* has to be deemed the most significant reform wrought on the College by John XXIII. He never issued a written communiqué of any sort officially documenting this change.

Figure 17: The coat of arms of the pope featuring the round, 'waisted', crenellated tower, on a red base, that also appeared in his episcopal coat of arms. The 'Lion of St. Mark' pertains to his 'Patriarchate of Venezia'.

At the December 15, 1958 consistory, Pope John created the first cardinal from Mexico, José Garibi Rivera, the Archbishop of Guadalajara, and the first (and as yet only) cardinal from Uruguay, Antonio María Barbieri, O.F.M.Cap., the Archbishop of Montevideo.

76) How many more cardinal creating consistories would the pope hold, how many cardinals in total did he create and how prolific was he when it came to creating cardinals?

There were to be four more cardinal creating consistories during the 4.6 year reign of this pope; all of them also on Mondays as was the norm at that time.

The second consistory, at which he created eight cardinals, was on December 14, 1959, one day short of the anniversary of his first. Three cardinals had died in the interim. So the College was 79 strong following this consistory. The average age of the eight created was 72.5 years. The average age of the twenty-three created at the first consistory had been 68.2 years.

The third consistory, at which he created seven cardinals, took place on March 28, 1960 – three months and two weeks after the second. The average age of the seven created was 62.0 years. At this consistory he created Peter Tatsuo Doi, Archbishop of Tōkyō, the first cardinal from Japan; Rufino Jiao Santos, Archbishop of Manila, the first cardinal from the Philippines, and Laurean Rugambwa, Bishop of Rutabo, the first cardinal from Tanganyika. At this juncture, one year and five months into his papacy, John XXIII had created thirty-eight cardinals. One cardinal had died in February. So the College was up to 85 once these seven red hats had been given out. The College was already 21% above the Sixtus V limit. So, per his goal of making the College more international, he had now extended cardinalates to five new countries across three continents.

The fourth consistory took place nine and a half months after the third, on January 16, 1961. He created just four cardinals, there average age 64.5 years. Four cardinals had died between these two consistories. So the College stayed at 85. Since the pope had not set any limits for the size of the College it is not clear whether there was supposed to be any correlation between the drop in the number by four and the addition of four new cardinals.

The pope's fifth, and last, consistory took place on March 19, 1962, one year and two months after his last. This was the longest gap between his cardinal creating consistories. The pope created ten cardinals this time around, with three more *in pectore*. The names of these three were never published during the life of the pope or in his will. So, they never got created. The average age of the ten that were created was 65.6 years. Eight cardinals had died since January 1961. So the College was 87 strong – 24% larger than what had been the 70 limit. It could have got up to 90 if the three created *in pectore* had been named.

The pope had created a total of **52 cardinals** in the space of three years and four months. **Pius XII** (#261) had been pope for 16.2 additional years and had only created four more (albeit in just two consistories)!

The average gap between John's five consistories was 9.25 months.

This was a faster rate than was normal at the time – setting aside Pius XII's atypical record. **Pius XI** (#260) during his 17.3 year reign held seventeen cardinal creating consistories – the gap between them, on average, 10.75 months. **Benedict XV's** (#259) five consistories were, on average, 16 months apart, while **Pius X's** (#258) seven were, on average, 20.8 months apart.

John XXIII created 10.4 cardinals per consistory, his most 23, his least 4.

A metric created by this author, on his *popes-and-papacy* blog, in 2010, was that of: *number of cardinals created per months as pope.*

John XXIII was pope for 55 months. He created 52 cardinals. So his *number of cardinals created per months as pope* score is **0.95**.

Pius XII was pope for 235 months and created 56 giving him a score of 0.24. So, by this measure John was nearly four times more 'prolific'.

Pius XI was pope for 204 months and created 56 giving him a score of 0.37.

Benedict XV was pope for 88 months and created 32 giving him a score of 0.36.

Pius X was pope for 132 months and created 50 giving him a score of 0.38.

Leo XIII (#257) created 147 cardinals and **Pius IX** (#256) 123. But their papacies were, respectively, 305 and 379 months long; their scores, as such, respectively, being 0.48 and 0.32.

John Paul II (#265), as is fairly well known, created an unprecedented 231 cardinals over nine consistories. He, however, was also pope for 26.4 years, i.e., 317 months. So his score comes in at 0.72 – still below that of John.

Somewhat unexpectedly it is **Benedict XVI** (#266), who surprised so many by resigning on February 28, 2013 after 7.8 years as pope that comes closest to John – actually equaling John. Benedict XVI created 90 cardinals in five consistories during his 94 months as pope. So his score is also 0.95.

So, it can be said that John XXIII was one of the most prolific among modern popes in terms of creating cardinals – and during his lifetime the most prolific of recent popes.

77) Though his implicit override of Sixtus' long honored 70 limit for the size of the College was the most pivotal, John XXIII made three other changes to the workings and nature of the College – two quite profound while the other was not as 'earth shattering'. All three of these changes, as is the override of the size of the College, all of which affected the dynamics of the College, are still in effect. What were these three additional College of Cardinals related changes implemented by John XXIII – each one of these changes, unlike the 'tacit' override of *Postquam verus*, however, done via a published proclamation, i.e., a *motu proprio* (on his own impulse)?

On March 10, 1961, 2.3 years into his pontificate, John XXIII again decided to override another **Sixtus V** (#228) edict from the 1586 *Postquam verus* constitution. This had to do with *Jus optionis* (right of option), the unilateral preferment mechanism of the College where cardinals with seniority could seek promotion or obtain a more prestigious title, as a right, rather than through papal intervention. Per *Postquam verus* the senior most cardinal priest or deacon had the right to opt for a vacant *suburbicarian* see [i.e., to seek promotion to be a cardinal bishop]. This right, by then three centuries old and widely used, had even been embodied in Canon 236 of the 1917 Code of Canon Law. John, with a *motu prorio, Ad Suburbicarias dioeceses*, decreed that this right was being rescinded.

Henceforth, the filling of a vacant *suburbicarian* see would be the exclusive prerogative of the pope, who could do so by creating a new cardinal or by promoting any of the existing cardinals, irrespective of their seniority. This made sense. There were only six cardinal bishop slots, the Dean of the College always getting the see of Ostia in addition to any other titles he already held. Now the pope could decide who would be the cardinal bishops rather than letting it be decided by *Jus optionis.* The pope had already witnessed one such preferment during his reign. Gaetano Cicognani, the onetime nuncio to Spain, who was created a cardinal priest at the same consistory as the 'pope', albeit just ahead of the 'pope', had in December 1959 opted for the *suburbicarian* see of Frascati when it became vacant following the death of Federico Tedeschini, a month earlier. John's *Ad Suburbicarias dioeceses* followed three months later.

John, with his characteristic flair for making a point, with style, when he so wished, demonstrated the new norm, quite dramatically, just sixteen days after the *motu prorio*. On March 26, he promoted Cardinal Priest Giuseppe Antonio Ferretto to be the Cardinal Bishop of the see of Sabina e Poggio Mirteto – though he, the last named cardinal, created just three months prior at the January 1961 consistory, was the most junior of the cardinals. That see had become vacant on March 6th, four days prior to the *motu prorio*, at the death of Cardinal Marcello Mimmi who had opted for it in June 1958. While this sure made the point, it does, however, beg the question as to why he did not take this opportunity to promote, and thereby reward, Domenico Tardini, his Secretary of State -- who was also one of his main collaborators in the preparations for Vatican II.

Prior to the 1917 Code of Canon Law, it was possible to be a cardinal, albeit just a cardinal deacon, without being in Holy Orders; i.e., never been ordained a deacon, priest or bishop. Teodolfo Mertel [1806 to 1899], a lawyer, was created a cardinal deacon in March 1858, though he had never been ordained a deacon or priest. Two months later he was, however, ordained a deacon by the pope, **Pius IX** (#256). He, nonetheless, was never ordained a priest. So at his death in July 1899 he became the last cardinal not to have been ordained a priest.

On April 15, 1962, in what must have been an effort to further bolster the stature and standing of the College, John XXIII issued a *motu prorio, Cum gravissima*, which required all cardinals to receive episcopal consecration --

unless an explicit exemption is granted by the pope, typically on the grounds of age. With this requirement, logical as it was, the prerequisites to being a cardinal had been significantly elevated over a 'short' period of forty-five years – cardinals, as they are now known, having existed since 769.

Though the 1917 Code only required priestly ordination, only a few (possibly less than 30) non-bishops had been created between 1917 and 1962, John himself creating around eleven. On April 19th, four days after the *motu prorio* the pope himself consecrated twelve cardinals, one of them Alfredo Ottaviani, who were not bishops. Since John's ruling only fifteen non-bishop cardinals had been created up until the end of the year 2013. The first of these was Henri de Lubac, S.J., created a cardinal deacon in February 1983 by **John Paul II** (#265). The last, up until year-end 2013, was Karl Josef Becker, S.J., created a cardinal deacon in February 2012 by **Benedict XVI** (#266).

Ad Suburbicarias dioeceses and *Cum gravissima* were the two 'biggies', in addition, of course, to the override of the 70-limit, when it came to the College of Cardinals reforms enacted by John XXIII. A third change decreed on April 11, 1962, four days ahead of *Cum gravissima*, was, by comparison, more mundane and furthermore was just applicable to the cardinal bishops. This change, implemented with *motu prorio Suburbicariis sedibus* had to do with the administration of the *suburbicarian* sees.

In April 1910, **Pius X** (#258), wished to ensure that the diocesans of the *suburbicarian* sees would receive undivided pastoral care unimpeded by the other duties of the cardinal bishops – many of whom happened to be senior curial or Vatican officials. They would typically have gotten precedence when created, thus giving them the seniority required for these sees per the then prevailing *jus optionis*. Pius X, thus, stipulated that these sees would have a 'suffragan' (surrogate) bishop who would have complete administrative authority over the see. The cardinal bishoprics would thus be strictly titular.

Benedict XV (#259), however, for reasons that were never clear other than for the sake of reducing some marginal costs, in February 1915, just under five months into his papacy, overturned Pius X's requirement for suffragan bishops. Cardinal bishops were again placed at the head of the *suburbicarian* sees irrespective of the practicality.

Forty-seven years later, John issued a *motu prorio, Suburbicariis sedibus*, which, quite sensibly, overturned Benedict XV's provision and reenacted Pius X's edict. So, once again, this time per John, cardinal bishops would be strictly titular when it came to the *suburbicarian* sees whose titles they held. This, as with all of the other College of Cardinals related reforms instituted by John XXIII, is still the norm.

78) There had never been legal or logistical reasons for popes to be *'prisoners of the Vatican'* following the fall of the Papal States in 1870. The *'Lateran Pacts of 1929'* ensured that this would never have to be the case, irrespective. Nonetheless, **Pius XI** (#260) and **Pius XII** (#261) did not show much enthusiasm for venturing into Rome though the fundamental basis for their authority as 'pope' was their standing as Bishop of Rome. John XXIII, on the other hand, not only relished visiting Rome at every opportunity, even late at night, gaily communing with his diocesans, but preferred to walk around so as to be more approachable. Suffice to say that the Romans, who were predominantly Catholic at the time, loved their new avuncular pope, 'Papa Giovanni', who had the 'common touch'. They devised a nickname for this perambulating pope which amply reflected their fondness and respect for him. What was this nickname?

'Johnnie Walker' after the then most popular brand of blended Scotch whisky; which in addition to the name was also known for its iconic logo of a formerly attired gentleman taking large strides. Some others called him **'John Outside the Walls'** – a clever twist on the Papal Basilica of St Paul Outside the Walls (*Basilica Papale di San Paolo fuori le Mura*).

By then, quite early into his papacy, he was also getting referred to, particularly by those in the Vatican that saw him in action on a regular basis, as *'il buon Roncalli'* (the good Roncalli) – a precursor to the *'Good Pope John'* appellation by which he would often be referred to after his passing.

79) In addition to the College of Cardinals related reforms discussed above, Pope John XXIII made one change, a crucial one at that, to papal election rules. What was that change?

This ruling was made on September 5, 1962, five weeks ahead of the opening of Vatican II, with a *motu prorio, Summi Pontificis electio*. By now, though it had yet to be confirmed by doctors, the pope had a fairly good idea that he was gravely ill and that his days were severely limited. With this *motu prorio*, the pope overrode **Pius XII's** (#261) controversial 1945 override of the previously sacrosanct two-thirds majority for papal election by insisting on two-thirds plus one, at all times. John reinstated the 1179 ruling requiring just a two-thirds majority if the number of electors participating was divisible by three – with two-thirds plus one only needed when a rounding up was required when the number of electors was not divisible by three. It would also now be possible, at least in theory, for a candidate to vote for himself since there were no admonitions against doing so – though it was assumed that most would not resort to voting for themselves.

Paul VI (#263) thirteen years later again instituted the two-thirds plus one majority only to have it overruled twenty-one years later by **John Paul II** (#265). John Paul's override, which brought things back to what was mandated by John, remains the norm; i.e., the majority required to be elected pope is *'two-thirds'*.

80) Though it was by no means his only major achievement as pope, his papal encyclical *Mater et Magistra* (mother and teacher (of all nations)) [1961] and his reforms to the College of Cardinals, at a minimum, among his other incontrovertible successes, John XXIII is now best remembered for **Vatican II** (and his *'good pope'* persona). When is he said to have first intimated his intention to hold such a Council, who did he first convey it to, how was it made public, and what other event was grouped with it when it came to the announcement?

Per the official record, the pope's first intimation that he intended to convene an ecumenical council took place during the morning of Tuesday, **January 20, 1959**. He was in the midst of his routine, near daily audience with his 'second-in-command', the Secretary of State, Cardinal Domenico Tardini. Thus, Cardinal Tardini, as would be appropriate, given that he was the pope's closest collaborator at the time, is said to be the first one to have heard of the pope's desire, attributed to the *"Lord's will"*, to summon the Second Council of the Vatican. Per the pope, though Tardini himself never commented on it, the Secretary of State's reaction was one of immediate, jubilant concurrence. He did not need the endorsement or support of any to go ahead with his plan. The pope, nonetheless, took Tardini's unreserved assent as a good sign of how the other prelates, in particular the cardinals, would react to this bold initiative – one that could profoundly shake and possibly shatter the *status quo* when it came to the Church.

On that Tuesday morning when the notion of Vatican II came to be, John XXIII had been pope for 84 days. None of the recent popes, as mentioned in #75, had even held a cardinal creating consistory that early in their papacy. This pope, elderly no doubt, had not only created twenty-three cardinals 36 days earlier but had also, in doing so, overridden a centuries old norm that appeared to have been sacrosanct. He who was meant to be a 'caretaker' pope was indeed taking care of quite a few important matters in a hurry.

On the Sunday following his disclosure to Tardini, i.e., January 25, 1959, the pope attended Mass at *Basilica Papale di San Paolo fuori le Mura* (Papal Basilica of St Paul Outside the Walls) – one of Rome's ancient papal basilicas, founded by Emperor Constantine the Great [306 to 337] over what is said to be the burial place of St. Paul. It was one of the pope's favorite churches in Rome. A

Benedictine Abbey, founded in the 6th century, is attached to this Basilica. Following the Mass, the pope, accompanied by an entourage of seventeen cardinals, retired to this Abbey.

It was at this Benedictine Abbey, that the seventeen cardinals accompanying the pope were told of the pope's plan to convene an Ecumenical Council of the Universal Church. This was the first official announcement of Vatican II.

Despite its towering import the pope did not announce Vatican II on its own. Instead it was combined and prefaced with the announcement of another council, a 'Diocesan Synod for Rome'. A synod, in general, is an ecclesiastical gathering. What differentiated the diocesan synod from the Ecumenical Council was one of scale and scope. The former, headed by the diocesan bishop [in this case the pope], was restricted to priests and clerics of that diocese. Whereas over 2,600 bishops, from around the world, would be invited to attend Vatican II.

That the pope intended to summon a diocesan synod surprised the assembled cardinals. Roman synods (or at least synods held in Rome) had been popular during the Middle Ages as a means to establish, rectify or ratify doctrine, canon law, procedural protocols or major disciplinary issues. But, they had fallen into disuse. When it came to the Diocese of Rome, the pope, as the Bishop of Rome, had been resolving issues related to 'Rome', for quite a while by then, without the need for a synod. This would be the *first* Diocesan Synod for Rome since the fall of the Papal States – and in reality the first synod specific to the Diocese of Rome. While the cardinals were still getting over this unexpected news the pope informed them that the diocesan synod would be followed by an Ecumenical Council.

Announcing the synod and the Council together, one after the other, in the same sentence, was a masterly touch by the pope – another example of his extraordinary interpersonal skills. It sure had the shock value the pope no doubt intended to achieve. The cardinals, and soon after that much of the Catholic world, were stunned. The laity and non-prelates, however, were quick to recognize, and embrace, the enormous latent promise of what the Council represented. Nobody though, lay or cleric, curialist or general public, was sure what the Council was supposed to address, let alone resolve. The pope, astute as ever, was very careful not to set any expectations, define any parameters or put forward any issues he had in mind. He, basically, though not in those exact words, stressed, repeatedly, that there were to be *'no scared cows'*. Anything and everything to do with the Church, whether it be doctrinal, liturgical, social, legislative or cultural, could (or should) be discussed and debated at the Council. But, the pope did make it clear that he wanted to see everything discussed in terms of their relevance and standing in the 20th-century (post-WW II) rather than what they meant or stood for in the past. That was key.

There was yet another initiative announced in addition to the synod and Council. That was the pope's intention to revise the 1918 Code of Canon Law. [This, however, would not get completed in the pope's lifetime. In reality it would be 1983 before the new Code came to be.]

81) How and where did *Concilium Oecumenicum Vaticanum Secundum* (i.e., Ecumenical Second Vatican Council) stand relative to the other ecumenical councils recognized by the Catholic Church?

John XXIII's Vatican II would be the **twenty-first** ecumenical council recognized by the Roman Catholic Church.

The first ecumenical council was the **First Council of Nicaea** [today's Turkey], convened by Emperor Constantine the Great [306 to 337], that was in session between May 20 to August 25, 325, and is best known for repudiating *Arianism* (i.e., that Christ was *not* of the same substance as the Father).

The prior council, i.e., the twentieth, had been **First Council of the Vatican** that was in session for 316 days between December 8, 1869 and October 20, 1870. It was the first ecumenical council to be held at the Vatican. The previous five councils held in Rome, the first in 1123 and the last between 1512 to 1517, had been held at the Lateran Basilica and as such are known as the *'Lateran Councils'*. Vatican I was convoked by **Pius IX** (#256) on June 29, 1868. It is best known for its dogmatic definition of papal infallibility and papal primacy.

In terms of the convocation of the two councils, the gap between Pius IX's convocation and that of John XXIII was **90.5 years**.

The gap if measured between when Vatican I ended and January 25, 1959, i.e., when Vatican II was announced, was 88 years and 3 months.

Eighty-eight years, or even 90 years, is by no means a record when it comes to the hiatus between ecumenical councils recognized by the Roman Catholic Church. The gap between the nineteenth council, i.e., the **Council of Trent** (famous for its Counter-Reformation measures) and the twentieth, i.e., Vatican I, was 324 years in terms of 'start-to-start' or 306 years when measured 'end-of-one to the start-of-other'. That, though the longest gap, was not a total 'one-off'. The gap between the ninth and tenth councils, i.e., **Fourth Council of Constantinople** and **First Council of the Lateran**, was 254 years, start-to-start. The gap between the sixth and seventh, i.e., Third Constantinople and Second Nicaea, was 107 years.

The average gap, start-to-start, between the twenty councils that preceded Vatican II was **81.3 years**. So, Vatican II really could not be deemed 'unreasonable', at least in terms of timeframe. The gap between the eighteenth and nineteenth, **Fifth Lateran** and Trent, had been thirty-three years, while that between the sixteenth and seventeenth, i.e., **Constance** and **Basel** et. al., had been just seventeen years.

82) As the pope would wryly note sometime later, the seventeen cardinals at the Benedictine abbey on January 25th, upon being told of his intent to call a Council did not, as he would have liked, crowd around him to express their enthusiastic approval and proffer good wishes on this boldly ambitious endeavor. Instead he was met with impressive silence. But within days, some of it but knee-jerk reactions to the unexpectedness of it, a few other cardinals were unabashed in being harshly critical of the Council. The major problem was that most prelates could not fathom the need for a Council at that juncture in history. As far as they could see there were no Church-related problems major enough to warrant the summoning of an ecumenical council. So, who were some of the better known cardinals who went on public record with some rather harsh assessments of the pope's acumen in summoning this Council?

The newly created Cardinal Montini, who as **Paul VI** (#263) would play a pivotal role in ensuring the success of Vatican II, upon being asked for his reaction to the pope's announcement referred to it as *"a hornets' nest"* – though he would in time become part of the pivotal behind-the-scenes 'cabinet' that helped John XXIII bring it to fruition.

Cardinal Giacomo Lercaro, the leading liberal *papabile* at the 1958 conclave, possibly still a bit irked that he was bypassed, was unbecomingly harsh. *[q.v. #7.]* He thought the pope's intent *'rash and impulsive'* and due to the pope's *'inexperience and lack of culture'*! He was put out that the pope, less than three months in office had had the audacity to convoke a new council when there had been none for a hundred years. His math, certainly, and his logic, apparently, was in need of some attention. But, he too, like Cardinal Montini would soon have a major change of heart and appreciate the merits of a 20th century council. He too would be a part of the 'kitchen cabinet' that labored tirelessly, behind the scenes, to ensure that no amount of 'political' wrangling or logistical missteps would derail the start of the Council.

Yet another cardinal whose initial criticism of the Council bordered on the impertinent was New York's Francis Joseph Spellman. As mentioned in #47 Spellman in the past had been a Roncalli friend and benefactor. He had even visited and stayed with him when he was the Patriarch in Venice. But, after the election he had been callously rude about the new pope -- mostly likely aggrieved that he, a very distant *papabile* at best, had received but short shrift. He was again aggravated when he heard about the news. He had heard about it from journalists prior to receiving any communiqués from Rome. This displeased him since he felt that he, as a cardinal, should have been told of it before it made it to the press. On the day he heard about it, he told a French diplomat, on the record, that it was *'premature, senseless and doomed'*. He went onto opine, independent of any facts, that the pope must have been coerced into calling this Council by 'people' who had misconstrued earlier statements by the pope.

Though these brutal remarks must have stung, the pope did not rebut, respond or retaliate. He, as he had done many times in the past, serenely held his peace. Later in his papacy he was asked by an American prelate as to how he managed to remain unperturbed in the face of obvious curial machinations against many of his initiatives. He replied that he was sure that when he met Christ, he, as a bishop, was more likely to be asked as to how many souls he had saved rather than how he got along with the curia. No doubt that this was the mindset that enabled him to maintain his equanimity, with nary an exception, during the lead up to the Council. What is more perplexing, however, is how the cardinals (and later on curialists) realized that they could get away, with impunity, with the type of intemperate behavior they exhibited. It seems unlikely that they would have been so disrespectful of another pope – and certainly not **Pius XII** (#261). They certainly were banking on his known good-nature.

But, there were to be at least two cardinals who exuberantly expressed their support for the Council as soon as it was announced, and even demanded some credit (whether justified or not) for it being called. These two cardinals were Ernesto Ruffini, Archbishop of Palermo (Sicily) and archconservative curialist, Alfredo Ottaviani, Pro-Secretary of the Supreme Sacred Congregation of the Holy Office. They had both served on a commission created by Pius XII to investigate a suitable agenda for a possible Council. They both claimed that they had, individually, briefed Cardinal Roncalli, during the conclave, of what the commission had concluded and, moreover, suggested that the pope should consider convening a new Council.

83) Diocesan Synod of Rome was seen by one and all as a mini dress rehearsal for Vatican II. As such, there was much interest in how the pope would interject himself into the proceedings, as the belief was that this would provide a preview of how the pope might run affairs come the Council. So, how did the pope comport himself during this synod – given that, of course, the pope knew that he was being watched for clues as to what could happen during Vatican II?

The synod assembled for their first session on Sunday, January 24th, 1960, at St. John Lateran – the cathedral church of the Diocese of Rome. Eight days prior the pope released a chirograph formally summoning the synod, under the patronage of the Virgin Mary, and stating that the theme would be the *'health of the Roman people'*. He stated that he wanted to see a rejuvenation of the

Catholic faith in Rome, so that it could flourish a new and be an example to others. He wished, in the main, to see Christian morals strengthened across Rome and a more disciplined, better trained cadre of clergy that was capable and willing to respond to the contemporary (as opposed to the no longer pertinent) needs of the Romans .

As had been the case for nearly nine centuries, the administration of the Diocese of Rome was entrusted, by the pope, to a Vicar General; a Cardinal Vicar General as of 1558. There was also a Vicar General for the Vatican City State, albeit post 1929. The Cardinal Vicar of Rome is assisted by a series of vicegerents, each, typically an auxiliary bishop. The pope intended that the cardinal vicar and the auxiliary bishops would take the lead when it came to the synod.

The Cardinal Vicar of Rome at the time of the synod was Cardinal Clemente Micara [1879 to 1965]. He had been created in 1946 and had become Cardinal Vicar on January 26, 1951. He was slightly older than the pope. He was set in his ways and had been Cardinal Vicar for eight years when the pope announced the synod. He really was not sure why the pope felt the need to call a synod. He believed that he had everything under control. The Vicegerent of Rome since December 1936 had been Archbishop Luigi Traglia [1895 to 1977]. He was more tractable and was named President of the Synod Committee.

One of the pope's main concerns about Rome was the consequences of its rapid growth of 'late' – what he referred to as its urban sprawl. In 1939 Rome had a population of 700,000 and 62 parishes. By 1958 the population had nearly tripled as had the number of parishes. Though there had never been a paucity of clerics in Rome, many, in reality, worked in the Vatican or were involved with academia. Of the over 3,000 priests in Rome at the time of the synod only about 20% were involved in the Diocese. The pope clearly felt that this was an issue. He communicated this to Traglia, in writing, in October 1959.

The synod lasted from January 24th to June 29th, 1960. The pope, as he would with Vatican II also, paid close attention to the proceedings. But, he kept a low profile and did not try to enforce his opinions, let alone his will, on the deliberations other than on the matter of clerical celibacy, albeit even that *sotto voce* to an extent. Consequently, the synod did not rise to the heights hoped for by the pope. But, he accepted that. What was important was that he had allowed the principals of the diocese to go about trying to determine their own future without papal directives.

A few months after the conclusion of the synod he would comment, with irony, that the synod had been more of an *opus bonum* rather than an *opus perfectum* [i.e., it had been 'good', if not perfect]. The principals involved appear to have, at a minimum, lacked vision and imagination, if not will and courage.

Rather than attempting to tackle anything ambitious they confined their scope to laying down petty prohibitions to do with clerical and lay behavior. They forbade priests in Rome from going to the movies, theater or opera – and even tried to dissuade them from being seen in bars or restaurants as well as watching too much television. They probably had forgotten that this pope, when Patriarch of Venice, had overturned a long held ban on clerics attending the *Biennale*.

Some priests anticipating that the synod will, inevitably, look at behavioral restrictions, took the opportunity, pre-synod, to openly question the dogmatic validity of the ever thorny issue of clerical celibacy. A priest of note even took it to the media, in print. Now, in hindsight, it is clear that these priests were being very naive.

The Church's long-held stance on clerical celibacy was not anything new to this pope. As a young man he had struggled with what had been expected of him – and prevailed. Now nearing eighty, he, who always thought of himself as a traditionalist when it came to doctrine and dogma, was unlikely to tackle this delicate issue without much more input. Just a few months earlier, on August 1, 1959, in an encyclical to honor St. John Vianney, the patron saint of all priests, he had highlighted and praised clerical chastity. The priests had also miscalculated in thinking that the synod was the right forum to have this matter aired. The forthcoming Council, with its universal participation, however, would have been the appropriate setting – provided, of course, that enough bishops felt that it merited deliberation.

Though he did not want to be heavy handed, the pope knew that he had to address the celibacy issue and put it in perspective to preclude it becoming the unnecessary *cause célèbre* of this synod. So, two days into the synod, on January 26, 1960, he gave his second allocution to the synod. In it he said: "*It deeply hurts Us that . . . anyone can dream that the Church will deliberately or even suitably renounce what from time immemorial has been, and still remains, one of the purest and noblest glories of her priesthood. The law of ecclesiastical celibacy and the efforts necessary to preserve it always recall to mind the struggles of the heroic times when the Church of Christ had to fight for and succeeded in obtaining her threefold glory, always an emblem of victory, that is, the Church of Christ, free, chaste and Catholic*". He left it at that, and clerical chastity was not a topic that the synod tried to mandate upon.

John XXIII's third cardinal creating consistory took place on March 28, 1960, prior to the official conclusion of the synod. The first to be created at that consistory was Luigi Traglia who became a cardinal priest. That same day he was appointed Pro-Vicar General of Rome; though he would not replace

Micara for another five years. One thing was very clear. Luigi Traglia had impressed the pope in his involvement with the synod.

84) Early in his pontificate, at the urging of his secretary, Loris Capovilla, the pope had restored and modernized a medieval structure at the Vatican. What was this structure and what was it used for?

The pope, true to his *'Johnnie Walker'* appellation, was a habitual walker. Whenever he got a chance, with no set routine, he liked to walk in the tranquility of the picturesquely laid out Vatican Gardens – some of the soil in this garden said to be from Golgotha, brought back from the Holy Land, c. 327, by Saint Helena, the mother of Constantine the Great. Unlike prior popes he did not ignore the gardeners; they, historically, having been instructed to hide when they saw the pope approaching. John XXIII would seek out the gardeners and make a point of talking to them – most often about their families.

On one of these walks, towards the very western edge of the Gardens, he, accompanied that day by Capovilla, came across the ruins of a stark but stout brick tower. It was the **Torre San Giovanni** (St. John's Tower) built at the behest of **Nicholas III** (#189) c. 1279, as part of a new walled fortification against a possible attack by Saracens [i.e., Muslim invaders]. It is not clear as to which *'St. John'* it is named after. It definitely was not named for the 'John' that will be made a saint on April 27, 2014 – though in years to come this fact might get blurred given that most references to this tower invariably mentions John XXIII. He, moreover, has a tower, albeit not this one, as discussed in #42, on his coat of arms. It is possible that it honors either John the Evangelist (the author of the Fourth Gospel) or **Pope St. John I** (#53), a much venerated martyr in the Middle Ages.

Nicholas III was the son of Senator Matteo Rosso *'il Grande'* Orsini, the enforcer of the first sequestered papal conclave. He was created a cardinal in 1244, and participated in seven conclaves, before getting elected, at the last, in 1277. He was the Archpriest of the Vatican Basilica when elected, having been appointed as such just over a year earlier in October 1276. Rather than taking up residence at the Lateran Palace he chose to move into the Vatican Palace – thus becoming the first pope to reside at the Vatican. He immediately started an ambitious program of renovation and expansion at the Vatican, starting with the Basilica and the Palace, but then extending it to encompass the then fledgling Vatican Garden. He acquired land adjoining the Vatican to make the Gardens bigger. He, as such, was the architect of the Vatican Gardens as it is now known. The *Torre San Giovanni* had been built as part of this initiative to be a watch tower and guard post at the perimeter of the expanded Vatican grounds, one of many on this perimeter. The tower had a diameter of 55' for most of it height and the walls, at ground level, were 15' in thickness.

Figure 18: San Giovanni (St. John's Tower), in the middle,
framed by two 'Vatican Radio' antennas.

The location of the tower appealed to the pope. It was in the most tranquil part of the Gardens, far from the bustle of St. Peter's Square. But, at the same time it was close to the edge of Rome; the tower thus providing an ideal vantage point to watch life in Rome from afar, and above. Capovilla suggested that the pope have the tower restored with an apartment built inside for his use. This appealed to the pope and he, at once, ordered the work to be done. To this end, foundations had to be strengthened, electricity and telephone wiring had to be brought in and an elevator installed for the aging pope. The apartment was on multiple levels. The main living area was on the fourth floor, consisting of a round living room, bedroom, study, dining room and chapel. The kitchen, laundry and utility areas were on the third floor. The fifth floor housed a small guest room and quarters for the staff. The first two floors were open halls. In the end, it cost more than had been hoped, was more elaborate than intended and took longer to complete than had been anticipated. But, when it was finished it became the pope's favored retreat; a place where he could get away from the demands of his office, contemplate, get some rest and best of all, with the aid of a pair of binoculars, watch, with pleasure, his Roman diocesans getting on with their lives.

The accommodation within the tower has since become a select guest quarters for VIPs – typically cardinals requiring temporary housing. Cardinal Tarciscio Bertone, when appointed Secretary of State in June 2006 stayed at the Tower while the prior Secretary, Angelo Sodano, the Dean of the College, continued to occupy the official residence assigned to the S.S. In 1971 Hungarian Cardinal József Mindszenty, who had spent fifteen years confined witin the U.S. embassy in Budapest, in political asylum, was permitted by **Paul VI** (#263) to stay in the Tower during his stay in Rome prior to moving to Vienna [Austria] as an exile. In 1979 **John Paul II** (#265) opted to live in the Tower while the Papal Apartments were being renovated. Since then the Tower has been designated as an alternate Vatican residence for the pope when maintenance work needs to be done to the Vatican Palace.

85) On Christmas Day 1958, his first Christmas as pope, John XXIII, to the astonishment of many, essentially on the spur-of-the-moment without any preplanning, revived a much cherished papal custom that had not been enacted since 1870. What did the pope do that Christmas afternoon, after he had celebrated Mass at St. Peter's and delivered a radio broadcast to the world (per the tradition established by his predecessor, **Pius XII**)?

The custom had been that popes would make pastoral visits on Christmas day, typically going to see indisposed and disadvantaged parishioners in Rome.

That Christmas Pope John decided to visit, without notifying the staff in advance, the children suffering from polio at the *Ospedale Pediatrico Bambino Gesù* (Baby Jesus Children's Hospital). The hospital was located in the Janiculum Hill in western Rome; an area administered by the Holy See per the extraterritorial rights granted by the 1929 Lateran Pacts. The nursing staff was perplexed to find the pope, unannounced, in their ward. They were not sure what they should do, or where the pope should sit. Not so, the kids and the pope. The kids, overjoyed, called out to the pope. The pope responded and started going from bed to bed, sometimes sitting on the beds. One boy told him that his name was 'Angelo'. The pope, obviously moved replied wistfully that he too used to be called as such at one time.

Figure 19: The hospital visit on Christmas Day 1958.

source: PIME

The next day he visited, again extemporaneously, Rome's Regina Coeli (Queen of Heaven) prison – though this time trailed by a bevy of Vatican staff, as well as journalists and photographers from around the world. A visit to a prison had been part of the old tradition. He, with his irrepressible good nature informed the prisoners, loudly, that he had come to see them because they couldn't come to see him. Suffice to say that he could not have been more welcome – even before he went on to add, addressing them as *'dear sons and brothers'*, that he had, anyway, wanted to see them. Then to the consternation of the Vatican staff, he, conspiratorially, informed them that one of his brothers had been incarcerated for poaching. The *L'Osservatore Romano*, despite the pope's admonishment for it to be more '20th century', opted to omit this revelation in its reporting of the pope's visit to the prison. He ordered internal prison doors to be opened so that all prisoners, even those convicted of violent crimes, got a chance to meet him.

On both these visits, and on subsequent visits of such pastoral nature, the pope would make a point of not referring to himself with the royal *'we'*. During his first days as pope he had had trouble remembering to use the *'we'*. Now he was doing it to show solidarity – a trait that would be copied by subsequent popes, in particular **John Paul II** (#265).

Three weeks after the groundbreaking Christmas visits, on January 20, 1959, the pope, aided by his driver and factotum Guido Gusso, took off, unannounced, from the Vatican, when they were supposed to be just going to the Vatican Gardens. He had decided to visit a retirement home for priests on Monte Mario to spend some time with 'old friends'. As with the prisoners he was going to see them because they couldn't come to see him.

86) During his 4.6 years as pope John XXIII published eight encyclicals as listed in the figure below. Of these, two are considered to be epic and are cited alongside Vatican II in terms of the outstanding achievements of his papacy. What are these two 'part of the legacy' encyclicals?

The two encyclicals of his that are deemed to be supreme are *Mater et Magistra* (mother and teacher (of all nations)) published in 1961 and *Pacem in Terris* (peace on earth) in 1963.

Mater et Magistra was published to coincide with the 70th anniversary of **Leo XIII's** (#257) *Rerum Novarum* (of new things) published on May 15, 1891, as well as the 40th anniversary of **Pius XI's** (#257) *Quadragesimo Anno* (of *Rerum Novarum*) (in the 40th year) published on May 15, 1931.

Rerum Novarum was the landmark encyclical that dealt with social inequality and the need for social justice within the context of the rights and duties of business owners (i.e., capital investors) and labor. *Quadragesimo Anno* went onto update Leo XIII's concerns in terms of the ethical ramifications of both burgeoning capitalism *or* communism and their conflicting concepts of human freedom and dignity. Always eager to show that his papacy was not meant to be a radical departure from the path followed by **Pius XII** (#261), John also made sure that his encyclical referenced to social teachings advocated by his immediate predecessor – in particular remarks made during a radio broadcast one June 1, 1941.

The theme of *Mater et Magistra*, as stated at the start of the document, was that of Christianity vis-á-vis social progress – and its purpose was to reexamine how people, especially the workers, were faring, socially and economically, in the resurgence of nations following WWII. It was a subject near and dear to his heart. It harked all the way back to his great-uncle Zaverio's steadfast belief in the role of Catholicism in ensuring an ethical way of life for workers and the disadvantaged. *[q.v. #19.]* In writing this encyclical the pope, furthermore, also had the advantage of what he had learnt from *Azione Cattolica*, Radini-Tedeschi, his time in Bergamo, 'worker-priests' in France and his brothers who continued to toil as relatively-poor farmers. The world, as the pope noted in

	Date [Time as pope]	Title of Encyclical	Dealt with: [Length of *Latin* text]
1.	June 29, 1959 [0.7 year]	*Ad Petri Cathedram* (To the chair of Peter)	A paternal, pastoral message on truth, unity and peace motivated by charity. *[8,429 words]*
2.	Aug. 1, 1959 [0.8 year]	*Sacerdotii Nostri Primordia* (From the beginning of our priesthood)	100th anniversary of the death of French, St. Jean-Baptiste-Marie Vianney, the patron saint of all priests. *[8,204 words]*
3.	Sep. 26, 1959 [0.9 year]	*Grata Recordatio* (With joyful recollection)	Urging the devout recitation of Mary's rosary especially during the month of October per a tradition promoted by **Leo XIII** (#257). *[1,283 words]*
4.	Nov. 28, 1959 [1.1 year]	*Princeps Pastorum* (The prince of the shepherds)	Celebrating the success of Catholic missions in recruiting and training local clergy, and the role of lay Catholics as role-models in non-Catholic countries. *[7,679 words]*
5.	May 15, 1961 [2.6 years]	*Mater et Magistra* (Mother and Teacher)	A contemporary update on Catholic teaching on the rights of workers, the role of government, common good and the dignity of agricultural work. *[18,191 words]*
6.	Nov. 11, 1961 [3.0 years]	*Aeterna Dei Sapientia* (God's eternal wisdom)	To commemorate the 1,500 year anniversary of the passing of **Leo 'the great' I** (#45). *[4,934 words]*
7.	July 1, 1962 [3.7 years]	*Paenitentiam Agere* (Penance for sins)	Calling Catholics to practice penance ahead of Vatican II. *[2,784 words]*
8.	Apr. 11, 1963 [4.5 years]	*Pacem in Terris* (Peace on earth)	On establishing universal peace and recognizing human rights. *[11,303 words]*

this encyclical, had changed quite markedly over the prior three decades. The Great Depression and WW II were over but the Cold War persisted. Major strides in technology, science, transportation and mass communications were impinging upon all aspects of life – automation, modern industrialization and scientific farming continually eroding the demand for labor, though, overall, the expectations were for a broad based increase in the standard of living.

In this encyclical the pope stresses the import of individual dignity and rights -- and how private initiatives and private ownership must always be given priority with governments, thus, encouraging and supporting individual freedom, rights and initiatives. The desirability for private and public cooperation at all times is stressed, albeit with the caveat that care should be taken that any public regulations do not unnecessarily curtail individual liberties. In this context (per a principle known as 'subsidiarity') the pope urges as much decentralized 'government' as possible with public authorities making decisions as lower down within an organization as possible to ensure appropriate empathy with the 'citizenary'.

The pope, understandably, speaks out against conspicuous economic disparity within and between countries and urges generosity from the wealthy nations towards those that are emerging, but to do so such that there are: 'no strings attached'.

'Common good', across the spectrum, is a recurrent motif of this encyclical whether it has to do with the rights of individual workers employed by one business, the policies specific to a nation or the interrelations between nations. Just wages and the ability for workers to 'organize' [e.g., unionize], including the prospect of shared ownership, is stressed within this framework, with the pope maintaining that the true prosperity of a nation is not its 'gross domestic product' (GDP) but an equitable distribution of its 'wealth' across its population.

Given his own personal background, the pope, unabashedly, promotes the dignity and ideal of agricultural endeavors (in particular family farms) and urges public authorities to help farmers by giving them the necessary utilities, infrastructure, tax incentives, technology, subsidies and financial help.

The detailed, well reasoned *Mater et Magistra* which is still regarded with awe half century after its publication served as a papal level-setting precursor to Vatican II which came to be sixteen months later.

Pacem in Terris, published 53 days prior to the pope's passing, deals head-on with the pope's unease as to the political realities and tensions of the Cold War – following what had been the dangerous brinkmanship of the October 1962 Cuban missile crisis and the erection of the Berlin Wall in 1961. This encyclical which is titled: *'On Establishing Universal Peace in Truth, Justice, Charity and*

Liberty', starts off with the sentence (per the English translation): *'Peace on Earth—which man throughout the ages has so longed for and sought after—can never be established, never guaranteed, except by the diligent observance of the divinely established order'.*

The encyclical garnered immediate attention (not to mention respect) in that it was the *first ever*, which rather than being addressed just to Catholics, also included *'all Men of Good Will'*. This was yet another masterly touch by a pope who excelled at connecting with the common people.

On October 26, 1962, twelve days into the *Cuban missile crisis* (and two weeks into Vatican II), the pope broadcast a message, in French, over Vatican Radio, directed to all the pertinent heads of state, advocating restraint. What was not disclosed at the time was that the pope had not done this impromptu, in isolation. Through intermediaries, one of them a U.S. journalist, the pope had let both Washington D.C. and Moscow know that he would be happy to make a call for peace that would give both sides the 'cover' they needed to gracefully deescalate the confrontation. U.S. President John F. Kennedy and Soviet Leader Nikita Khrushchev immediately, but independently, agreed that this would indeed be quite helpful. That same day, the state-controlled Soviet news media printed extracts from the broadcast augmented with their own headlines to ensure that Soviets citizens knew of the speech. Two days later Khrushchev announced that the missiles were being withdrawn from Cuba. Many of the experts at the time believed that the pope had played a decisive role in making this happen. The defusing of this powder-keg event appears to have been the inspiration for *Pacem in Terris* which was issued five and a half months later. By then the pope knew, for certain, that his days were numbered. With this encyclical he was leaving a vital message knowing that he would not be around, in person, to intervene at the next 'crisis'.

Though the Cold War would sputter to an end three decades later with the dissolution of the Soviet Union with the nuclear deterrence doctrine still prevailing and intact – this was by no means a given in 1961 or 1962. Especially after the shenanigans of the Cuban missile crisis, many, including the pope, genuinely feared bloated egos, hotheadedness and itchy fingers. So the overarching message of *Pacem in Terris* was that of resolving conflicts by means of negotiation and mediation rather than through recourse to arms. One could argue that though the recourse to arms has continued unabated, that the pope at least, indirectly though it maybe, had the satisfaction of preventing nuclear Armageddon -- which was the real fear at the time that this encyclical was written.

87) In the three decades that preceded his papacy, this pope had repeatedly demonstrated his avid desire for Christian harmony and unity, irrespective of provocations, particularly when it came to the Orthodox. It was an unconditional and uncomplicated commitment to inter-faith cooperation. As pope he got the chance to take his ecumenical beliefs and aspirations to a higher, more concrete level. What are some of the key ecumenical initiatives that this pope is rightly famous for?

In reality Vatican II, which was by definition and design an *'Ecumenical Council'*, the twenty-first recognized by the Catholic Church, was by far his greatest and profoundest of efforts to foster inter-religious discourse. He ardently hoped that the Council would lead to some degree of reconciliation. On **Christmas Day 1961**, when the pope formally convoked the Council 'for sometime in 1962' he said: *'...To this chorus of prayers, we invite also all Christians of Churches separated from Rome, that the Council may be also to their advantage. We know that many of these sons are anxious for a return of unity and of peace, according to the teachings and the prayer of Christ to the Father. And we know also that the announcement of the Council has been accepted by them not only with joy but also that not a few have already promised to offer their prayers for its success, and that they hope to send representatives of their communities to follow its work at close quarters. All this is for us a reason of great comfort and of hope, and precisely for the purpose of facilitating these contacts we instituted some time ago the secretariat for this specific purpose. ...'*. The pope could not have been any clearer.

The *'secretariat'* mentioned above was the *'Secretariat for Promoting Christian Unity'*, established on **June 5, 1960** (the day of the Pentecost), with his *motu proprio, Superno Dei nutu factum*, as one of the ten specialized preparatory commissions for the Council. The *'Christian Unity Secretariat'* was headed up by recently created German Jesuit cardinal, Augustin Bea. He, at one time **Pius XII's** (#261) confessor, was a renowned Biblical scholar and was noted for his friendly relations with Christians of all stripes.

This was the first time that the Holy See had had a curial office explicitly dedicated to deal with ecumenical affairs. In the *motu proprio*, in establishing the secretariat, the pope states that his rationale for doing so is: *'Demonstrating Our love and kindness to those who call themselves Christians, but are separated from this Apostolic See, so that they can continue the work of the council and easily find the way to achieve the unity ...'* Yet again the pope left nothing to doubt as to what he would like to see happen. [In June 1988, **John Paul II** (#265) in his *Pastor Bonus* Apostolic Constitution which restructured the Roman curia, changed this secretariat to be the *'Pontifical Council for Promoting Christian Unity'*.]

One of the first major accomplishments of this secretariat was to set up the historic meeting in **November 1960** between the pope and the principal leader of the Church of England, the Archbishop of Canterbury, at that time Geoffrey

Francis Fisher [b: 1887, Archbishop Jan. 1945 to May 1961]. It was a milestone; the first ever meeting between a pope and the Archbishop of Canterbury since the English Reformation in the 16th century. The visit, seen around the world as an icebreaker, was also pivotal in that it signaled that other Christians would, per the pope's ardent wish, attend the Council, albeit as observers.

There were at least two other ecumenical 'firsts' of a similar vein. Exactly a year later, in **November 1961**, Arthur C. Lichtenberger, Presiding Bishop of the U.S. Protestant Episcopal Church, stopped over in Rome to meet with the pope. It was the first time a U.S. Episcopal chief prelate had met with a Pope. That Lichtenberger was on his way to New Delhi for the Third General Assembly of the *'World Council of Churches'* added piquancy to this meeting. The pope was sending five official observers to this Assembly. Lichtenberger's meeting, as with Fisher's, would convey the new amity at the Vatican, ahead of the Council. The Lichtenberger meeting too had been orchestrated by Cardinal Bea. In 1959 the pope had met with Archbishop Iakovos, the Primate of the Greek Orthodox Archdiocese of North and South America – the first meeting between a Greek Orthodox archbishop and a pope in 350 years.

When meetings were not possible he sent envoys: one to Istanbul with his open-arms greetings to Ecumenical Patriarch (of Constantinople) Athenagoras I (who had been living in the U.S. during Roncali's time in Istanbul) and the other to Moscow with his felicitations to Patriarch Alexy I, Primate of the Russian Orthodox Church. In both instances the envoys conveyed the pope's sincere wish that they would not hesitate to send observers to the Council. For political expediency, Athenagoras I, was asked, to take the lead in forwarding the official invitations to the Orthodox Churches and coordinate their planned participation.

Behind the scenes he had trusted collaborators, Cardinal Tisserant and Dutch Cardinal Johannes Willebrands in particular, feverishly working the 'back channels', especially in the Soviet Union and China. They set out to 'grease-the-skids' to overcome as many hurdles as possible, whether they be political, diplomatic or religious. Cardinal Willebrands was even dispatched to Moscow, in secret, at the eleventh-hour, with more assurances that the Orthodox delegates would not be in any way confronted or even embarrassed at the Council. That in the end two representatives from the Russian Orthodox Church, Archpriest Vitali Borovoi (who was based in Geneva) and Archimandrite (superior abbot) Vladimir Kotliarov (from Jerusalem), arrived on October 12, 1962, to attend the Council, albeit a day after the opening, was a notable accomplishment for the 'team' and a testament to the widespread trust and respect commanded by the pope. There was, however, no participation from China.

In a nod to the Eastern Rite Catholics with whom he had had so much dealings with when an Archbishop, the pope, on Sunday, November 13, 1960, celebrated Mass in the Byzantine-Slav Rite. He as the head of that Rite had the right to do so.

All of these initiatives notwithstanding, when it comes to ecumenism, this pope, in many circles, is best known for his expunging of, as of his first Holy Week, the derogatory and inappropriate *'perfidious'* (Latin for 'faithless') from the *'prayer for Jews'* in the Good Friday liturgy. The old prayer, at the time, went: *'Let us pray for the faithless Jews: that almighty God may remove the veil from their hearts …'*. On March 21, 1959, six days ahead of Good Friday, the pope issued an edict that the word *'perfidious'*, many times confused incorrectly with *'perfidy'* (treacherous), should no longer be used. That the pope, well aware that Jesus had been a Jew, felt a special kinship with the Jews was well known; his efforts on their behalf during WW II near legendary by this time. As Dr. Isaac Herzog, the Chief Rabbi of Jerusalem had said during the War: *'Cardinal Roncalli is a man who really loves the People of the Book'*.

Along the same lines the pope asked for the baptismal ceremony for new Catholic converts to be revised so that it no longer required a denunciation of the convert's prior faith. There were also certain changes made to some passages in the *'Consecration to the Sacred Heart'* liturgical prayer to eliminate unsavory references to non-Catholics.

On April 12, 1963, on what would be the pope's last Good Friday, a cardinal celebrating the Good Friday liturgy at St. Peter's, using an old text that had been given to him, intoned, without realizing it and per habit, the 'old prayer' with: *'Oremus et pro perfidis Judaeis …'*. The pope, without hesitation, stopped him in mid-track and asked him politely to redo it the new way. It is unlikely that such an interruption, especially for such a cause, had happened too often, if ever, at a papal Holy Week celebration at St. Peter's. But, that, was Pope John XXIII; committed as ever to eradicate, while he had a say, as many of the 'bad habits' that he felt that the Church had acquired over the years especially in the area of tolerance.

88) The opening of Vatican II was scheduled for Thursday, **October 11, 1962**. Though it would be November before its exact nature, i.e., inoperable stomach cancer was conclusively determined, the pope and his inner circle, though a very few outside, knew that he was very and fatally ill. But the pope was resolute as ever to press on. What did the pope do, a week ahead of the opening, that caught many by surprise and yet again established some more new papal milestones?

The eighty-year old pope, no doubt now contemplating what lay ahead, had decided to reenact the pilgrimage he had undertaken sixty-two years earlier, as a young eighteen-year old seminarian, in September 1900. He was going to visit the tomb of St. Francis in Assisi and then proceed to Loreto to worship at the shrine of the Holy Virgin. Furthermore, as he had done in 1900, he was going to make this '250 mile' pilgrimage by train — leaving Rome on the morning of October 4, 1962 and returning late that night. The government of Italy lent the pope the presidential train for this journey. As mentioned in #26 this was the first time a pope, while pope, had travelled by train in 99 years. It had been even longer that a pope had travelled this far from Rome by any form of transport.

The building of a Vatican City State railway station and the linking of the City State to the Italian railway system had been guaranteed by the Lateran Pact of February 11, 1929. Construction to make this a reality started in April of that year. The first locomotive officially entered the Vatican in March 1932. The Vatican railway station was opened on October 2, 1934 and was used mainly for freight. John XXIII, aware that the Vatican station had yet to be used by a *living* pope, chose, symbolically, to begin his pilgrimage from there — thus inaugurating papal use of this ornate, marble-clad station.

When Cardinal Giuseppe Melchiorre Sarto, Patriarch of Venice, left in July 1903 to attend the funeral of **Pope Leo XIII** (#257) and the conclave that followed, his last words to the Venetians who had come to the railway station to see him off were: *'I shall come back, alive or dead'*. Given that he was elected pope at that conclave and chose to be a 'prisoner of the Vatican', he, during his 11.5 year papacy, never did go back. In early 1959, John XXIII, another Patriarch of Venice that had left with the assumption that he was coming back, decided to make his predecessor's pledge come true — especially since **Pius X** (#258) had been canonized five years earlier. He arranged for Pius X's body to be ceremoniously returned to Venice for a month, for public veneration — from April 12 to May 11, 1959. The prior pope's body, in an elaborate crystal casket, was transported in a special seven-coach train that left the Vatican station the night of April 11th. This was the first time a passenger train had graced the Vatican station since its opening; its primary purpose till then having been for freight. The pope, accompanied by twenty cardinals, arrived at the station and paid homage to the body prior to the train's departure. It is possible that **Pope Francis** (#267) or another pope may decide to recreate this *'back to Venice'* gesture but this time with the body of **Pope Saint John XXIII** (#262) — and do so with a train that departs the Vatican station.

All along the route to Assisi and Loreto crowds gathered around the railway line to cheer on their beloved pope — ahead of what they all knew by then was to be a monumental achievement of courage, commitment and tenacity. Fifty thousand awaited his arrival in Loreto where he prayed, at the shrine of Our Lady, for the success of his Council. He was back in the Vatican that night around 11 p.m. On the way back, he had stood up in the train, for long periods of time, belying any fatigue, to wave back at the crowds, as he had also done that morning and afternoon.

Back at the Vatican he did not go back to the Apostolic Palace as had been assumed. Instead he opted to spend the days ahead of the Council, in meditative retreat, in quiet seclusion of the *Torre San Giovanni*. Capovilla was told to cancel all of the meetings and audiences that had been scheduled for that week.

89) On Thursday, **October 11, 1962**, the feast of the *'Maternity of the Blessed Virgin Mary'*, a day that started off dreary with rain but was soon replaced with sunshine, the **Second Vatican Council**, the *twenty-first* of the ecumenical councils, opened in St. Peter's Basilica, with considerable due pomp and ceremony. Of 2,908 invited to participate, 2,540 were present that morning at the Vatican; just under half were from Europe, there were 240 from the U.S., 600 from Latin America and 250 from Africa. 2,381 of them were bishops. There were 86 other dignitaries, clerical and civil, from various countries as well as 33 'delegate-observers' representing 17 different non-Catholic Christian denominations. [The ranks of these 'observers', who were not allowed to speak in the public sessions or vote, but could convey their thoughts to Cardinal Bea's 'Secretariat for Promoting Christian Unity', would eventually swell to be in excess of 90 – with the two Russians, for example, arriving the day after the opening.] It was, by far, the largest gathering of Fathers at any council in the history of the Church; 744 having been the highest attendance at Vatican I, 92 years earlier. What functions did the ailing pope perform on this august day, one that he had worked towards for over three and a half years?

The public proceedings of the day started at 8:30 a.m. with a mesmerizing procession, more celebratory than solemn, of 2,500 Church Fathers, nearly all wearing copes and tall white double peaked miters. The pope, in his *sedia gestatoria*, brought up the rear. This procession vended its way across St. Peter's Square, in a long snaking column, six to eight abreast, into the wide-open doors of St. Peter's Basilica. The procession began at the elliptical section of the Bernini Colonnades (below the Papal Apartments), cut across the square and then made a right-angle turn to head towards the Basilica -- the number of Fathers marching abreast thinning out to the six to eight across as the turn was being made. Crowds, estimated to be 150,000 strong, thronged the lower part of the square. The procession made its way through these crowds before reaching an open area, prior to the steps of the Basilica. This transition permitted the white-clad line of Fathers to be observed, unobscured (especially on TV), emerging from the throng. It took over an hour for the procession to pass through the Square into the Basilica.

As those in the procession walked across the Portico (or Atrium) of the Basilica they would step across a stylized version of the John XXIII coat of arms that had been embedded into the floor of the Portico to mark the start of the Council.

Figure 20: The procession of the bishops at the start of Vatican II.

The staging for this dramatic, iconic procession was done, starting at 8 a.m., in the Apostolic Palace, albeit with the cardinals, in the main, congregated in the Hall of Benedictions (the long room above the Basilica's Portico). The pope vested in a heavy white mantle and wearing a jeweled miter set things in motion when he entered the Pauline Chapel, in the Apostolic Palace, where the Blessed Sacrament was on display. He, aided by his entourage, started intoning the hymn *'Ave Maris Stella'* (Hail Star of the Sea) and leading the way towards the great *Scala Regia* (Royal Staircase) that led out to the Square. Bishops, cardinals, abbots and patriarchs emerged from various halls falling in line behind the pope. The pope led them down the stairs and past the famous bronze doors heading towards the elliptical section of the Colonnades. The pope, as the Bishop of Rome, insisted upon, and delighted in, walking along with his brother bishops at this stage. But, once they reached the edge of the Colonnades, from where they were going to start walking across the Square, the pope, per the plan, got into his *sedia gestatoria*. He was carried aloft with a canopy above him. He waved to the crowds as much as possible, sometimes using both hands. His tiara and ceremonial miter were also included in the procession carried by members of the pope's staff.

The pope alighted at the entrance of the Basilica and walked, slowly but purposefully, through the entire length of the knave, the Church Fathers now seated in steeply banked tiers of seats on either side. The pope proceeded up to the altar, before the tomb of St. Peter, where he began intoning the second hymn, *Veni Creator Spiritus* (Come Creator Spirit) – this chant for Holy guidance taken by the Fathers packed into the Basilica. Following the hymn the pope sat at a papal throne placed close to the altar. He, realizing that he had to preserve his energies, had decided that he would not personally celebrate the solemn Pontifical Mass that was to initiate the Council. He delegated this task to his trusted collaborator, a friend from his time as nuncio, the Dean of the College of Cardinals, the 78-year old, Eugène Tisserant.

At the conclusion of the Mass the pope removed his mantle and miter and donned his choir dress vestments. A reading from the Gospels, using the same podium that had been used in Vatican I, took place. Then an oversized book of the Gospels was placed in the center of the altar to be a symbolic focal point for the duration of the Council. The cardinals and Eastern Rite patriarchs then approached the pope to pay homage. Having all of the other Church Fathers following suit, given the numbers involved, was not feasible. Instead a delegation consisting of two archbishops, two bishops and two abbots paid homage as representatives of the gathered assembly. More liturgical ceremonies, including the chanting in Greek of the Gospel, followed.

Finally it was time for the pope's allocution that would in essence be the first act of this Council. He, wearing gold-rimmed glasses and articulating his words strongly, read out his declaration **Gaudet Mater Ecclesia** (Mother Church Rejoices). It was a message of hope and promise for the future, disagreeing *'with those prophets of doom, who are always forecasting disaster as though the end of the world were at hand'*. He stressed that the main task of this Council was to defend and spread the doctrine. He wanted the Council to promote unity in the Christian family and among all humans. He had the rapt attention of the Fathers present in the Basilica as well as the world; his words broadcast live on television.

Following his allocution the pope left the Basilica, in his *sedia gestatoria*, accompanied only by his personal entourage. The Church Fathers stayed in their seats until the pope had departed. That concluded the formal portion of the Vatican II opening ceremony.

That night, under lights, a crowd of over 50,000, some carrying torches, were still congregated in and around St. Peter's Square enthusiastically celebrating that historic day and expressing their great affection for the 'Good Pope'. The pope did not disappoint them. He made an appearance from the central balcony of St. Peter's and addressed them paternally, sans formality, ending his remarks with the touching request that they now go back to their homes, give their little children a hug and tell them that it was from the pope. This speech has come to be known as the *'Speech to the Moon'*.

90) Following the opening day on Thursday, October 11, 1962, when did the pope next meet with a group of the invited delegates attending the Council?

In the fairly early stages of the conciliar preparations, and certainly well before the full extent of his stomach cancer was known, the pope had made a conscious decision, which he had conveyed to the organizers, that he did not intend to participate on a regular basis, if that, in the deliberative sessions of the Council. He wanted this to be a council of the bishops, run and managed by the bishops, without them feeling coerced in any way by what they perceived as papal pressure, if not interference. He, however, intended to follow as much of the proceedings as he could from the Papal Apartments via a specially installed closed-circuit TV. Suffice to say that this was the first time that a pope had followed the working of a council, in real time, from afar – let alone on television.

There were no official Council events scheduled for Friday, October 12, 1962. That was a day set aside to transition from the opening day ceremonies to the actual working sessions. The first working session was to be on Saturday, October 13th.

The pope did not attend the first working session. Instead he met, in the large Consistory Hall in the Apostolic Palace, with the thirty-five or so non-Catholic delegate-observers attending the Council – two representing the Russian Orthodox Church having arrived the day before. Chairs for the attendees had been arranged in a square configuration as was the norm when the pope held a consistory ('sitting together') with his cardinals. A papal throne was present for the pope, at the 'head' of the square. The pope opted, extemporaneously, to sit on one of the chairs rather than on the throne. These delegates are said to have left that meeting with one shared opinion – *viz.* that the pope was a good man.

The first session, known formally as the *'First General Congregation'*, however, did not go according to expectations.

The Preparatory Committees that developed the framework for the Council intended that most of the work of this Council would be done under the direction of ten permanent *'Conciliar Commissions'* – each consisting of sixteen elected and eight appointed members. So, a total of 160 members had to be voted in by the Church Fathers to man these ten permanent commissions. The curialist-heavy Preparatory Committees had assumed that the Church Fathers would, without demur, rubber-stamp a list of 160 names compiled by them. So, they had put together such a list of names, they themselves, and as such the curia, unabashedly to the fore.

The first agenda item of that first working session was to be the approval of this list so that the ten permanent commissions could be established. Much to the surprise and the chagrin of the curialists present, the Church Fathers balked at this. They, rightly, pointed out that they could not vote for members that they had not chosen or had a chance to research – particularly so given that these 160 members would be in charge of the overall administration and structure of the Council. Per a motion by French Cardinal, Achille Liénart (Bishop of Lille), seconded by a German Cardinal, Josef Richard Frings (Archbishop of Cologne), the first session was adjourned, forthwith, without a vote, so that the Church Fathers could come up with their own recommendations as to who should be on these commissions. The first working session of Vatican II had lasted less than twenty minutes.

The media called it the *'Revolt of the Bishops!'* The bishops, somewhat to their surprise, realized that they, per what the pope had always maintained, indeed did have control of this Council. It was a defining, and exhilarating, moment for the bishops, that then set the tone for at least the remainder of that period of the Council, the so called *'First Period of 1962'.*

The pope is said to have witnessed the 'revolt' in its entirety on TV. He, obviously, did not intervene or even make a public comment. Given his proven acumen and his keen appreciation of Church politics it is even possible that he knew that this push-back from the bishops was likely. One could even postulate that maybe he set this up so as to see if the Church Fathers realized, upfront, that they had the power, with his blessings, to have their say when it came to this Council.

91) Despite his intentions not to interfere with the proceedings of the Council, the pope felt obligated in just one instance to override a vote that had been taken by the Council members. What was the topic in question and how did this happen?

The pope's singular intervention happened on November 21, 1962, during the first period of the Council – 39 days into the deliberative sessions. It happened when the schema for the *'On the Sources of Revelation'* was being debated. The schema had been prepared by a commission made up of many curial old-guards. This commission had been presided over, furthermore, by none other than the staunch traditionalist, Cardinal Alfredo Ottaviani, Secretary of the Holy Office (today's Congregation of the Doctrine of the Faith). He was one who strongly opposed, on principle, any and all of the changes being sought by the Council, though he often claimed that he had suggested the Council to the future pope during the 1958 conclave.

The pope had been following the proceedings on closed-circuit TV from the Papal Apartments. He watched what was transpiring with this schema – the second schema to be debated at the Council.

He saw that many of the prelates attending were unhappy with the schema as presented. It had stubbornly adhered to the traditional Catholic beliefs without making any attempts to be even moderately inclusive when it came to other contemporary viewpoints – in particular the Protestant belief that the Bible was the only source of revelation (whereas Catholics also subscribed to 'Apostolic Tradition' as another source). This was counter to the spirit of ecumenism that the pope had desired for this council; a desire embraced, at the time, by quite a few of those participating.

A vote requested on November 20, 1962 to *reject* this rigid Ottaviani schema clearly indicated that the majority of those present were not happy with it. The vote was 1,368 to 822 in favor of rejecting the schema. But, akin to papal elections, a simple majority, in this case 62%, did not suffice. A two-thirds super-majority was required to reject a schema.

The pope, disquieted, mulled over what had transpired. He slept on what he should do. The next morning he was sure as to what needed to be done. He sent a message down to St. Peter's that he, as pope, irrespective of the outcome of the vote, was withdrawing Ottaviani's schema and was requesting that a new commission be formed, at the Council, to draft a new schema. This decisive intervention by the pope, that sent an unmistakable message to the traditionalists like Ottaviani that wished to obstruct change, imbued the council with a renewed sense of possibility and purpose. As would be the case with his *Pacem in Terris encyclical* the pope was making a statement which was meant to be a part of his enduring legacy and as such would influence the course of the Council even when he was no longer around.

92) What and when was the pope's last formal interaction with the *Conciliar* attendees?

The pope's health had continued to deteriorate since October. On the same day that the 'Ottaviani schema' vote described above was been taken, i.e., on November 20, 1962, the Vatican announced that the pope had chosen Professor Antonio Gasbarrini [b. 1882], from Bologna, as his personal physician;

Dr. Filippo Rocchi the prior appointee having died nine days earlier. Gasbarrini, noted for his familiarity with the latest in modern medical practices, had treated **Pius XII** (#257) towards the end of his long illness. Furthermore, the pope had known him, on a friendly basis, for many years and liked his values and style. They were similar in age, the pope the tad older of the two.

Gasbarrini had immediately ordered another round of X-rays and tests. Finally they found conclusive evidence that the pope, like his sister Ancilla and brother Giovanni Francesco, was suffering from inoperable, malignant, stomach cancer. It was thought unlikely that he would live much beyond six months. The indications are that the pope already knew, well ahead of hearing the damning prognosis from Gasbarrini.

A talented young anesthesiologist from Rome, Dr. Piero Mazzoni, at the behest of Prof. Gasbarrini, moved into the Apostolic Palace to be close to the pope; Gasbarrini needing to return to Bologna.

While the appointment of a physician from Bologna, rather than Rome, was somewhat incongruous, Gasbarrini's renown and his known fellowship with the pope prevented too much being read into this news *per se*. That a new doctor had been appointed was also not in itself unusual given Dr. Rocchi's death. Rumors, however, had already been circulating since the start of the Council that the pope was ill.

Sunday, November 25, 1962, was the pope's 81st birthday. He celebrated it with an early morning Mass at 7 a.m. at the *Collegio Urbano of Propaganda Fide* (a Roman college associated with the Propagation of the Faith) attended by a large gathering of cardinals, bishops and seminarians; his very first job in Rome, forty-one years earlier, having had to do with *Propaganda Fide*. During this gathering he provided a hint that his mortality was on his mind with this cryptic statement: *'any day is a good day to be born and any day is a good day to die'*. When he got back to the Vatican the Square was crowded with well-wishers wanting to say *'Buon Natale'* (Happy Birthday). Though fatigued from the morning activities, the pope nonetheless addressed the crowds later on that day. The events of the day were to take a toll. Dr. Mazzoni requested that the pope spend Monday in bed getting some rest.

On the night of Tuesday, November 27th, the pope suffered a huge intestinal hemorrhage. Luckily Dr. Mazzoni was at hand to administer suitable treatment, including a blood transfusion and morphine for the pain. A public audience scheduled for Wednesday, obviously, had to be cancelled. The Vatican Press Office, as it is wont to do, released two vague and inconsistent bulletins as to why the audience was cancelled. Vatican-watchers who knew, all too well, how the Press Office struggled and stumbled when a pope was indisposed immediately realized that something of consequence had happened. The rumors amplified. On Thursday, November 29th another bulletin was released. This for the first time mentioned 'gastropathy' and 'anemia'. People started putting two and two together, particularly in light of the pope's family history of cancer. There was talk that the pope had already been operated upon. Others predicted the worst within the week.

But, three days later, at noon on Sunday, December 2nd, the pope, to the amazement of all watching, appeared, as usual, at his study window to recite the *Angelus*. He told the cheering crowd that his health, which had threatened to desert him, was back.

The growing awareness that the pope was very ill had cast a palpable pall over the Council. The Church Fathers in attendance genuinely loved and respected this pope. They knew that the Council would not have been possible without him and his recent intervention had, moreover, confirmed that the pope really wanted this to be a different type of Council – one where the bishops had a say in how they wanted to see their Church in the future. The ardor in which the deliberations were being done had noticeably declined. The bishops, confronting the loss of their pope, had lost their pep.

Then there was the ever thorny issue of a *sede vacante* while a Council was in session. Canon 229 of the then applicable 1917 Code of Canon Law (as does the equivalent Canon 340 in the 1983 Code) did address that with no ambiguity, viz. *'If the Apostolic See becomes vacant during the celebration of a council, the council is interrupted by the law itself until the new Supreme Pontiff orders it to be continued or dissolves it'*. But, most likely the pope nor his inner circle of advisors wanted the Council suspended in that manner. Plus, Christmas was approaching.

Wednesdays was the day for the pope's regular public audience in St. Peter's. Whereas the audience on November 28th had been cancelled altogether, an announcement was made that at noon on Wednesday, December 5th, the pope would offer a public blessing to those in St. Peter's Square from his study window (as he had done three days earlier). The council was adjourned early so that the Church Fathers could attend this blessing. The pope yet again as he had done just a few days earlier recited the Angelus. When he finished there was great jubilation. The pope waited for the commotion below to die down. Then he started talking: *'My children, Providence is with us. You see, every day there is progress, not down, but towards improvement. ... We help each other so that everyone can move on. ...'*. Then with no preamble or warning he said that the Council will be suspended for several months. He did not elaborate. He just reminded all that they will always remember in their hearts the image of unity afforded by the Council. He didn't have much more to say. It was a short speech.

The 36th General Congregation of the Council (i.e., the 36th working session) scheduled for the next day, Friday, December 7th, was deemed to be the last day of deliberation prior to the suspension. Archbishop Pericle Felici, the Secretary General of the Council, started the proceedings for that day by announcing that the pope had appointed Cardinal Gaetano Cicognani (who was created at the same time as the pope) to head up a new coordinating committee tasked with making preparations for the second session which was scheduled to begin on September 8, 1963. Then with no warning the pope entered St. Peter's, where the Church Fathers were meeting, via a side door. They could immediately tell that the pope was ill, very ill. But, they could not help cheering – though this was St. Peter's. The pope sat in the papal throne.

The pope spoke briefly, just 624 words of Latin. He expressed his appreciation for the work that had been done and thanked them. He, however, diplomatic as ever, did not mention that the Council had yet to approve a single schema. When the pope left most assumed that that would be the last time they would see him. They were wrong.

The closing Mass for the first period was held on Saturday, December 8th, the Feast of the Immaculate Conception. This also happened to be the anniversary of the opening day of Vatican I ninety-three years earlier.

The Mass was celebrated by Cardinal Paolo Marella, the Archpriest of St. Peter's. The Mass finished soon after 10 a.m. The pope, yet again, came into St. Peter's – this time walking the length of the nave, in between the seated ranks of Church Fathers, just as he had done during the opening ceremony in October. Again he sat on his throne, put on his gold rimmed glasses and read an address. This one was longer than that of the previous – nearly three times longer. He as was to be expected focused on the future, noting that the first session had been but a 'slow and solemn introduction'. He noted that a good beginning had been made. He pointed out that in marked contrast to previous Councils, 'modern communications' would make it possible for the Church Fathers to continue some of the work of the Council during the recess. He expected the eventual outcome of the Council to herald a new Pentecost.

He concluded his address with a Holy Kiss.

That was the last time that the Church Fathers attending the Second Vatican Council got to see the pope.

VIII.
THE SAINT

Following the suspension of Vatican II, the pope, though gravely ill and often in severe pain, continued to soldier on into 1963, with nary a respite, exhibiting a remarkably rugged constitution often attributed to his sharecropper heritage. He celebrated Mass, at St. Peter's, on Christmas 1962 and continued working on the lengthy and profound *Pacem in Terris* encyclical that was published on April 11, 1963. *[q.v. #86.]*

He, most likely exploiting skills acquired during his decades in 'foreign service', had, more or less from the start of his papacy, a surprisingly accurate and unfiltered 'ear' as to what was being said in the ever-chattering Vatican grapevine. He was distressed and frustrated to learn that many in the upper echelons of the Church believed that most of his initiatives, including the Council, would fizzle away with his passing. So, once *Pacem* had been dealt with, he started writing an Apostolic Exhortation, *Novem Per Dies,* which, referring to the Council in terms of a new Epiphany as well as a new Pentecost, asked the faithful to pray for the success of the Council. It was published on May 20, 1963; fittingly the pope's last major written communiqué to the world.

During the course of 1963 the pope was not reticent about making pointed remarks pertaining to his curtailed lifespan. He told the parish priest of Sotto il Monte, when informed that there were folks back home that wanted to come and see him, *'Well tell them to come quickly. Are they waiting till I am dead?'* When concluding a meeting with Cardinal Wyszynski of Poland, on the day the Exhortation was published, and been told *'Until September'* (when the Council was scheduled to resume), the pope, smilingly, replied that in September the cardinal would either find him at the Vatican or another. He then went onto marvel that these days 'they' (meaning the cardinals) could do it all, i.e., have a funeral for one pope and elect a new one, within a month.

In 1962 the International Balzan Prize Foundation, established in 1959 along the lines of the Nobel Prize Foundation, by the Italian family of Eugenio Balzan (1874 – 1953), had awarded the pope its prize for Peace, Humanity and Fraternity among Peoples. The pope was the second recipient of this prize, the Nobel Foundation having been awarded it the year before for their commitment to honor those fostering global peace. The award ceremony for the pope was held in St. Peter's on May 10, 1963, with Giovanni Gronchi a former President of Italy and now the Chairman of the Foundation performing the honors. The pope was awarded $230,000 (U.S.) which he intended to use to create a new foundation to foster peace between nations.

The following day, May 11th, the four other Balzan prizes, for mathematics, biology, history and music, were being awarded at the Quirinal Palace in Rome. The Quirinal, once a papal residence until the fall of the Papal States in 1870, was now the official residence of the President of Italy. No pope had stepped into the Quirinal since Italy became a Republic in 1946. This did not deter John. He, against the objections of Dr. Mazzoni and to the surprise of many, agreed to be present at the award ceremony; the awards being presented that day by the Italian President, Antonio Segni, who welcomed the pope at the entrance to the Palace. This turned out to be the pope's last public *engagement* -- and his last appearance outside of the Vatican.

He had suffered another hemorrhage on April 30, 1963, similar to that on November 27th, but this one requiring more plasma transfusions and treatment. Again, defying the odds, he had recovered, and was trying to maintain a 'normal' routine in May – the Balzan ceremonies, the meeting with Cardinal Wyszynski and other audiences at St. Peter's ensuing. But during the night of May 20th, the day of his meeting with Wyszynski and the publication of the *Novem Per Dies* Exhortation, he again hemorrhaged and was in need of multiple transfusions. He could no longer digest solid food and had to be sustained intravenously. Two days later it was again time for the pope's usual Wednesday public audience at St. Peter's. The pope fainted, briefly, while trying to get ready for that. The audience had to be cancelled. Yet the pope insisted on appearing at his window and letting the crowds know, in his gentle paternal way, that he still wanted them to see him – even if it was from further away.

The next day, May 23, was Ascension Thursday. The pope, as scheduled, appeared at his window and blessed a crowd of 15,000 that had gathered. He looked very frail, his voice quivered and the toll on his body as he articulated the words, which in the past had come so naturally, was plain for all to see. The large crowd below, in St. Peter's Square, instinctively realized that this was momentous. There wasn't the usual jubilation that had marked past appearances at the window. The crowd was still. It, in what proved to be the pope's *last* public appearance, was solemn.

Three days later there was yet another hemorrhage – the most serious of them all. Professor Gasbarrini came rushing over from Bologna. Yet again the pope's indomitable constitution prevailed; on May 29th, he, astonishing the doctors, was showing signs of recovery. Gasbarrini went back to Bologna, and Dr. Mazzoni, for the first time in a week, got a chance to leave the Vatican for a few hours. That night, however, luckily after Dr. Mazzoni had returned, things, suddenly, took a turn for the worse. The cancer had erupted inside his stomach. His body was getting poisoned from within. He drifted in and out of a coma. When conscious he was in excruciating pain. On the 30th, per compact that they had struck when he had moved into the Vatican, Dr. Mazzoni informed the pope that the end of nigh. The pope was serene; not so Capovilla who couldn't stop crying. The pope comforted the doctor and the secretary, told them that he was ready and asked them to show courage.

The pope asked for his confessor and told Capovilla to get the 'people' together. He received his last rites. In the afternoon his nephew Battista arrived. Later in the evening his sister Assunta and his brothers Francesco Zaverio, Alfredo and Giuseppe Luigi arrived – but the pope had been in a coma much of that day. Cardinal Montini (the future **Paul VI** (#263)) who was present with a contingent of other cardinals did his best to help the Roncallis feel at ease in the dark, crowded and somber, papal bedchamber. During the night the pope regained consciousness and was able to embrace his family members.

On Sunday, June 2nd he was running a very high fever, his pulse racing at 140; his body trying to fight the infections it was beset with. On Monday, **June 3rd**, he slipped into a fatal coma – his breathing labored. That evening, at sunset, Cardinal Luigi Traglia, Vicar General of Rome, celebrated an outdoor Mass at St. Peter's Square to a crowd of 80,000. At 7:49 p.m. Rome time, just as the Mass was drawing to an end, the pope breathed his last.

He had lived for 81 years, 6 months, 1 week and 2 days. He had been pope for 4 years, 7 months and 6 days. He had only been pope for *5.6% of his life.*

The pope had requested a less elaborate papal funeral than that followed in the past. Aware that the final, private, burial ceremony involving three separate coffins, the innermost of cypress, the next of engraved lead and the outermost of burnished pine, was a lengthy process, the pope specified that the assembled dignitaries, including the bulk of the cardinals present, should be allowed to leave once the cypress coffin was sealed. Only those 'officials' required to perform and certify the burial, which included a few cardinals, needed to stay on after that. During the beatification process for John XXIII it came to light that the pope, in his will, had *requested* that he be buried in St. John Lateran, the cathedral church of Rome. But given that a pope's body is deemed to belong to the Church, the College of Cardinals, when meeting in 'General Congregations' to arrange for the funeral, had opted to suppress this request, wanting this pope, beloved by so many, to be buried in St. Peter's – the epicenter of the Church. [John Paul II (#265) had indicated a wish to be buried in Poland. But again it was felt imperative that this pope too be buried in St. Peter's for the good of the Church.]

Two million people paid their respects to the pope during the day and a half that his body was on public display. His funeral took place on Thursday evening, **June 6, 1963**. The Russian Orthodox Church sent three representatives to the funeral. The U.S. delegation to the funeral was led by Vice-President Lyndon B. Johnson, a Protestant. Around thirty cardinals were present at the funeral ceremony, thirty-two having been in Rome on Wednesday.

The interment of the pope's body began around 6:30 p.m. on June 6th. The body was placed in a crypt in the Vatican Grottoes below St. Peter's. His resting place was across the aisle, separated by the central altar, from that of **Pius XI** (#260) – the pope who had made him an Archbishop and sent him to Bulgaria. An old crucifix that the pope had found thirty-seven years earlier in an antique store was buried with him, per his request. The pope's two nearest neighbors in the Grottoes were two of the three women buried there, viz. Queen Christina of Sweden and Queen Charlotte of Cyprus. The Pope, however, is no longer interred in the Grottoes.

Figure 21: The funeral.

93) How and when did the 'cause for canonization' for Pope John XXIII come to pass?

To many clerics and laity alike, irrespective of their stripe of Christianity, that Pope John XXIII was a saint was a foregone conclusion even ahead of his passing. Media reports of his death invariably alluded to his saintliness. But, since the institutionalization of the *'Congregation for the Causes of Saints'*, in January 1588, by **Sixtus V** (#228), it was no longer possible to have a saint proclaimed, sans any Vatican involvement, through *vox populi* [i.e., spontaneous local acclamation]. Plus, it was customary that five years had to pass from the time of the potential saint's death before a cause for canonization could be initiated – typically by the bishop of the diocese where the designee died. In the case of John XXIII, however, there were quite a few influential prelates, all of them involved with Vatican II given their seniority, that felt that these requisites should not apply to the *'Good Pope'*.

When the Council reopened on **September 29, 1963**, there was a significant contingent of Church Fathers in attendance that believed that it was incumbent on the Council to canonize John as a formal act of the Council – thus forever tying the canonization of the pope with the Council. There was, however, no precedent, other than the rather generic *vox populi* of old, for a conciliar canonization. So some of the Fathers, Belgian Cardinal Léon Joseph Suenens among them, started exploring means by which they could make this happen.

One of the major objectives of the 'Second Period' was to work on schemata dealing with the Church, bishops and dioceses – essentially the framework for what got promulgated as *Lumen Gentium* (Dogmatic Constitution on the Church) in 1964 and *Gaudium et Spes* (Pastoral Constitution on the Church in the Modern World) in 1965.

During the last week of October 1963, following a day that was devoted to honoring John XXIII, the council, within the context of the schemata on the Church, started debating *'The Vocation to Sanctity in the Church'*. This provided an opening for Cardinal Suenens to stand up and complain that the current canonization process lacked a sense of urgency -- thereby depriving the faithful of the chance to venerate contemporary figures of holiness. Though he never mentioned the name, there was nobody who was in any doubt that the main 'contemporary' that he had in mind was John XXIII. This was not lost on **Paul VI** (#263) or the *Congregation for the Causes of Saints*.

Paul and the 'Congregation for the Causes', however, knew that there were some important issues that had to be addressed upfront to ensure that John's canonization process retained the *gravitas* that it warranted. Paul, in particular, was anxious to make sure that it would never be perceived merely as a 'political' maneuver by the liberal factions of the Council.

The canonization of popes is not as prevalent as it appears at first sight. In 1963, as was still the case at the start of 2014, there were 78 popes that had been canonized. However, of these, all but three were pre-12th century popes.

Of the three post-12th century: the first was **Celestine V** (#193), the hermit monk who became a kind of 'accidental' pope in 1294 to bring to an end a conclave that had lasted 2.3 years. Though his piety was never in doubt, and he is the godfather of 'modern' sequestered conclaves, it is widely held that his canonization had to do with a vendetta being pursued by Philip IV of France against **Boniface VIII** (#194). In essence Philip IV coerced **Clement V** (#196) to canonize Celestine V, in 1313, to make Boniface, who succeeded Celestine, look bad. This was especially so since Boniface imprisoned Celestine upon his abdication, even though it was he, as a noted canon lawyer, who had advised Celestine of the appropriateness of abdicating.

The Celestine canonization was germane to the dilemma facing Paul VI. Paul worried that some of the 'liberal' Church Fathers may be trying to force through the John XXIII canonization to embarrass Pius XII (#261). Paul knew that even a perception of this was not good for either pope or to the Church. **Pius X** (#258), another Patriarch of Venice, was the last pope to have been canonized at that stage. Given that he too had been very popular the calls for his canonization also had started as soon as he died. However, his cause for canonization had only been initiated 8.5 years after his death. In the case of John conciliar members were trying to initiate the process even prior to the first year anniversary of the pope's passing. To cap it all, the members of 'Congregation for the Causes', suffice to say, were also rather perturbed that a willful Council may try to hijack what had been their exclusive prerogative for 375 years. Consequently, per contemporaneous accounts, there were quite a few backroom discussions that took place as to how this matter should and could be best handled.

The 'Second Period' of the Council ended on December 4, 1963, with no public conciliar discussions or papal announcements regarding the canonization. The 'Third Period' began on September 14, 1964. *Lumen Gentium* was approved and promulgated by the pope on November 21, 1964 – the last day of this period. Though Cardinal Suenens had been heavily involved in getting *Lumen Gentium* passed he had made no attempts during this 1964 'period' to initiate a public debate on the canonization.

The fourth and last 'Period' of the Council began on September 14, 1965. *Gaudium et Spes* was expected to be voted upon in late November or December. Many felt that this constitution, which dealt with contemporary social issues, would be one that would have been very dear to John XXIII. So, there was a feeling that John's memory would be much invoked when this constitution was being discussed. Moreover, Cardinal Suenens was once again a major sponsor. With the Council drawing to an end there was an undercurrent of feeling that Cardinal Suenens might try to bring up John's canonization, to the floor, when *Gaudium et Spes* was brought to the floor. Paul VI was aware of this possibility.

To forestall any attempts by the Council to force the issue and to ensure that his former mentor Pius XII was not disrespected, Paul VI, on **November 18, 1965**, formally opened the causes for canonization for both John XXIII and Pius XII. It was a deft move by an astute pope who would become noted for his wont at making such preemptive executive decisions.

The canonization process was thus started 899 days, i.e., *2.46 years*, after the pope's death. So it was more than three times faster than that for Pius X. It was not what some had wanted. The pope had not been made a Saint by an act of the Council. Nonetheless there was at least the satisfaction that the process had been initiated while the Council was still in session. Though it was never voiced, it is likely that the Fathers appreciated, deep down, that having the canonization handled in the conventional way would ensure that it would never be perceived, in the eyes of future historians, as but just a 'gimmick' of an overzealous Council. [The canonization process for John Paul II (#265) was initiated 37 days after his death, while that for Mother Teresa was started just prior to the two year anniversary of her demise.]

Gaudium et Spes, approved by an overwhelming vote of 2,307 to 75 was promulgated by Paul VI on December 7, 1965 – one day ahead of the Council's conclusion.

94) Who were the postulators who handled the John XXIII canonization process and what were the key milestones leading up to the canonization?

A postulator is a subject-matter expert, who has to be Catholic, who is appointed by the Vatican to manage and guide a specific cause for canonization through the intricate, multistep judicial process dictated by the Church. The petitioner seeking the canonization is permitted to nominate a postulator provided that person, who does not necessarily have to be a cleric, meets a set of stringent qualifications specified by the *'Congregation for the Causes of Saints'*. The major religious orders, such as the Franciscans, Jesuits and Dominicans, maintain a roster of their members who have been trained to act as postulators and refer to these as 'postulators-general'. Given that these postulators-general are continually in demand, some, over time, amass a wealth of experience making them even more sought after – especially for high-profile causes.

It being a celebrity cause, petitioned by the reigning pope as opposed to a diocesan bishop, it was a given that the Vatican would chose a proven postulator-general. That indeed proved to be the case. Msgr. Angelo Dell'Acqua who helped John XXIII on his first day as pope write his plea for world peace address, recommended Antonio Cairoli, a Franciscan friar of the Province of the Friars Minor of Umbria, He was indeed a very experienced postulator who by the time he died in 1989 was being referred to as the 'prince of postulators'.

Given John's long and varied career, spanning many geographies, Cairoli had a lot of ground to cover. He appointed tribunals to scrutinize Angelo Roncalli's 'record', policies and virtues in Bergamo, Bulgaria, Turkey, France and Venice. On the other hand evaluating his papacy was going to be relatively easy. It had been short, recent and in the main transparent – Vatican II, indubitably, his most controversial act. There was also no difficulty in finding miracles attributed to the pope. Right at the start of his investigations Cairoli was made aware of three promising, potential miracles: one in Naples [Italy], the other in Sicily [Italy] and the third in Chicago [U.S.A.]. For logistical, cost and linguistic reasons he opted to start by pursing the two Italian miracles rather than getting on a plane to visit Chicago.

The miracle from Naples, said to have taken place in 1966, concerned the healing of an Italian nun suffering from near fatal intestinal hemorrhages. The Sicilian miracle, said to have occurred a year later, related to the cure of a female who was suffering from a severe tubercular (TB) related infection which was exacerbating a heart ailment. The Archdiocese of Naples submitted an official report of the former to the Vatican in mid-1966. According to this report the nun who was near death had a vision of the former pope at her bedside telling her that she would recover – which she had.

The term "devil's advocate" comes from a step in the canonization process where a canon lawyer designated 'Promoter of the Faith' (Promotor Fidei) argues against the canonization of the candidate (to ensure that all the pros and cons have been suitably explored). As Cardinal Suenens had correctly complained about, the modern day canonization process was byzantine, laborious, bureaucratic, wordy, and interminable. The tribunals appointed by Br. Cairoli gathered testimony from over 280 witnesses, the transcripts of which were over 20,000 pages long. Cairoli and his team also found 6,000 documents that were deemed pertinent to the case. Getting all of this done took over twenty years! Br. Cairoli was getting ready to write the Positio super Virtutibus (the 'positio'), the declaration of the findings that support the candidate being deemed 'Venerable', when he died in March 1989. He had been working on John XXIII's cause for 23 years.

Cairoli was replaced by another Franciscan postulator-general, Br. Juan Folguera Trepat from the (Spanish) Catalan Province of St. Salvatore of Horta OFM. He made progress on the positio prior to passing away in 1995. Br. Luca M. De Rosa, of the Neapolitan Province of the Sacred Heart, another

Franciscan postulator-general, took his place. He worked on the cause until his death in 2009. The fourth postulator to be assigned to the cause was yet another Franciscan postulator-general, this time Giovangiuseppe Califano, who like the original Cairoli, was from the Friars Minor of the Province of Umbria.

With John XXIII there was no *'Servant of God'* step *per se* since his cause was not presented to the *'Congregation for the Causes of Saints'* by a diocesan bishop following a diocesan-level investigation into the justification for canonization. In a sense it can be interpreted that John's status as a *'Servant of God'* was taken as a given and did not need to be substantiated. So, in the case of John, the first stage, i.e., that of the *'Servant of God'*, of the four-stage process leading to canonization was by-passed.

So, the next stage in the process was that of the *'heroic virtues'* of the candidate, i.e., John XXIII, being so proclaimed by the reigning pope based on the evidence presented in the *positio*. It is then that the candidate starts being referred to as *'Venerable'*. The determination of the *positio* is, of course, done by the 'Congregation for the Causes of Saints' who then recommend to the pope the validity of the *'heroic virtues'* stature. In the case of John XXIII this validation was completed in 1999.

John XXIII was deemed '**Venerable**' on **December 20, 1999**, by **John Paul II** (#265). It had been *36.5 years* since the pope's death [and 34 years since the 'cause' had been initiated].

Pius X (#258) had become 'Venerable' in 1943 after 28.5 years, though it took **Pius IX** (#256) 107.4 years to reach that milestone in 1985. It would take **Pius XII** (#261) 51.2 years to be deemed as such, while John Paul II was so venerated in 4.8 years and Mother Teresa in 5.3 years.

John Paul II, as Karol Wojtyla, had been made a titular bishop in September 1958, at the age of thirty-eight, and had attended all of the sessions of Vatican II – where he was actively involved, among other things, in the drafting of *Gaudium et Spes* (discussed above). In June 1962 he was appointed Vicar capitular (i.e., acting administrator) of Kraków [Poland]. **Pope John XXIII had to have approved this appointment in some form.** Thus it is fair to say that these two popes knew each other, though there is no record of them having met personally.

In the case of John XXIII the next stage of the canonization, i.e., beatification, occurred very fast, i.e., within eight months – given that the submitted *positio* already had all of the requisite justifications.

John XXIII was beatified on September 3, 2000. It had been *37.3 years* since the pope's death [and 34.8 years since the 'cause' had been initiated]. He was as of that day **Blessed John XXIII**.

Pius IX, who had died three years before John was born, was also beatified that same day. His beatification had taken 122.5 years.

Following **Paul VI's** (#263) grouping of the two papal 'causes' in 1965 succeeding popes also appear to be trying to combine papal honorifics – especially now that there are more papal 'causes' in the pipeline. On December 19, 2009 both John Paul II and Pius XII were deemed 'Venerable' and on April 27, 2014 John XXIII will be canonized alongside John Paul II. Hence post-1965 there are now three instances of double 'honorifics'.

Following the beatification, on January 16, 2001, the marble sarcophagus in the Vatican Grottoes containing John XXIII's remains was opened, in the presence of the Holy See Secretary of State. His body was then removed from the three coffins in which it had been placed in during the funeral. This was to enable his mortal remains to be identified – another requisite step in the path to canonization. The body was found to be remarkably well preserved; this being attributed to the air tightness of the triple coffin and the efficacy of the original embalming.

The identification of the pope's body, that day, was but a formality. The body then had to be 'stabilized' and prepared for *permanent* public display. Once this was done the body was to be transferred from the Grottoes to the main level of St. Peter's so that the faithful would have greater access – the pope's popularity even further enhanced by the beatification.

It had been decided that the pope's body would be moved to the space below the Altar of St. Jerome, a prime location on the central aisle, close to the central Papal Altar and the *Baldacchino* and just behind the famous bronze statue of the seated **St. Peter** (#1) – the one with the worn down right toe from centuries of physical veneration of the Saint's feet by pilgrims. A pope from peasant stock, who had a short but momentous papacy, was being given pride of place befitting his continued acclaim.

His body in white papal vestments, in a new bronze and crystal casket, his face covered in a lifelike wax mask, was moved to its new location on Sunday, **June 3, 2001** – the thirty-eighth anniversary of his death. Prior to being placed beneath the altar, the casket was brought out to St. Peter's Square where John Paul II, in front of a crowd of 30,000, celebrated Mass for the feast of Pentecost recalling, in his homily, John's sanctity.

Four years later the space in the Vatican Grottoes that had been occupied by John XXIII's sarcophagus was repurposed so that it could be used as the burial site for John Paul II – this pope, following the example of **Paul VI** (#263), requesting in his will that he be buried in the ground rather than above it. Thus John XXIII and John Paul II who are to be canonized on the same day have shared the same burial site – albeit both having their remains moved to the main floor of the Basilica post-beatification.

95) What were the two miracles said to have been performed by John XXIII, demonstrating intercession after death, to validate his canonization – which is set to occur on Sunday, April 27, 2014?

That was a trick question, the *only* one in this book. John XXIII will be canonized with just *one* approved miracle per the wishes of **Pope Francis** (#267).

On **July 5, 2013**, 114 days into his papacy, Francis met with Cardinal Angelo Amato, S.D.B., prefect of the 'Congregation for the Causes of Saints', to ratify the Congregation's approval on a slate of twelve 'causes', seven for canonization, through martyrdom or miracles, and the other five for 'heroic virtue' (i.e., designation as 'Venerable'). At the top of the slate was the approval of the second miracle attributed to **John Paul II** (#265). The ratification of this paved the way for his canonization – at a date to be determined by the pope.

Appended to the slate was the recommendation from the Congregation, based upon an internal vote of its prelate-level members three days earlier, that John XXIII be canonized, forthwith, without seeking validation of a second miracle. Francis concurred and suggested that both popes would be canonized at the same time – the date for which would be set at a future consistory. That consistory took place on **September 30, 2013**, with Pope Francis decreeing that the names of John XXIII and John Paul II be inscribed in the *'Book of Saints'* on **Sunday, April 27, 2014**, the second Sunday of Easter, Divine Mercy Sunday.

The papal waiver on the second miracle was not due to the unavailability of one. There had never been a paucity of miracles attributed to the 'Good Pope', the incidents of which, moreover, having increased since his beatification to the point that the Vatican supposedly had twenty *'most promising'* possibilities. The 'Congregation for the Causes' had recommended the waiver so as to finally expedite this canonization. As Cardinal Suenens had contended fifty years earlier, the normal process for canonization was way too languid; this made even more conspicuous by the haste in which John Paul II's saintliness was getting fast tracked.

October 2012 had been the fifty year anniversary of the opening of Vatican II. December 2015 would mark fifty years since its conclusion. Given the movement that had been afoot to try and canonize the pope as an act of the

Council the Vatican appreciated the symbolic significance of having John XXIII sainted prior to the last possible fifty year commemoration of that Council. Some had already pointed out that the canonization was the only remaining unfulfilled act that had been sought by the Church Fathers.

Plus, the delay in his canonization was becoming an embarrassment in the face of the already strong universal cult pertaining to the pope – with the Vatican already having to concede, on a regular basis, requests from around the world for permission to celebrate the feast of his beatification. For many faithful around the globe 'Good Pope John XXIII' was already a venerated *de facto* Saint.

Then there was the issue of the 'fast-tracking' of John Paul II's cause. Canonizing John Paul II ahead of John would have appeared, at a minimum, incongruous. The Vatican was essentially facing the same dilemma that **Paul VI** (#263) had faced fifty years earlier vis-à-vis **Pius XII** (#261) and John. And, basically in 2013 they too opted for the same expediency: grouping the two popes together to mitigate unflattering comparisons.

The one verified miracle attributed to the pope was the 'Naples cure', discussed in #94 above. It had been reported to the Vatican by the local Archdiocese in 1966. This had been verified and sanctioned, as required, ahead of the September 2000 beatification.

This miracle relates to a Catholic nun, **Sister Caterina Capitani**, born in Cosenza [southern Italy] c. 1944. She belonged to the religious order *'Company of the Daughters of Charity of Saint Vincent de Paul'* and worked as a nurse at a children's hospital in Naples. In 1962, when she was around 18 years of age, she became extremely ill hemorrhaging large amounts of blood due to severe stomach ulcers. Her condition was so critical that it warranted drastic measures. So, an eminent Neapolitan doctor performed two surgeries to remove three-quarters of her stomach, her pancreas and spleen.

Figure 22: Sister Caterina Capitani.

source: PIME

In May 1966 she suffered a major relapse. She had developed a peptic ulcer in what was left of her stomach. This resulted in an open sore through which contents of her stomach oozed out. She was in severe pain and was back in the hospital. She was running a high fever and had trouble breathing. She was again thought to be dying and, at her request, administered the last rites. She asked to be left alone in her hospital room to pray. Another nun gave her a relic of Pope John XXIII which she placed on her stomach. The relic, obtained from Rome, was a piece of the bed sheet upon which the pope had died.

On May 25, 1966, while asleep she felt the pope appearing at her bedside calling her name and placing his hand on her stomach. She woke up and saw the pope, resplendent and smiling, telling her not to be afraid and that she was fully cured. The pope stayed with her for nearly ten minutes. After the pope departed she got up from bed and was amazed to realize that she was no longer in pain. She called for the nurses and asked for something to eat, the first time that she had been able to ingest solid food in a long time. Her temperature was back to normal and there was no pain. Within forty-eight hours she was regaining her strength. Doctors pronounced her fully cured and she went back to work as a nurse soon afterwards. It was at this juncture that the Neapolitan archdiocese reported the miracle to the Vatican.

Thirty-four years later, at the time of the pope's beatification, Sister Capitani was still alive and well, not in pain, and able to perform her expected duties as a nun. She has not had a recurrence of her stomach ailments since the miracle. In October 2002, thirty-six years after the miracle she, looking sound, radiant and happy, provided a video testimony of the miracle. Multiple copies of this video can be found on YouTube by doing a search on *'Caterina Capitani'*.

Coincidentally or otherwise both the popes being canonized on April 27, 2014 are associated with the miraculous cure of conditions similar to those that had ailed them: John XXIII with stomach hemorrhages in the case of Sister Capitani and **John Paul II** (#265) with Parkinson's disease in the case of both his miracles, that of French Sister Marie Simon-Pierre and an ex-mayor from Colombia, Marco Fidel Rojas.

96) What is the feast day assigned to Pope John XXIII?

The feast day for Pope Saint John XXIII is **October 11th**, the anniversary of the opening of his Council, rather than June 3rd, the anniversary of his death – as would typically have been the case. The October 11th feast day was specified at the time of his beatification and has been observed by a growing number of communities since, well ahead of his canonization.

The pope is also venerated by the Anglican Communion, albeit on **June 4th** – in lieu of the June 3rd anniversary.

IX.
THE SAYINGS

John XXIII, by any measure, was an extraordinary, exemplary human being throughout what was a long, varied and productive life. He left his mark, always positively but with growing avuncularity over time, wherever he went; it in essence the *'welcoming candle in the window'* per his parting remarks in Sofia [Bulgaria]. He knew no strangers. His humanity and humility was legendary; his piety indubitable; his tact and diplomacy unsurpassable. He was scholarly and perspicacious; down-to-earth and canny. His wisdom, profound, has stood the test of time.

All that said, the trait that most set him apart, especially as a pope, was his irrepressible, often incisive wit. Hence, it would not be just remiss, but an inexcusable error to conclude a book such as this without even a few examples of his delightful insights and wit. The five listed here are but the tip of a huge iceberg in terms of the breadth of his sayings. These are but random examples that hopefully illustrate the scope of his repertoire.

It should be noted that the pope did not speak English. On December 6, 1959, U.S. President Dwight D. Eisenhower, originally a Jehovah's Witness who later became a Presbyterian, met with the pope at the Vatican. The pope had a greeting in English composed for the occasion and rehearsed it, painstakingly, a few times beforehand. Nonetheless, the pope managed to mangle it when the time came. He immediately acknowledged it, as such, by exclaiming, with a huge grin: *'Era di belli!'* (that was a beauty!). The President knew exactly what he meant (without a need of translation) and his laughter, head thrown back, and the glee on the faces of the rest of the U.S. delegation – with the pope standing in the middle, grinning along with them, the sheet with the greeting still in his hand – was immortalized for the world the next day by a press photographer. *[See below.]* This was the second meeting between an incumbent U.S. president and a reigning pope. The first of its kind had taken place nearly forty-one years earlier when Woodrow Wilson, another Presbyterian, visited **Benedict XV** (#259), at the Vatican, on January 4, 1919 – ahead of the 1919 Peace Conference in Paris [France]; WW I having ended on November 11, 1918.

On March 11, 1962, he had a private audience with the U.S. First Lady Jacqueline Kennedy. They conversed in French.

Italian, of course, was the pope's mother tongue. Given his long years as a seminarian, despite his slow and painful start as mentioned in #21, he was a Latinist – who decreed, to the dismay of many, that all of the Vatican II public

Figure 23: With U.S. President Dwight D. Eisenhower acknowledging his limitations when it comes to English.

debates had to be in Latin. He was fluent in French even ahead of his nunciature; it the *lingua franca* among European diplomats of that era. He had learned Bulgarian and Turkish and given his scholarship probably knew some Greek. He is said to have had some familiarity with Spanish.

So, all five of the following sayings would have been in Italian. What is shown here are but the English translations. All five probably sounded even better in the original Italian. None of them are believed to be apocryphal though there is a possibility that a bit of 'gloss' may have been added over time or in translation. Try to factor in the look of amusement on the pope's face when reading these papal gems.

97) Shortly after becoming pope, John XXIII received a letter from an eight-year old Italian boy, 'Bruno', who told the pope that he was having difficulty making up his mind about whether he wanted to be a policeman or pope, and asking the pope for advice. The pope responded. What did he say?

"My dear Bruno, in my opinion it is better to be policemen because there are standards you have to meet to do so. On the other hand anyone can become

pope. I am the proof. If you are ever in Rome, please stop by and I will be glad to talk this over with you."

98) *"See everything, overlook a great deal, correct a little"* is a famous John XXIII adage. He definitely put this into practice vis-á-vis the Roman curia during his papacy. Despite his low-key style of management, John XXIII, as pope, always appeared to have a knack of knowing much more than he let on about what was happening in the Vatican. But, on occasion he would, however, have his say. It had come to his attention that his Secretary of State, the loyal, efficacious but gruff, Domenico Tardini, had a habit of referring to the pope, especially when conveying papal directives, as *'the one up there'*, pointing up towards the Papal Apartments and rolling his eyes at the same time – the Secretary of State's office being below and to the side of the Papal Apartments. How did the pope let the Secretary of State know that he was aware of this uncalled for mannerism?

After one of their near daily meetings, he gently chided Tardini, to his bemusement: *"Dear Tardini, we have to get something cleared up. 'The one up there', that you refer to, is the good Lord. I am only the 'one up of the fourth floor'. Tardini, I implore you, please don't add to the confusion among the staff."*

99) As mentioned in #84 the pope was a 'walker'. He relished the opportunity to perambulate in the tranquility of the Vatican Gardens whenever he got a chance, with no set schedule and irrespective of the hour. This was in marked contrast to the ever regimental **Pius XII** (#261) who had a set time for his daily walks. John's *ad hoc* schedule perturbed the Vatican officials in charge of security. During the reign of Pius XII they had closed access to the dome [i.e., cupola] of St. Peter's Basilica ahead of the pope's set time for walking so that there would be no public visitors in the dome or on the roof when the pope was walking. They conveyed their dilemma to the pope and wished to know how they were supposed to control access to the dome if they did not know in advance when the pope intended to go for a walk. What was the pope's response?

"Please, don't worry about it at all. I promise not to do anything that will scandalize the faithful."

100) On his first full day as pope, shortly after he had broadcast his appeal for peace to world leaders the pope met with a delegation from Bergamo that had arrived to congratulate him and receive his blessing. The pope was still wearing the hastily modified white vestments he had worn for his first public appearance from the balcony of St. Peter's. He was still trying to come to terms with the protocols a pope was supposed to follow, including that of always using the royal 'we'. A journalist who was a part of the delegation recorded the pope's remarks as to the challenges he faced. The pope, humble as ever, started by asking for forgiveness because he had yet to master the protocols and rituals expected of him. What did he then go onto add as to the gifts of the Holy Ghost when it comes to a new pope?

Figure 24: Pope John XXIII papal coin from 1962.

"As you may know, the gifts bestowed by the Holy Ghost do not, alas, include the gift of papal style."

101) That the pope was not happy with the ineffective cumbersome bureaucracy of the Roman curia is no great secret. He, however, knew that it would not be possible to convoke a Council and reform the curia at the same time. Furthermore, once he had decided upon having a Council he wanted the Church Fathers to have an opportunity to put forward their recommendations as to how they would like to see the curia function in the 'modern' world. So he opted to set aside curial reform till after the Council; preparations for the Council providing more than enough work to keep the curia busy.

Ahead of the Council a journalist asked the pope: *'Holy Father, how many people work at the Vatican'*. What was the pope's unhesitant response?

"About half."

୪୭୪ ୨୦୨୦

Appendix A:
List Of Popes In
Chronological Order

Notes:

▶ **266, 265, 264 or 263**: This list, the basis for all the statistics quoted in this book (unless otherwise stated), contains **266** popes – up to and including Pope Benedict XVI (#266), who was elected April 2005. The current Vatican list has one less pope – *viz.* the original Stephen II (#92; March 752) who died 4 days after being elected. This Stephen, however, did appear in Vatican lists till 1961. He also appears in the papal list maintained by Wikipedia, the increasingly popular online encyclopedia. He is thus included in this list for completeness. The three separate terms of Benedict IX (#146, #148 & #151) are also listed separately, rather than as a single, grouped entry. Thus the differences in the numbers used in various lists are due to:

   266 = includes the original Stephen II (#92) and Benedict IX's 3 terms.

   265 = without the original Stephen II, but with 3 entries for Benedict IX.

   264 = with the original Stephen II, but with Benedict IX listed just once.

   263 = without the original Stephen II and with Benedict IX listed but once.

▶ The start and end dates for papacies tend to be the most inclusive, i.e., the longest possible. The scope of this book limits the option of listing multiple alternate dates when there are deferring opinions about the dates. The start date in general refers to when the pope was elected (or received Imperial approval) rather than the date when the pope was consecrated.

▶ The lengths of the papacies, though probably the most accurate to-date, are still approximations in the main. They were calculated using fixed 30 day months with no rounding up of the months; i.e., months shown represent completed months. Thus a papacy whose duration was 4 years, 10 months and 23 days will be shown as 4y 10m.

► Start/End ages for the popes are based on the best available dates, to the nearest year, starting as of 1404. Dates prior to that are unavailable or unreliable. That said, there is uncertainly as to the dates for Innocent VII (#205), Gregory XII (#206), Martin V (#207), Eugene IV (#208) & Innocent VIII (#214). Hence the lighter font.

► # - sequence number. ~ = approximately. ? = uncertainty.
c. = circa; about. solid line denotes century splits.
shading denotes, per context:
'# Sequence Number Column' – consecutive use of the same name.
'From Column' – non-Italian.
'Length Column' – exceptionally long or short papacies.

► Abbreviations:
'nc' column – documented name change (nc).
y – years, m – months, d – days, w -- weeks

#	Papal Name	Start of reign	End of reign	Length	From	Age Start/End	'nc'
1	St. Peter	c. 42/57	c. 64/67	~25y	Holy Land		
2	St. Linus	c. 64/67	c. 76/79	~12y	Italy		
3	St. Anacletus	c. 76/79	c. 88/92	~12y	Greece		
4	St. Clement I	c. 88/92	c. 97/101	~9y	Italy?		
5	St. Evaristus	c. 97/101	c. 105/109	~9y	Greece ?		
6	St. Alexander I	c. 105/109	c. 115/116	~11y	Italy?		
7	St. Sixtus I	c. 115/116	c. 125/128	~10y	Italy?		
8	St. Telesphorus	c. 125/128	c. 136/138	~11y	Greece ?		
9	St. Hyginus	c. 136/138	c. 140/142	~4y	Greece		
10	St. Pius I	c. 140/142	c. 154/155	~15y	Italy?		
11	St. Anicetus	c. 154/155	c. 166/167	~11y	Syria		
12	St. Soter	c. 166/167	c. 174/175	~9y	Italy		
13	St. Eleutherius	c. 174/175	c. 189	~15y	Balkans		
14	St. Victor I	189	198/199	~10y	N. Africa		
15	St. Zephyrinus	199	217	~18y	Italy		
16	St. Callistus I	217	222/223	~5y	Greece ?		
17	St. Urban I	222/223	230	~8y 11m	Italy		
18	St. Pontian	21 July 230	28 Sep 235	5y 2m	Italy		
19	St. Anterus	21 Nov 235	3 Jan 236	43 days	Greece ?		
20	St. Fabian	10 Jan 236	20 Jan 250	14y	Italy		
21	St. Cornelius	Mar/Apr 251	June 253	~2y 3m	Italy		
22	St. Lucius I	25 June 253	5 Mar 254	9m	Italy		
23	St. Stephen I	12 May 254	2 Aug 257	3y 3m	Italy		
24	St. Sixtus II	30/31 Aug 257	6 Aug 258	11m	Greece		
25	St. Dionysius	22 July 260	26 Dec 268	8y 5m	Greece ?		

#	Papal Name	Start of reign	End of reign	Length	From	Age Start/End	'nc'
26	St. Felix I	5 Jan 269	30 Dec 274	6y	Italy		
27	St. Eutychian	4 Jan 275	7 Dec 283	8y 11m	Italy		
28	St. Caius	17 Dec 283	22 Apr 296	12y 4m	Croatia		
29	St. Marcellinus	30 June 296	304	~8y	Italy		
30	St. Marcellus I	~306/308	~308/309	11m	Italy		
31	St. Eusebius	18 Apr (310?)	21 Oct (310?)	6m	Greece ?		
32	St. Miltiades	2 July 311	10 Jan 314	2y 6m	Italy		
33	St. Silvester I	31 Jan 314	31 Dec 335	21y 11m	Italy		
34	St. Mark	18 Jan 336	7 Oct 336	8m 20d	Italy		
35	St. Julius I	6 Feb 337	12 Apr 352	15y 2m	Italy		
36	Liberius	17 May 352	24 Sep 366	14y 4m	Italy		
37	St. Damasus I	1 Oct 366	11 Dec 384	18y 2m	Portugal		
38	St. Siricius	Dec 384	26 Nov 399	14y 11m	Italy		
39	St. Anastasius I	27 Nov 399	19 Dec 401	2y 22d	Italy		
40	St. Innocent I	22 Dec 401	12 Mar 417	15y 3m	Italy		
41	St. Zosimus	18 Mar 417	26 Dec 418	1y 9m	Greece ?		
42	St. Boniface I	29 Dec 418	4 Sep 422	3y 8m	Italy		
43	St. Celestine I	10 Sep 422	27 Jul 432	9y 10m	Italy		
44	St. Sixtus III	31 July 432	19 Aug 440	8y 19d	Italy		
45	St. Leo I *the Great*	29 Sep 440	10 Nov 461	21y 42d	Italy		
46	St. Hilarius	19 Nov 461	29 Feb 468	6y 3m	Italy		
47	St. Simplicius	3 Mar 468	10 Mar 483	15y 7d	Italy		
48	St. Felix III	13 Mar 483	1 Mar 492	9y	Italy		
49	St. Gelasius I	1 Mar 492	21 Nov 496	4y 8m	Italy		
50	Anastasius II	24 Nov 496	19 Nov 498	2y	Italy		
51	St. Symmachus	22 Nov 498	19 July 514	15y 8m	Italy		

#	Papal Name	Start of reign	End of reign	Length	From	Age Start/End	'nc'
52	St. Hormisdas	20 July 514	6 Aug 523	9y 17d	Italy		
53	St. John I	13 Aug 523	18 May 526	2y 9m	Italy		
54	St. Felix IV	12 Jul 526	22 Sep 530	4y 2m	Italy		
55	Boniface II	22 Sep 530	17 Oct 532	2y 25d	Italy		
56	John II	2 Jan 533	8 May 535	2y 4m	Italy		✓
57	St. Agapetus I	13 May 535	22 Apr 536	11m	Italy		
58	St. Silverius	8 June 536	11 Nov 537	1y 5m	Italy		
59	Vigilius	29 Mar 537	7 Jun 555	18y 2m	Italy		
60	Pelagius I	16 Apr 556	4 Mar 561	4y 10m	Italy		
61	John III	17 July 561	13 July 574	13y	Italy		✓
62	Benedict I	2 June 575	30 July 579	4y 1m	Italy		
63	Pelagius II	Aug 579	7 Feb 590	10y 6m	Italy		
64	St. Gregory I *the Great*	3 Sep 590	12 Mar 604	13y 6m	Italy		
65	Sabinian	13 Sep 604	22 Feb 606	1y 5m	Italy		
66	Boniface III	19 Feb 607	12 Nov 607	8m 3w	Italy		
67	St. Boniface IV	15 Sep 608	8 May 615	6y 8m	Italy		
68	St. Deusdedit	19 Oct 615	8 Nov 618	3y 19d	Italy		
69	Boniface V	23 Dec 619	25 Oct 625	5y 10m	Italy		
70	Honorius I	27 Oct 625	12 Oct 638	13y	Italy		
71	Severinus	28 May 640	2 Aug 640	2m 5d	Italy		
72	John IV	24 Dec 640	12 Oct 642	1 y 9m	Croatia		
73	Theodore I	24 Nov 642	14 May 649	6y 5m	Palestine		
74	St. Martin I	5 July 649	10 Aug 654	5y 36d	Italy		
75	St. Eugene I	10 Aug 654	2 Jun 657	2y 10m	Italy		
76	St. Vitalian	30 July 657	27 Jan 672	14y 6m	Italy		
77	Adeodatus (II)	11 Apr 672	17 Jun 676	4y 2m	Italy		
78	Donus	2 Nov 676	11 Apr 678	1y 5m	Italy		
79	St. Agatho	27 June 678	10 Jan 681	2y 6m	Italy		
80	St. Leo II	17 Aug 682	3 July 683	10m 20d	Italy		

#	Papal Name	Start of reign	End of reign	Length	From	Age Start/End	'nc'
81	St. Benedict II	26 June 684	8 May 685	10m 16d	Italy		
82	John V	23 July 685	2 Aug 686	1y 10d	Syria		
83	Conon	21 Oct 686	21 Sep 687	11m	Balkans		
84	St. Sergius I	15 Dec 687	9 Sep 701	13y 9m	Italy		
85	John VI	30 Oct 701	11 Jan 705	3y 2m	Greece		
86	John VII	1 Mar 705	18 Oct 707	2y 7m	Greece		
87	Sisinnius	15 Jan 708	4 Feb 708	20 days	Syria		
88	Constantine	25 Mar 708	9 Apr 715	7y	Syria		
89	St. Gregory II	19 May 715	11 Feb 731	15y 9m	Italy		
90	St. Gregory III	18 Mar 731	28 Nov 741	10y 8m	Syria		
91	St. Zacharias	3 Dec 741	15 Mar 752	10y 3m	Italy		
92	Stephen (II)	23 Mar 752	26 Mar 752	4 days	Italy?		
93	Stephen II (III)	26 Mar 752	26 Apr 757	5y 1m	Italy		
94	St. Paul I	29 May 757	28 June 767	10y 1m	Italy		
95	Stephen III (IV)	7 Aug 768	24 Jan 772	3y 5m	Italy		
96	Hadrian I	1 Feb 772	25 Dec 795	23y 10m	Italy		
97	St. Leo III	26 Dec 795	12 June 816	20y 5m	Italy		
98	Stephen IV (V)	22 June 816	24 Jan 817	7m 2d	Italy		
99	St. Paschal I	24 Jan 817	11 Feb 824	7y	Italy		
100	Eugene II	June 824	Aug 827	~3y 1m	Italy		
101	Valentine	Aug 827	Sep 827	~1m	Italy		
102	Gregory IV	late 827	25 Jan 844	~16y	Italy		
103	Sergius II	Jan 844	27 Jan 847	3y	Italy		
104	St. Leo IV	10 Apr 847	17 Jul 855	8y 3m	Italy		
105	Benedict III	29 Sep 855	17 Apr 858	2y 6m	Italy		
106	St. Nicholas I *the Great*	24 Apr 858	13 Nov 867	9y 6m	Italy		
107	Hadrian II	14 Dec 867	Nov/Dec 872	5y	Italy		
108	John VIII	14 Dec 872	16 Dec 882	10y 2d	Italy		
109	Marinus I	16 Dec 882	15 May 884	1y 5m	Italy		

#	Papal Name	Start of reign	End of reign	Length	From	Age Start/End	'nc'
110	St. Hadrian III	17 May 884	mid-Sep 885	1y 4m	Italy		
111	Stephen V (VI)	late-Sep 885	14 Sep 891	6y	Italy		
112	Formosus	6 Oct 891	4 Apr 896	4y 6m	Italy		
113	Boniface VI	Apr 896	Apr 896	15 days	Italy		
114	Stephen VI (VII)	May 896	Aug 897	1y 2m	Italy		
115	Romanus	Aug 897	Nov 897	~3m	Italy		
116	Theodore II	Nov 897	Nov(/Dec) 897	20 days	Italy		
117	John IX	Jan 898	Jan 900	~2y	Italy		
118	Benedict IV	May/June 900	Aug 903	~3y 3m	Italy		
119	Leo V	Aug 903	Sep 903	~2m	Italy?		
120	Sergius III	29 Jan 904	14 Apr 911	7y 2m	Italy		
121	Anastasius III	June 911	Aug 913	~2y 1m	Italy		
122	Lando	Aug 913	Mar 914	6m 11d	Italy		
123	John X	Mar/Apr 914	May 928	~14y	Italy		
124	Leo VI	May 928	Dec 928	~6m	Italy		
125	Stephen VII (VIII)	Dec 928	Feb 931	~2y 2m	Italy		
126	John XI	Feb/Mar 931	Dec 935/Jan 936	~4y 9m	Italy		
127	Leo VII	3 Jan 936	13 July 939	3y 6m	Italy		
128	Stephen VIII (IX)	14 July 939	late-Oct 942	~3y 3m	Italy		
129	Marinus II	30 Oct 942	early-May 946	~3y 6m	Italy		
130	Agapetus II	10 My 946	Dec 955	~9y 7m	Italy		
131	John XII	16 Dec 955	14 May 964	8y 5m	Italy		✓
132	Leo VIII	4 Dec 963	1 Mar 965	1y 2m	Italy		
133	Benedict V	22 May 964	23 June 964	32 days	Italy		
134	John XIII	1 Oct 965	6 Sep 972	6y 11m	Italy		
135	Benedict VI	19 Jan 973	July 974	~1y 5m	Italy		
136	Benedict VII	Oct 974	10 July 983	~8y 9m	Italy		
137	John XIV	Dec 983	20 Aug 984	~8m	Italy		✓

#	Papal Name	Start of reign	End of reign	Length	From	Age Start/End	'nc'
138	John XV	mid-Aug 985	Mar 996	~10y 7m	Italy		
139	Gregory V	3 May 996	18 Feb 999	2y 9m	Germany		✓
140	Silvester II	2 Apr 999	12 May 1003	4y 1m	France		✓
141	John XVII	16 May 1003	6 Nov 1003	5m 25d	Italy		
142	John XVIII (XIX)	25 Dec 1003	June/July 1009	~5y 6m	Italy		
143	Sergius IV	31 July 1009	12 May 1012	2y 9m	Italy		✓
144	Benedict VIII	17 May 1012	9 Apr 1024	11y 11m	Italy		✓
145	John XIX	19 Apr 1024	20 Oct 1032	8y 6m	Italy		✓
146	Benedict IX – 1st term	21 Oct 1032	15 Sep 1044	~11y 11m	Italy		✓
147	Silvester III	20 Jan 1045	10 Mar 1045	49 days	Italy		✓
148	Benedict IX – 2nd term	10 Mar 1045	1 May 1045	52 days	Italy		✓
149	Gregory VI	1 May 1045	20 Dec 1046	1 y 7m	Italy		✓
150	Clement II	24 Dec 1046	9 Oct 1047	9m 19d	Germany		✓
151	Benedict IX – 3rd term	8 Nov 1047	16 July 1048	8m 11d	Italy		✓
152	Damasus II	17 July 1048	9 Aug 1048	23 days	Germany		✓
153	St. Leo IX	12 Feb 1049	19 Apr 1054	5y 2m	Germany		✓
154	Victor II	13 Apr 1055	28 July 1057	2y 3m	Germany		✓
155	Stephen IX (X)	2 Aug 1057	29 Mar 1058	7m 29d	France		✓
156	Nicholas II	6 Dec 1058	27 July 1061	2y 7m	France		✓
157	Alexander II	30 Sep 1061	21 Apr 1073	11y 6m	Italy		✓
158	St. Gregory VII	22 Apr 1073	25 May 1085	12y 1m	Italy		✓
159	Bl. Victor III	9 May 1087	16 Sep 1087	4m 10d	Italy		✓
160	Bl. Urban II	12 Mar 1088	29 July 1099	11y 4m	France		✓
161	Paschal II	13 Aug 1099	21 Jan 1118	18y 5m	Italy		✓
162	Gelasius II	24 Jan 1118	29 Jan 1119	1y 5d	Italy		✓
163	Callistus II	2 Feb 1119	14 Dec 1124	5y 10m	France		✓
164	Honorius II	21 Dec 1124	13 Feb 1130	5y 1m	Italy		✓
165	Innocent II	14 Feb 1130	24 Sep 1143	13y 7m	Italy		✓

#	Papal Name	Start of reign	End of reign	Length	From	Age Start/End	'nc'
166	Celestine II	26 Sep 1143	8 Mar 1144	5m 13d	Italy		✓
167	Lucius II	12 March 1144	15 Feb 1145	11m	Italy		✓
168	Bl. Eugene III	15 Feb 1145	8 July 1153	8y 4m	Italy		✓
169	Anastasius IV	8 July 1153	3 Dec 1154	1y 4m	Italy		✓
170	Hadrian IV	4 Dec 1154	1 Sep 1159	4y 9m	England		✓
171	Alexander III	7 Sep 1159	30 Aug 1181	21y 11m	Italy		✓
172	Lucius III	1 Sep 1181	25 Nov 1185	4y 2m	Italy		✓
173	Urban III	25 Nov 1185	20 Oct 1187	1y 10m	Italy		✓
174	Gregory VIII	21 Oct 1187	17 Dec 1187	57 days	Italy		✓
175	Clement III	19 Dec 1187	late-Mar 1191	3y 3m	Italy		✓
176	Celestine III	14 Apr 1191	8 Jan 1198	6y 9m	Italy		✓
177	Innocent III	8 Jan 1198	16 July 1216	18y 6m	Italy		✓
178	Honorius III	18 July 1216	18 Mar 1227	10y 8m	Italy		✓
179	Gregory IX	19 Mar 1227	22 Aug 1241	14y 5m	Italy		✓
180	Celestine IV	25 Oct 1241	10 Nov 1241	16 days	Italy		✓
181	Innocent IV	25 June 1243	7 Dec 1254	11y 5m	Italy		✓
182	Alexander IV	12 Dec 1254	25 May 1261	6y 5m	Italy		✓
183	Urban IV	29 Aug 1261	2 Oct 1264	3y 1m	France		✓
184	Clement IV	5 Feb 1265	29 Nov 1268	3y 9m	France		✓
185	Bl. Gregory X	1 Sep 1271	10 Jan 1276	4y 4m	Italy		✓
186	Bl. Innocent V	21 Jan 1276	22 June 1276	5m	France		✓
187	Hadrian V	11 July 1276	18 Aug 1276	38 days	Italy		✓
188	John XXI	8 Sep 1276	20 May 1277	8m 12d	Portugal		✓
189	Nicholas III	25 Nov 1277	22 Aug 1280	2y 9m	Italy		✓
190	Martin IV	22 Feb 1281	28 Mar 1285	4y 1m	France		✓
191	Honorius IV	2 Apr 1285	3 Apr 1287	2y	Italy		✓
192	Nicholas IV	22 Feb 1288	4 Apr 1292	4y 1m	Italy		✓
193	St. Celestine V	5 July 1294	13 Dec 1294	5m 8d	Italy		✓
194	Boniface VIII	24 Dec 1294	11 Oct 1303	8y 9m	Italy		✓
195	Bl. Benedict XI	22 Oct 1303	7 July 1304	8m	Italy		✓

#	Papal Name	Start of reign	End of reign	Length	From	Age Start/End	'nc'
196	Clement V	5 June 1305	20 Apr 1314	8y 10m	France		✓
197	John XXII	7 Aug 1316	4 Dec 1334	18y 4m	France		✓
198	Benedict XII	20 Dec 1334	25 Apr 1342	7y 4m	France		✓
199	Clement VI	7 May 1342	6 Dec 1352	10y 7m	France		✓
200	Innocent VI	18 Dec 1352	12 Sep 1362	9y 9m	France		✓
201	Bl. Urban V	28 Sep 1362	19 Dec 1370	8y 2m	France		✓
202	Gregory XI	30 Dec 1370	27 Mar 1378	7y 2m	France		✓
203	Urban VI	8 Apr 1378	15 Oct 1389	11y 6m	Italy		✓
204	Boniface IX	2 Nov 1389	1 Oct 1404	14y 11m	Italy		✓
205	Innocent VII	17 Oct 1404	6 Nov 1406	2y 19d	Italy	67/69	✓
206	Gregory XII	30 Nov 1406	4 July 1415	8y 7m	Italy	60/69	✓
207	Martin V	11 Nov 1417	20 Feb 1431	13y 3m	Italy	48/62	✓
208	Eugene IV	3 Mar 1431	23 Feb 1447	15y 11m	Italy	47/63	✓
209	Nicholas V	6 Mar 1447	24 Mar 1455	8y 18d	Italy	49/57	✓
210	Callistus III	8 Apr 1455	6 Aug 1458	3y 4m	Spain	76/79	✓
211	Pius II	19 Aug 1458	15 Aug 1464	6y	Italy	52/58	✓
212	Paul II	30 Aug 1464	26 July 1471	6y 11m	Italy	47/54	✓
213	Sixtus IV	9 Aug 1471	12 Aug 1484	13y	Italy	57/70	✓
214	Innocent VIII	29 Aug 1484	25 July 1492	7y 11m	Italy	51/59	✓
215	Alexander VI	11 Aug 1492	18 Aug 1503	11y	Spain	61/72	✓
216	Pius III	22 Sep 1503	18 Oct 1503	26 days	Italy	64/64	✓
217	Julius II	1 Nov 1503	21 Feb 1513	9y 3m	Italy	59/69	
218	Leo X	11 Mar 1513	1 Dec 1521	8y 8m	Italy	37/45	✓
219	Hadrian VI	9 Jan 1522	14 Sep 1523	1y 8m	Netherlands	62/64	
220	Clement VII	19 Nov 1523	25 Sep 1534	10y 10m	Italy	45/56	✓
221	Paul III	13 Oct 1534	10 Nov 1549	15y 1m	Italy	66/81	✓
222	Julius III	8 Feb 1550	23 Mar 1555	5y 1m	Italy	62/67	✓
223	Marcellus II	9 Apr 1555	1 May 1555	22 days	Italy	53/53	
224	Paul IV	23 May 1555	18 Aug 1559	4y 2m	Italy	78/83	✓
225	Pius IV	25 Dec 1559	9 Dec 1565	5y 11m	Italy	59/66	✓
226	St. Pius V	7 Jan 1566	1 May 1572	6y 3m	Italy	61/68	✓

#	Papal Name	Start of reign	End of reign	Length	From	Age Start/End	'nc'
227	Gregory XIII	14 May 1572	10 Apr 1585	12y 11m	Italy	70/83	✓
228	Sixtus V	24 Apr 1585	27 Aug 1590	5y 4m	Italy	63/68	✓
229	Urban VII	15 Sep 1590	27 Sep 1590	12 days	Italy	69/69	✓
230	Gregory XIV	5 Dec 1590	16 Oct 1591	10m	Italy	55/56	✓
231	Innocent IX	29 Oct 1591	30 Dec 1591	62 days	Italy	72/72	✓
232	Clement VIII	30 Jan 1592	5 Mar 1605	13y 1m	Italy	55/69	✓
233	Leo XI	1 Apr 1605	27 Apr 1605	26 days	Italy	69/69	✓
234	Paul V	16 May 1605	28 Jan 1621	15y 8m	Italy	52/68	✓
235	Gregory XV	9 Feb 1621	8 July 1623	2y 4m	Italy	67/69	✓
236	Urban VIII	6 Aug 1623	29 July 1644	20y 11m	Italy	55/76	✓
237	Innocent X	15 Sep 1644	1 Jan 1655	10y 3m	Italy	70/80	✓
238	Alexander VII	7 Apr 1655	22 May 1667	12y 1m	Italy	56/68	✓
239	Clement IX	20 June 1667	9 Dec 1669	2y 5m	Italy	67/69	✓
240	Clement X	29 Apr 1670	22 July 1676	6y 2m	Italy	79/86	✓
241	Bl. Innocent XI	21 Sep 1676	12 Aug 1689	12y 10m	Italy	65/78	✓
242	Alexander VIII	6 Oct 1689	1 Feb 1691	1y 3m	Italy	79/80	✓
243	Innocent XII	12 July 1691	27 Sep 1700	9y 2m	Italy	76/85	✓
244	Clement XI	23 Nov 1700	19 Mar 1721	20y 4m	Italy	51/71	✓
245	Innocent XIII	8 May 1721	7 Mar 1724	2y 10m	Italy	65/68	✓
246	Benedict XIII	29 May 1724	21 Feb 1730	5y 8m	Italy	75/81	✓
247	Clement XII	12 July 1730	6 Feb 1740	9y 6m	Italy	78/87	✓
248	Benedict XIV	17 Aug 1740	3 May 1758	17y 8m	Italy	65/83	✓
249	Clement XIII	6 July 1758	2 Feb 1769	10y 6m	Italy	65/75	✓
250	Clement XIV	19 May 1769	22 Sep 1774	5y 4m	Italy	63/68	✓
251	Pius VI	15 Feb 1775	29 Aug 1799	24y 6m	Italy	57/81	✓
252	Pius VII	14 Mar 1800	20 Aug 1823	23y 5m	Italy	57/81	✓
253	Leo XII	28 Sep 1823	10 Feb 1829	5y 4m	Italy	63/68	✓
254	Pius VIII	31 Mar 1829	30 Nov 1830	1y 8m	Italy	67/69	✓
255	Gregory XVI	2 Feb 1831	1 June 1846	15y 4m	Italy	65/80	✓
256	Bl. Pius IX	16 June 1846	7 Feb 1878	31y 7m	Italy	54/85	✓
257	Leo XIII	20 Feb 1878	20 July 1903	25y 5m	Italy	67/93	✓

#	Papal Name	Start of reign	End of reign	Length	From	Age Start/End	'nc'
258	St. Pius X	4 Aug 1903	20 Aug 1914	11y 16d	Italy	68/79	✓
259	Benedict XV	3 Sep 1914	22 Jan 1922	7y 4m	Italy	59/67	✓
260	Pius XI	6 Feb 1922	10 Feb 1939	17y 4d	Italy	64/81	✓
261	Pius XII	2 Mar 1939	9 Oct 1958	19y 7m	Italy	63/82	✓
262	**St. John XXIII**	**28 Oct 1958**	**3 June 1963**	**4y 7m**	**Italy**	**76/81**	✓
263	Paul VI	21 June 1963	6 Aug 1978	15y 1m	Italy	65/80	✓
264	John Paul I	26 Aug 1978	28 Sep 1978	33 days	Italy	65/65	✓
265	St. John Paul II	16 Oct 1978	2 Apr 2005	26y 5m	Poland	58/84	✓
266	Benedict XVI	19 Apr 2005	28 Feb 2013	7y 10m	Germany	78/85	✓
267	Francis	13 Mar 2013			Argentina	76 ->	✓

SELECT REFERENCES

📖 Elliott, Lawrence, *I Will be Called John*, Reader's Digest Press, 1973.

📖 Hatch, Alden, *A Man Named John*, Hawthorn Books, 1963.

📖 Cahill, Thomas, *Pope John XXIII*, Viking Penguin, 2002.

📖 Hebblethwaite, *Peter, John XXIII: Pope of the Century*, Continuum, 2005.

📖 Kelly, J.N.D., *The Oxford Dictionary of Popes*, Oxford University Press, 2006.

📖 Pham, John-Peter, *Heirs of the Fisherman*, Oxford University Press, 2004.

📖 Gurugé, Anura, *The Next Pope: 2011*, WOWNH LLC, 2011.

⌨ 'Papa Giovanni' by *Il Pontificio istituto missioni estere* (PIME) [Pontifical Institute for Foreign Missions] at www.papagiovanni.com.

⌨ The official Website of Sotto il Monte, hometown of John XXIII at www.papagiovannisottoilmonte.org.

⌨ The Vatican Web site at www.vatican.va.

⌨ 'The Hierarchy of the Catholic Church' by David M. Cheney at www.catholic-hierarchy.org.

⌨ 'Giga-Catholic' Information by Gabriel Chow at www.gcatholic.com.

⌨ 'Popes and the Papacy' at www.popes-and-papacy.com.

⌨ Wikipedia at www.wikipedia.org.

⌨ 'Our Sunday Visitor' at www.osv.com.

⌨ 'Eternal World Television Network' at www.ewtn.com.

⌨ 'Conciliaria' at www.conciliaria.com.

⌨ 'Service of Documentation & Study on Global Mission' at www.sedosmission.org.

⌨ 'California Catholic Conference' at www.cacatholic.org.

⌨ 'Archdiocese of Indianapolis' at www.archindy.org.

Partial Index

Made in the USA
Lexington, KY
25 April 2014